How to Raise Kids Who Aren't Assholes

Praise for Melinda Wenner Moyer

'Most parents say we want our children to be kind, compassionate people. Yet everything in the culture urges us to teach something else. . . . Melinda Wenner Moyer weaves cutting-edge science with accessible stories and actionable tips to help us rebalance those crucial scales, to be the parents we know we can be.'

Peggy Orenstein, author of Girls & Sex and Boys & Sex

'I can't think of a more important life lesson than 'Don't be an asshole.' Unfortunately, many kids don't learn it—because many parents fail to teach it. Thanks to this book, they no longer have an excuse. It's a smart, engaging, honest, and surprisingly useful read about how to nurture decency and generosity.'

Adam Grant, author of Think Again

'How can parents raise kids who believe in themselves and in building a better, more compassionate future? This book provides the road map. Filled with actionable, sometimes surprising, always data-driven ideas, Melinda Wenner Moyer has given us an invaluable resource.'

Madeline Levine, PhD, author of
The Price of Privilege and Ready or Not

'If you are a parent who wants to know that your parenting energies are tried and true, tested and trusted, this book is the place where you can plant your flag.'

Mark Mcconville, PhD, author of Failure to Launch

How to Raise Kids Who Aren't Assholes

Science-Based Strategies for Better
Parenting – from Tots to Teens

Melinda Wenner Moyer

First published in 2021 by HEADLINE HOME
an imprint of HEADLINE PUBLISHING GROUP

5

Cataloguing in Publication Data is available from the British Library

Book design by Katy Riegel

Trade paperback ISBN 978 1 4722 8878 3
eBook ISBN 978 1 4722 8879 0

Offset in 11.96/17.68 pt Minion Pro by Jouve (UK), Milton Keynes

Printed and bound in Great Britain by Clays Ltd, Elcograf S.p.A.

HEADLINE PUBLISHING GROUP
An Hachette UK Company
Carmelite House
50 Victoria Embankment
London EC4Y 0DZ

www.headline.co.uk
www.hachette.co.uk

For my children, who teach me every day

Contents

How to Raise
Kids Who
Aren't Assholes

Introduction

MY FRIEND MILLIE still remembers, in cringing, Technicolor detail, the time her then five-year-old son said something blatantly racist. It was three years ago, and she and her husband, who are both white, were on vacation with their kids in Florida. After a week of intense together time, they'd hired a babysitter so they could enjoy a night out. The babysitter happened to be Black.

The next day, Millie asked her son whether he had fun with his babysitter. "No, I didn't like her," he replied. When Millie pressed for more info, her son said matter-of-factly, "I didn't like her because she had dark skin."

Millie was mortified and had no idea how to respond. She and her husband thought they were raising their kids to be respectful and, you know, *not racist*, but now? Now they weren't so sure. And they had no idea what to do about it.

Most parents—myself included—want their kids to grow up to become kindhearted people. In 2020, *Parents* magazine surveyed more than 1,200 parents around the country about what they wanted most for their kids. In response, 73 percent of mothers and 68 percent of fathers said that kindness was the quality they most wanted to instill in their children, above intelligence, individuality, and work ethic. Similarly, in 2016, Sesame Workshop, the nonprofit organization behind the show *Sesame Street*, interviewed more than two thousand American parents of children ages three to twelve, as well as five hundred pre-K through sixth grade teachers. Approximately three-quarters of parents and teachers said they felt it is more important for kids to be kind than it is for them to be academically successful.

Yet in that same 2020 *Parents* magazine survey, 76 percent of mothers and 58 percent of fathers said that kids today are not as kind as kids from years past. The parents in the Sesame Workshop survey felt similarly: 67 percent said most children today are disrespectful, while 43 percent said they didn't think their own kids were very thoughtful. Clearly, despite *wanting* to foster goodness, many parents aren't sure how to do it.

For the past nine years, I've been using my science journalism background to educate myself about the research on child development and parenting. I've written a science-based parenting column for *Slate* and dozens of parenting articles for *The New York Times*. I dig into the published academic research on complicated parenting questions, vet it with experts, and translate it into straightforward parenting advice—advice that the science truly supports. And I've often been surprised, if not flat-out shocked, by what the research actually suggests parents do . . . and how different that professional guidance is from what I had assumed it would be.

Take, for instance, the issue of race, which became a much

more pressing issue in many parents' minds after the police officer–involved deaths of George Floyd, Breonna Taylor, and other Black Americans in 2020. Although parents of color typically have regular conversations with their kids about race—they have to—most white parents, my friend Millie included, avoid the topic in a well-meaning attempt to raise their kids to be "color-blind." If they don't mention race, these parents think, maybe their kids won't notice it. But the research clearly shows that children (even babies!) do see race—and that, when they aren't provided with a framework through which to make sense of it, kids make prejudiced inferences. They see that white people tend to have more power and wealth than people of other races, and then they assume that's because white people are somehow better or smarter.

When I interviewed primary school educator Naomi O'Brien, the coauthor of a series of books for parents about race, she explained that she regularly sees her white students saying and doing racist things, such as announcing they won't play with a particular peer because of his "dirty skin"—and that their parents are often oblivious to those judgments. Making matters worse, when white kids try to talk to their parents about race, O'Brien said, "They're hushed and they're shushed and told not to speak about it, and they just internalize it as talking about color is bad, having color is bad." The truth is—and the research clearly shows—that white parents *need* to talk to their kids about race in explicit ways to prevent them from making racist assumptions.

Parents often unwittingly fuel sexist beliefs, too, by giving different messages to girls than to boys—messages that reflect our grown-up misogynistic reality. Like that appearance matters more for girls than for boys, and that boys aren't allowed to feel sad or afraid. And when we follow the age-old advice to let our kids work out sibling fights by themselves, we often make sibling rivalry worse and cause our kids to think that bullying and coercion are the best ways to resolve conflict.

Sometimes, of course, research confirms our deeply held parenting instincts, but other times it directly contradicts it in fascinating, thought-provoking ways—which is one of the reasons I decided to write this book. I wanted to share all the surprising science I've uncovered about raising kind kids.

SO MANY ASSHOLES

I wrote this book for another big reason, too. I believe our work as parents today is more crucial than ever. The world has been sending dangerous messages to our kids about how they should behave and treat one another—messages that we desperately need to challenge and counteract.

Before I explain, I first want to say that I think kids are sometimes *supposed* to act like assholes. They have to challenge boundaries in order to understand them, and they have to make social bloopers in order to learn from them. I've come to think of mortifying kid moments (and we have a lot of those in our house) as teaching opportunities—or, better yet, as wake-up calls that illustrate what we need to be working on as a family.

Unfortunately, right now, parents are being bombarded with wake-up calls, because people everywhere have been behaving pretty badly. In the fall of 2018, K–12 teachers and staff reported to the Southern Poverty Law Center that they had observed more than 3,200 hate-related incidents in their schools over the past few months. In Monroe, Louisiana, for instance, a white student was arrested for putting a noose around a Black classmate's neck.

And things appear to be getting worse. Between 2015 and 2018, according to the FBI, the number of hate crime incidents in the United States increased by 21 percent. Many of these incidents were perpetrated by adults, but kids have been involved as well. Bullying, too, seems to be escalating. In 2016 and 2017, the Human Rights Campaign surveyed more than fifty thousand American thirteen-to-eighteen-year-olds, and 79 percent of them said they thought school bullying incidents had recently gotten worse. When researchers at the University of California, Los Angeles, surveyed 1,535 public high school teachers in the summer of 2017, nearly 30 percent said that their students were making more derogatory remarks about their peers than they had the previous year.

This crisis of kindness may have many causes. Some researchers think it has been fueled at least in part by the ascendancy of Donald Trump. The notion that political figures could influence kids may seem like a stretch, since many kids aren't particularly interested in politics. But Trump's rhetoric—which has included lying, joking about sexual assault, mocking disabled individuals, and referring to majority-Black countries as "shithole countries"—was all over the TV and the internet for years, pervading many a dinner conversation, and it may have had a direct effect on our children.

There's even some evidence linking support for Trump with bullying behavior. In a study published in January 2019, educational psychologists Dewey Cornell and Francis Huang analyzed teasing and bullying patterns in Virginia middle schools before and after the 2016 presidential election using results from school surveys. Before the election, the schools had the same rates of bullying and teasing. Afterward, in schools in the pro-Trump districts, rates of teasing and bullying were 18 percent higher than in schools located in pro-Clinton districts. (It's important to note, too, that these findings followed a documented decline in school bullying. A 2017 study published in the journal *Pediatrics* noted that between 2005 and 2014, bullying dropped among fourth to twelfth graders, and had been declining faster and faster over time.)

In November 2016, the Southern Poverty Law Center compiled a list of 867 hate incidents that happened in the ten days following the 2016 presidential election. Many involved kids. One teacher in Washington State reported that students chanted "Build a wall" in her school cafeteria the day after the election; she also overheard one student say to another, "If you aren't born here, pack your bags." In Greenville, South Carolina, a twelve-year-old was surrounded by eight classmates who told her they "couldn't wait to see her ugly face deported," while in Cedar Falls, Iowa, a sixteen-year-old dropped out of school after classmates called her a fag and a queer and threatened to "grab her by the pussy." The teen had come out as gay four years earlier, and according to her parents, she'd never been harassed in this way. "All of a sudden, the ninth [of November] hits," one of her parents said, "and she's some kind of freak—she's a target."

In a 2019 paper published in the *Journal of Child Psychotherapy*, five US child psychologists lamented that many of their young, vulnerable patients are more terrified than ever because of the cruelty and oppression they feel every day. "Since the 2016 election, children's fears, once tied to their immediate ecosystem—

the school, local community, and the home—seem to have expanded," they wrote. One patient pretended to pack their doll's bags during a therapy session and said, "We are moving to Canada where it is safe. We can speak Spanish there and no one will hate us."

To be fair, these incidents are not controlled studies, and it's hard to say for sure that hate speech and bullying wouldn't have worsened no matter who was sitting in the White House. They may be symptoms of broader social patterns rather than evidence of a specific political shift. But kids do learn from bad examples. According to a well-accepted theory in psychology known as Social Learning Theory, developed in the 1960s by Stanford psychologist Albert Bandura, children (as well as adults) take cues on how to behave by observing the people around them. The people they most tend to emulate are the ones with high status—like the president of the United States.

In one well-known experiment, Bandura and his colleagues invited three-to-six-year-olds into a room where they, by themselves, watched another adult play. Some kids saw the adult hit, beat, and verbally assault a doll; others watched the adult play calmly with toys. Then the children were individually taken into a different room and made to feel frustrated: After playing with cool new toys for a couple of minutes, they were told they could no longer have them and were brought back to the original room, where they were allowed to play with other toys, including the doll, for twenty minutes.

The kids who had seen an adult harm the doll were much more likely than the other kids to attack it, too, and many assaulted it over and over and over again.

This experiment is, essentially, playing out in our country right now on a large scale: People in power have been the adults showing everyone that racism, sexism, bullying, and aggression are not just OK but *what powerful people do.*

As a result, young people's behavior and values have been shifting in worrying ways. Research has found that college students are less empathetic than they were a decade ago—they are less likely to feel for people who are less fortunate and to try to put themselves in other people's shoes. When a high school teacher heard that I was writing this book, she summarized her thoughts on today's kids this way: "So many assholes."

A BETTER TOMORROW

If all of this makes you want to throw up your hands and drown yourself in wine, I get it. I went through that phase, too. But now, I see all of this as a call to action. More than anything else, I want my kids to be happy and to feel loved. Yet as I observe the cruelty that is increasingly enveloping our country, a growing part of me wants something else for my kids, too: I want them to be kindhearted and to treat other people with respect and dignity. It's not something I used to actively think about, but now it feels pressing and essential.

And the great thing is, if parents focus on raising kind kids, we *can* eliminate the mounting cruelty in the world, or at least tamp it down. We're raising future lawyers, politicians, business owners, artists, health-care workers . . . future *everythings.* Of course, we aren't molding our kids out of clay. Many aspects of our kids' lives—their peers, their teachers, their genes, the experiences they have that we can't control—shape who they ultimately become, too. But we have considerable influence on the trajectories our kids take in life. In a 2019 study, researchers followed nearly 450 kids for three years in an attempt to tease out which factors most strongly shape kids' character and values. They found that although peers do have influence, especially during the transition to adolescence, parents "play a key role in the personal and social development of their children."

If you're worried that raising your kids to be good and kind will ultimately make them less happy or successful, you can relax on that front, too. Research consistently shows that when people (including kids) are kind and generous to others, they feel happier. And in a 2019 analysis of thirty years' worth of data that controlled for the effects of family economic status and child IQ, researchers found that boys who were kinder and more generous in kindergarten earned significantly more money as adults. In his research-based book *Give and Take*, Adam Grant, a Wharton School of Business organizational psychologist, argued that generosity and helpfulness are traits that often distinguish the extremely successful from the merely average.

By raising our kids to be kind, we'll ensure that they thrive. And they'll build a better, fairer, stronger world in the process.

MY GOALS AND HOPES, EXPLAINED

I'll be honest and admit that, at first, I wasn't comfortable with the idea of writing a parenting book. The whole premise felt kind of obnoxious. Who was I to tell other parents what to do? It's not like I'm anything close to a perfect parent, and if you think I have perfect kids, you are welcome to come over this weekend and see for yourself. I think of parenting as a 100,000-piece puzzle that you're trying to put together while also driving, making dinner, and keeping your kids from killing each other.

But one night, I changed my mind. What I was learning as a journalist about the science of character was changing how I interacted with my kids on a day-to-day basis—the kinds of details I brought into our conversations, the kinds of questions I asked them, how I reacted to their feelings and their explanations. Slowly, my parenting became infused with a subtle awareness of small things I could do to help my kids learn how to be empathetic and kind. And I started seeing changes in their behavior. My kids started fighting a bit less. They became better able to recognize and handle their emotions. They seemed more resilient. If what I was learning was helping me handle situations better—and helping my kids become better humans—wouldn't other parents want to know about it, too?

As you can see, I did end up writing the book, and now you're reading it. Here's how I've laid out the information for you. In part 1, I explore what the science says about shaping specific traits. How do you foster generosity, honesty, kindness, ambition, and resilience? How do you stamp out rudeness, entitlement, arrogance, sexism, and racism? (A note of warning: Some of the issues and scenarios I discuss might be hard to read if you've experienced related discrimination or trauma.) In each chapter, I provide simple, evidence-based approaches you can use on a daily basis with kids of various ages to bolster good character traits and eliminate the bad. In part 2, I provide science-backed strategies to help you deal with particularly gnarly situations and issues: What should you do when your kids fight? How should you manage technology and social media? What's the best way to talk to your kids about sex and pornography? There's also a notes section at the end of the book listing all the studies I've mentioned, in case you'd like to look them up and read more.

One thing I absolutely do *not* want this book to be is yet another reason for you to judge yourself. Today's parents endure far too much criticism as it is—we're ruining our kids because of *snowplow parenting* and *helicopter parenting* and *intensive parenting* and 843 other kinds of supposedly bad parenting that I don't really understand. Pediatrician Leonard Sax penned an entire book in 2015 called *The Collapse of Parenting*, which I reviewed for *Slate*, and let me just say I did not find his arguments evidence-based. I don't think that kids today are struggling with moral issues because we are doing a worse job than our parents did. I do, however, think that many of the role models that kids are learning from today are dangerous, and that we as parents need to do what we can to push against the pernicious messages they are sending.

I don't want my advice to feel like additional pressure, either— that I'm giving you more to worry about and squeeze into your busy life. Parents, especially mothers, are spread so very thin these days. As I write this, we're all having to keep our kids home and safe during a deadly pandemic, while also working and doing all the other things, which has deeply intensified our burden. We don't have time to do any more than we already do, and when we try, things often crumble. (For a few months while I was writing this book, I took on too much and got really stressed, and I noticed I was not being a very patient or empathetic mother. Oh the irony: I was spending so much time researching and writing about parenting that *I couldn't actually be an effective parent.*)

Instead of adding to your overflowing plates, I hope this book will clear a few things away and make you feel empowered. I want to save you time and effort by giving you the answers to questions you might have had in the back of your mind for years. I want to provide you with ways to handle the kinds of situations that make you think, *What the hell should I do now?* With my science background, I have digested and translated the complicated science on child development into simple advice that you can use on a daily basis. My hope is that this book makes your life as a parent just a little bit easier, and perhaps more enjoyable, too.

This all said, you're going to have to be patient, and you're going to have to be forgiving. Shaping a child's character (not to mention your own behavior as a parent) takes time, and the way children engage with the world is also strongly influenced by their temperament, hormones, mental health, and life history. Our children will have many experiences we can't control, and these will shape them in ways we cannot override. Kids—even those with big, wonderful hearts—can't always be generous, empathetic, and warm, and parents shouldn't jump to conclusions when children demonstrate inevitable hiccups.

Still, it is my firm belief that we can become better parents by educating ourselves, and that what we learn directly benefits our kids. When we understand how kids' brains develop, why they do the things they do, and how to best communicate with them, we can provide our children with the tools and coping strategies they need to gracefully and compassionately handle what the world throws at them.

From what I've learned, it all makes a difference: the boundaries we set, the conversations we have, the behaviors we respond to—and the ones we ignore. Parenting presents us with infinite opportunities to teach our kids values. The more we take advantage of these opportunities, and the more knowledgeable we are about what actually works, the more confident we can be that our children will grow into the kinds of people we want them to be—the kinds of people the world really needs.

PART I

Traits

CHAPTER 1

"It's All About ME!"

How to Raise Kids Who Aren't (Overly) Selfish

In April 2019, my friend Celia was driving her seven-year-old daughter, Ella, home from Target when her phone rang. It was Celia's mother-in-law—Ella's grandmother—and Celia answered the call using Bluetooth. They heard very sad news via the car speakers: Ella's great-grandmother had just passed away.

Ella, though, seemed unperturbed. Throughout the call, she piped up from the back seat with unrelated questions, like whether she could watch TV when they got home. At one point, she yelled unsympathetically, *"Who died?!"* Celia tried to take the call off speaker, but she couldn't figure out how; needless to say, the eight-minute drive home felt excruciatingly long.

When Celia finally got off the call, Ella asked her if she could give a speech at the funeral. Thinking she might want to share fond memories—she'd seen her great-grandmother at least once a year since she was born—Celia asked her what she would want to say. Ella then launched into a potential speech about how sorry everyone should feel for her for having lost her great-grandmother. At one point, Ella paused—"What was her name again?" she asked—and then turned back to her speech, which had nothing to do with her great-grandmother and everything to do with Ella.

Let's face it: Kids can be incredibly self-centered. They interrupt you during important work Zoom presentations to tell you poop jokes. They don't want to share their LEGO pieces—even though they have 4.8 million, not including the 642 strewn across the kitchen floor. They also have an astounding ability to put themselves at the center of every situation, even when doing so seems terribly inappropriate. Another friend of mine recently told me that when her son was opening presents on his first birthday, her three-year-old daughter sat down next to him, burst into tears, and wailed, "It's not all about me?!"

In situations like this, kids aren't (usually) trying to be assholes. They just can't help themselves. Toddlers and preschoolers don't have a particularly well-developed frontal lobe, the brain region responsible for planning, logic, reasoning, and self-control. I, too, get jealous when other people open amazing gifts in front of me, but I don't burst into tears, because I have perfected the skill of silently fuming (and doesn't my husband know it).

Young kids also haven't yet developed what's called *theory of mind*—the ability to put oneself in someone else's shoes and understand their perspective. Without theory of mind, it's hard to understand how your actions or words might affect others. Toddlers and preschoolers are basically living in an egocentric bubble, oblivious to the needs and experiences of everyone else. (Older kids have their selfish moments, too, of course—like another friend's seven-year-old nephew, who sat down to a lavish Mother's Day dinner that his grandmother had spent the afternoon preparing for the entire family, only to immediately start whining and to demand that she make him chicken nuggets instead.)

That said, some kids do seem more or less selfish than others. My two kids, for instance, couldn't be more different in this regard, and their Halloween baskets are a case in point. My son hoards his candy and rarely even shares the candies he dislikes. When I recently asked him for a Reese's Peanut Butter Cup, a candy he loathes, he paused and said, "Didn't I give you one like four months ago?" My daughter, on the other hand, gives most of her candy away—she wraps individual candies up in tissue paper and hands them out to friends, teachers, and acquaintances. How is it possible that these kids share the same home, parents, and half of their genes? I honestly don't know sometimes.

Still, researchers who study children's behavior say that regardless of a child's baseline inclination toward selfishness, we as parents can make a difference—we can inch our kids in the right direction, little by little, day by day, with simple strategies.

THE PUSHOVER MYTH

Before I delve into these strategies, I want to correct a popular misconception about kindness. In March 2019, the parenting website Fatherly published an article titled "Should Parents Want to Raise Nice Kids? Probably Not." The piece, written by science writer Joshua A. Krisch, opened with a few of Krisch's parental concerns. "When I teach my daughter not to interrupt a conversation, I wonder how she'll know when to break that rule when she needs to shut down an obnoxious mansplainer," he wrote.

"When I tell my son to share his cookies, I wonder: am I molding him into the sort of kid who gives away his lunch, his toys, his homework, to grade school bullies?"

Krisch has a point. If you teach your kids to be generous, aren't you increasing the chance that less generous people will take advantage of them? I certainly don't want my daughter to be too polite to speak up for herself or to claim what's rightfully hers. At the same time, I think that these concerns are largely overblown. While being thoughtful can involve a bit of a sacrifice (if you share your cookies, you inevitably end up with fewer for yourself), it doesn't require sacrificing *everything*, like the things you really want, the ideals you stand for, or your integrity. As a parent, you can teach your kids to think of others while also instilling in them a sense of self-worth and a fighting spirit. These character traits can all coexist.

Krisch then highlights another potential problem with kindness. "Maintaining a consistently happy-go-lucky attitude may not be as healthy as it seems," he wrote. I agree—but teaching kids to be generous isn't the same thing as teaching them to suppress their emotions. In fact, as I'll argue in a minute, by teaching kids to experience and accept the depth of their feelings, we can actually *make* them more generous.

These concerns about the "risks of kindness" miss another key point, too: Kindness reaps its own rewards. Research suggests that generous individuals live longer and have better health than stingy grumps. Being kind and helpful also reduces symptoms of depression, anxiety, and stress and causes people to feel more energetic in what is known as a "helper's high."

Being kind makes people happier, too, and that's true not just for adults but also for kids. In a 2012 study, psychologists at the

University of British Columbia gave toddlers crackers to eat and then gave them more to share with a monkey puppet. Watching their facial expressions, the researchers saw that the toddlers appeared much happier giving crackers away—even when they had to give up their own crackers to do so—than when the kids kept the food for themselves. I'm often surprised by the gleeful expression on my daughter's face when she offers me a piece of her Halloween candy, but it makes sense: Being generous really can feel good.

And—bonus—kindness also makes kids more popular. After researchers asked nine-to-eleven-year-olds to perform three acts of kindness each week for four weeks—such as giving friends hugs, cleaning up messes, or sharing their lunch with others— they were rated as more popular by their peers than kids who hadn't gone out of their way to be kind.

And again, if you're worried that by raising your kids to be generous you'll be setting them up for career failure, you don't need to be. A growing body of research suggests that "soft skills" like empathy and kindness predict long-term success far more than do "hard skills" such as academic scores and grades. A 2018 study reported that kids who were rated by peers as more helpful in middle school got better grades later in both middle school and in high school, and that their IQ had no bearing on those differences. And in a 2015 study, researchers followed a group of children from kindergarten to age twenty-five and reported that the kindergarteners who had cooperated well with peers, been helpful to others, and resolved problems by themselves were more likely than other kids to graduate from college and hold stable jobs as adults. What goes around really does come around—so by raising our kids to be selfless, we are, in fact, nudging them down the path toward a happy, successful life.

Selflessness Strategy #1
Talk about, validate, and help your kids manage emotions.

One sunny Tuesday in May 2019 at the Chambers Elementary School in Kingston, New York, fourteen kindergarteners took a break from their reading and math lessons to learn about feelings. Former teacher David Levine, the director of the Teaching Empathy Institute, sat in front of the class, frowning.

"Pretend I'm your classmate and I just moved here, I don't know anyone," Levine said to the students, who were sitting in rows on an alphabet rug. He called on a girl wearing a rhinestoned hair bow and asked if she would come up to the front of the class and try to connect with him as part of a role-play exercise.

The girl walked up to him shyly. "Hi," she said.

"Hi," Levine mumbled, looking down, shoulders slumped. "What's your name?"

"Amber," she said.

"My name's Howard," he said. "I don't have any friends in this school. I don't know anybody, and I don't like it here."

"I can be your friend," Amber replied.

"Really?" Levine's face perked up. His shoulders straightened. "Yeah."

"Why would you be my friend? You just met me," Levine said, but his demeanor was still brightening.

"Because that's being nice to other people," Amber said.

Levine stopped and addressed the class. "Look at me. Have I changed?" he asked.

"Yes!" the students all chimed in unison.

"How have I changed?" he asked. "Use words, describe. What's different about my face?"

"You're smiling," one girl said.

"What are my eyes doing?" he asked.

"Happy!" another student interjected.

Levine was teaching these students how to read, label, and understand emotions. That might not seem like a skill as important as arithmetic or literacy, but research is starting to suggest otherwise. Kids have to recognize and understand emotions in order to figure out and manage their own feelings. And "emotional regulation," as this skill is called, is strongly linked to academic success, the ability to have stable and healthy relationships, happiness, and other good outcomes.

Understanding the language of emotions is also a first step toward being generous and helpful. Think about it: If a child wants to do something nice for a friend, he first has to be able to perceive that friend's feelings and needs. He has to be able to read his friend's face and body language and translate that into an understanding of what his friend is going through and what he might want, without letting his own emotions or desires get in the way. When kids struggle with these skills, they understandably have more trouble connecting with others and being compassionate and helpful. This isn't just theoretical; research confirms that emotional literacy is powerfully linked with altruistic behavior.

In a 2013 study, Celia Brownell, a psychologist at the University of Pittsburgh, and her colleagues invited toddlers and their caregivers—mostly mothers—into their lab and asked the moms to read a book to their kids. As they read, the researchers recorded how frequently the moms paused their reading to label and explain the characters' feelings. (They presumed that the moms who stopped to discuss feelings while reading in the lab did the same when reading at home.) Then the toddlers were each invited to play with toys and a researcher in another room. While they played, they were given the opportunity to share toys, as well as to help when the researcher pretended to need assistance. In one situation, the researcher couldn't reach an object she wanted; in another, the researcher pretended to be cold, hoping the toddler would bring her a nearby blanket.

When Brownell and her colleagues compared the mothers' reading habits with the kids' behaviors, they found that the children of moms who engaged with their kids about feelings while reading—and who got their kids to talk about feelings, too—were much more likely to help and share while playing.

You don't have to read a book to talk about emotions, though; nor does this strategy apply only to toddlers and preschoolers. Ideally, parents should interject emotion talk into various parts of the day with kids of all ages. First, try to open up about your own feelings. *I'm upset today, because my boss criticized the report I spent so much time on.* Comment or ask about your kids' feelings, too. *Are you OK, sweetie? You look a little sad. Are you feeling sad?* These kinds of conversations "promote empathy and compassion, in the sense of understanding others' feelings and caring about them," said developmental psychologist Stuart Hammond, director of the University of Ottawa's Social Moral Development Lab. Even just naming and defining feelings can be helpful. Not so long ago, at dinner, my kids and I tried to brainstorm as many feelings as possible and talk about what they meant. It was a fun exercise, and I know they learned from it, because the next day I heard my daughter use the word *elated* while talking with her brother, which she'd never done before.

Bring feelings—and other people and their feelings—into your requests and encouragements, too. In one experiment, third and fourth graders were given money and then encouraged to donate it to children in need of food and toys. Some were told that sharing would help the other children and make them happy. Others were told that sharing is "the right thing to do." The kids who'd been encouraged to share because of how it would make the other children feel were much more likely to donate their money. Other research has shown that the more that mothers consider other people's feelings and encourage their children to do the same, the more empathetic their kids are, and the more helpful and kind they are at home and at school.

Emotions should become part of your disciplinary conversations as well. When your kids act out in ways that make other people sad or hurt, say so. When my daughter hits her brother, I now try to go beyond admonishing with *Don't hit!* and instead say something like *Hitting isn't OK because it really hurts your brother, and I suspect that's why he's so sad right now.* And then, instead of merely asking her to apologize, I ask her to check that her brother is OK and to figure out what she can do to make him feel better.

This idea is the foundation of a disciplinary approach known as *induction*, which was developed by child psychologists Martin Hoffman and Herbert Salzstein in the 1960s. Their research found that when parents discipline kids with explanations of how their actions affect others, kids are more likely to grasp the significance of their choices and amend their behavior. They empathize with the other person's distress and are made aware of their responsibility for it. Examples of these kinds of explanations include *When you throw snow on the neighbors' walkway, they have to shovel it all over again* and *Try to be quiet; if your brother can sleep a while longer, he'll feel better when he wakes up.* (For more on discipline, see chapter 8.)

In a 1996 study designed to test Hoffman's theory, researchers surveyed mothers of sixth and seventh graders about the ways in which they disciplined their kids and asked the kids how their parents disciplined them. The researchers also asked the kids' teachers to rate how altruistic and helpful the students were; gave tests to the students to assess their levels of empathy; and tested the kids' generosity by inviting them to give money to a charity. Kids whose parents used induction as a form of discipline—who explained to their kids how their actions affected others—were more generous and empathetic than kids whose parents disciplined in power-assertive ways, such as with punishments.

In another study, researchers found that the children of mothers who clearly explained to their kids how their transgressions harmed others were more interested in making reparations for their mistakes—and that they were more likely to help bystanders who appeared to be in distress.

Another key aspect of building emotional literacy is validating your kids' feelings, even when they seem over the top or don't make sense to you. This one is especially hard for me. My daughter is a meltdown machine: She'll react maniacally to things that don't seem like a big deal to anyone else. As an example, she now knows how to unstrap herself from her car seat, but she fluctuates between wanting me to open the car door for her and wanting to open it herself. Of course, she doesn't tell me which preference she has on a given day (and if I ask, she gets mad), so I'm left to make a best guess—and God help me if I open the car door on a day when she doesn't want me to. Then I have to deal with a full-on, sprawled-out-on-the-ground, kicking-and-screaming meltdown.

These moments are . . . challenging. Often, I'm in a hurry, or I'm tired, and everything inside me wants to say *Calm down!* or *This isn't a big deal!* But of course, it is a big deal to *her*. A five-year-old's world is very, very different from that of a forty-one-year-old; there are plenty of adult-world things that I consider mortifying that would elicit nothing more than a shrug from her if I tried to explain them. Like the time when, during the corona-virus pandemic, I forgot that I'd put my hair in ridiculous pigtails and then rediscovered them when I signed onto a Zoom inter-view with an esteemed physician and saw myself on the screen.

So despite how much we might want to tell our kids to calm down or buck up, when our children are upset, researchers say the best approach is to validate and acknowledge our children's feelings, by saying something like *Oh, you must be so frustrated that I opened the car door when you didn't want me to!* Research suggests that when parents are responsive to their children's feel-ings of distress, their kids become better able to handle their own negative emotions, and they behave more empathetically and helpfully toward others who are upset. (Parental responsiveness to distress is also a crucial component of attachment theory, which was developed by psychologists John Bowlby and Mary Ainsworth starting in the 1950s. The theory, which is backed by research, suggests that when parents respond sensitively and con-sistently to their children in times of need, those kids learn that they can depend on their parents for comfort and safety, and they grow into more independent and resilient children and adults.)

This doesn't mean, though, that you have to condone the way your child *handles* her feelings. It's totally fine to communicate to your kid—perhaps once she's stopped wailing—that although you know she was *so incredibly mad*, it wasn't OK that she knocked

over the kitchen chair in fury. (This is very
dismissing her feelings or telling her she shoul
so mad.)

Maybe you say, *What are some other ways y
made yourself feel better?* Some alternatives I've (
my daughter include taking slow deep breaths,
room or somewhere else that's appropriate, and
feet. And she's learning: Recently, when she got up:
up, walked outside, and screamed like a banshee fo
two. (My poor neighbors.)

When parents help their kids problem-solve ways
ation or make themselves feel better, their kids really
more considerate. In a multiyear study published i
searchers at Penn State and the University of California, Riverside, surveyed mothers about their toddlers' behavior and the way
they typically responded to their toddlers' negative feelings. They
also observed the moms and kids together in the lab after the
children were made to feel disappointed by being given a gift they
didn't want. They found that the kids whose moms helped them
problem-solve while upset developed better emotional regulation
skills over time and became more compassionate and helpful.

And in a 2019 study, researchers found that when mothers
made an effort to help their toddlers manage stressful situations,
those kids, one year later, were more likely than others to comfort
a researcher who acted like she had been hurt. It may well be that
when parents respond warmly to their kids in times of distress
and give them the tools to calm themselves down, kids learn to
understand their own emotions and then can recognize—and respond to—emotional needs they see in others.

This all said, it's not like emotionally literate kids are nice all the time. That would be too easy. In fact, the same emotional skills that help kids empathize and understand others' needs can be used to undermine others' well-being—something I see almost daily in my kids' interactions as they fling perfectly engineered insults at each other that hit right where it hurts most. But sibling conflict isn't evidence that your kids are evil; it's normal and natural, to a degree (for more on what you can do to help siblings get along, see chapter 9). And sometimes, kids can be unbearably obnoxious to their siblings but very considerate to their friends, in a Jekyll and Hyde sort of way.

To sum things up: Talk to your kids about feelings—yours, theirs, everybody's. Tie their actions and choices to other people's feelings. When they're upset, validate their feelings even when you just want to roll your eyes. But when they've calmed down a bit, discuss the kinds of emotional expressions you think are appropriate, and help them identify strategies they can use in difficult situations in the future.

Selflessness Strategy #2
Create opportunities for your kids to help.

One day not too long ago, my then five-year-old daughter really wanted to get a waffle out of the toaster herself. Great idea in theory, but allowing her to "help" meant that we had to find a stool, move the stool next to the toaster, move the toaster toward the edge of the counter, and then ensure she didn't burn herself as she pulled the waffle out. Her "help" required extra work and time on my end, which meant, of course, that it wasn't really helpful at all.

Researchers have invented the perfect phrase to describe this:

Unhelpful helping. Baking cookies with kids, compared with baking them alone, takes about three times as long and makes the kitchen eight times as messy. And how fun is it when they "help" without asking your permission? *Look, Mom, I refolded the clothes!* Oh God, please, no. *Hey, Dad, I washed your car!* Oh shit, is that a garden hose in my front seat? In a 2018 paper, Brownell and Hammond interviewed more than five hundred parents about their toddlers' unhelpfully helpful behaviors. One mom admitted that she has to check the trash several times a day because her daughter is always throwing away perfectly good things. "We believe she lost one of her favorite shoes that way," she said.

Sometimes, you just don't have time for your kids to unhelpfully help. As a working mom, I often fall into this camp: I'll say, *No, honey, not this time, I'm in a hurry* and then do it all myself, because *efficiency.* I've been trying to relax a bit on this front, though, because research suggests that the more opportunities parents create for kids to help—what researchers refer to as "scaffolding"—the more kids want to help and the better they become at it. This doesn't mean your kid has to participate in every step of the Sunday morning pancake-making process: You can preselect tasks that you think they'll be able to manage, like stirring the batter or pouring in premeasured ingredients. Over time, they'll learn skills that actually make them helpful.

Research directly supports this idea. In a 2015 study, Hammond and his colleague Jeremy Carpendale watched mothers interact with their toddlers when they were asked to clean up after a pretend tea party. The more the moms encouraged their kids to help, and the more they supported their kids' (sometimes counterproductive) attempts to help, the more their children offered to help researchers who pretended to encounter problems later on.

Joan Grusec, a developmental psychologist who is now a professor emerita at the University of Toronto, and her colleagues have found that when kids regularly help around the house—and especially when they do tasks that directly assist other people—they also become more compassionate. In a 1997 study, she and her colleagues interviewed mothers about the kinds of jobs their ten-to-fourteen-year-olds were expected to do around the house. (They asked fathers, too, but they rarely knew what their kids did around the house. Dads, I hope that today you'd do better!) Then the researchers asked the mothers to rate the level of concern their kids had for others, and also asked the moms to write down whenever their kids helped, shared with, comforted, or defended other people. They asked the kids' teachers, too, how helpful the kids were in the classroom and how kind they were to their fellow students.

Grusec and her team found that among older kids in particular (ages twelve to fourteen), those who were routinely expected to help around the house and whose jobs directly benefited the family—they set or cleared the table, helped to prepare meals, fetched things for others, and cleaned up shared spaces—were more helpful and compassionate compared with kids who weren't expected to help. And the types of tasks mattered. Kids who were expected to do only self-oriented tasks, like cleaning their own room or putting away their own clothes, were not rated as quite as helpful.

Interestingly, though, some research suggests that with younger kids, giving kids the *choice* to help might work better than forcing them to. In a 2017 study, researchers found that five-year-olds (particularly girls) who were given the choice to clean up a pile of spilled paper, but who were told they didn't have to, cleaned up *three times as much paper* as kids who were instructed that they had to help. Research by psychologist Edward Deci has shown that when people do things out of choice, they feel much more motivated and empowered; when they feel they've been strong-armed into doing them, they lose interest rather quickly. (For more on Deci's research, see chapter 2.) Also, when helping is framed as a personal choice, kids can take all the credit for it, which makes them feel pretty darn good.

You can create opportunities for your kids to help not just in your house but in your community, too. If your child is in pre-school or elementary school, consider adopting a family over the holidays that you buy gifts for (and have your kids help pick out the presents). Or have your family volunteer at a charity or home-less shelter. If you regularly give money to charities, discuss the organizations you choose and why, and encourage your kids to volunteer or donate to their favorite causes as well. You can even set up a formal system, like "Give," "Save," and "Spend" jars that they split their allowance into each week.

The teen years are also a great time for kids to get involved. At this age, kids are "figuring out who they are in the world," said Nancy Deutsch, director of Youth-Nex, the University of Virginia Curry School of Education's Center to Promote Effective Youth Development. They are hunting for causes to care about and latching on to immutable ideas about themselves—*I am this kind of person*, or *I am someone who believes in that*. Giving them op-portunities to do good can solidify their self-identities as com-passionate, do-good people.

Indeed, a 2014 meta-analysis of forty-nine studies found that teens who participate in community service and reflect on it have better attitudes toward others and do better in school compared with teens who don't. So if your teens volunteer, talk to them about how volunteering makes them feel and how it might be assisting the community. Certain kinds of community service may also be more influential than others. Studies suggest that when service is directed toward people who are vulnerable, when the work helps others' emotional or physical well-being, and when teens have direct personal contact with their beneficiaries, the volunteering makes more of an impression.

To help your tween or teen find opportunities that will suit them, explain the various options available, but ideally, let them make their own choices. Instead of pushing your kid to support the cause *you* care about, discuss with them a handful of issues they might find engaging to help them discover where their passion lies. My nephew developed a strong interest in animal welfare in elementary school, became a vegetarian, and has since donated money each year to animal rights organizations. When a child becomes involved in helpful, larger-than-oneself activities, it becomes "internalized into a view of themselves as a moral, caring kind of person," Grusec said, and they'll grow into more knowledgeable and confident adults for having participated in their society.

In many ways, teens and young adults are uniquely suited to effect social change, because they are at a point in their lives when they are primed to reject authority and take risks. "It's no surprise to me that young people are often at the forefront of social change movements," Deutsch said. "We tend to position adolescent risk-taking as a negative thing—it leading to fast driving, drug use, and drinking—but that same neurological system in the brain that contributes to negative risk-taking can also contribute to positive risk-taking." So yeah, they might drive too fast, but they also might change the world.

Selflessness Strategy #3
Make your expectations explicit,
and discuss them as a family.

We all have ideas about how we want our children to behave in particular situations and what values we want them to develop. Most of us want our kids to be kind, to treat others with respect, and to not physically hurt one another, for instance. But how many of us have actually made these expectations explicit? Parents often think that expectations like this are obvious, that they are things our kids should already know. But kids aren't born knowing these values—we have to be clear about them.

Case in point: When I first started introducing my children to adult friends, I expected that they would know to be polite, answer their questions, and look them in the eye. But did they? Of course not! They ran away, sometimes screaming. Later, I realized that I'd never actually walked them through introductions, which, let's be honest, can be all kinds of complicated. (I *still* struggle with them, which is one reason why I tend to avoid cocktail parties.)

It also helps to explain *why* you're asking your kids to do what you're asking—an idea that again goes back to Hoffman's theory of induction. I'm quite adept at barking orders like *Don't talk with your mouth full!* and *Hang up your coat!*, but it can help to take an extra few seconds and link requests to an explanation—ideally, an explanation that delves into how your request relates to you or them or others. So not just *Please pick up your LEGO pieces*, but *Please pick up your LEGO pieces because otherwise one of us will step on one and it will really hurt.*

One day a few months ago, I sighed while making dinner and confessed to my son—the one who doesn't share his Halloween candy—that I was really tired and wasn't sure I could get everything done that day that I needed to. He turned to me and said, "Mom, how can I help you? Let me do something." When I actually opened up to him about needing help and explained why, he was right there to offer it.

And sometimes, even though you think kids should "know better" about certain things, they really, honest-to-God don't. I remember a few years ago when, out of the blue, my son began giggling and speaking with an accent and said he was pretending to be Chinese. I felt instantly upset and wanted to snap at him, thinking he should know better than to do something so culturally insensitive, but then I realized: It's not obvious to a six-year-old why mimicking a Chinese person's accent isn't OK. He wasn't trying to be rude; he really, truly didn't know that kind of behavior was unacceptable. So instead, I took a deep breath, sat down with him, and started a conversation.

One way to make your values and expectations clear is to draw up a list of family rules or values with your kids, giving them the opportunity to contribute their own ideas, said developmental psychologist Marvin Berkowitz, who codirects the University of Missouri–St. Louis's Center for Character and Citizenship. You want less of a lecture, more of a family discussion—one that culminates in a list or outline you can put up on the refrigerator. It might include declarations like *We treat one another with respect* or *No matter how angry we are, we never physically harm each other.* Or they could be more specific, like *When someone's hurt, we always ask what we can do to help.* This approach works well in the teen years, too, to address new situations or evolving family expectations.

Then, when your kids break a rule (because they always do!), you can refer back to the list, discuss what went wrong, and explore ways they could have behaved differently.

Brace yourself, though: Your kids might start calling you out on your behavior, too.

Selflessness Strategy #4
Model kindness in your daily choices.

This advice might sound obvious, but it's amazing how hard it can be to follow. It can be really, really challenging to treat family members with respect all the time, particularly when we're tired, frustrated, or having a bad day. But think about it: If we want our kids to be kind, thoughtful, and compassionate, we do need to model that behavior. "We provide the blueprint for how to behave, what to say, what to do in what contexts—they're looking to us for this information," explained Jeffrey Froh, a psychologist at Hofstra University and the coauthor of *Making Grateful Kids.*

As regularly as you can, stop and think about whether your actions reflect what you want to see in your kids. Are you being as patient and respectful as you can with your spouse, or are you constantly needling them or putting them down? Do you talk about your friends behind their back? Children do as we do, not as we say. If we show them that we think it's OK to disrespect friends and loved ones, they will assume it's OK for them to do the same.

In a large 2014 study, researchers at Indiana University and the University of Indianapolis analyzed how effective it was for parents to talk to their teens about generosity and charitableness versus how effective it was when parents modeled generosity and charitable behavior themselves. They found that both were independently associated with teens' giving and volunteering—talking the talk and walking the walk *both* make a difference.

Modeling works in part because generosity is contagious. In a 2016 study, psychologists found that people donated more money to charities when they heard other people had donated a lot, too—and people donated less if they had heard others had been stingy. Those who'd learned about generous donations also wrote nicer notes to their coworkers, suggesting that when you model one form of generous behavior in front of your kids, they may respond by being charitable in other ways, too.

Kids aren't going to notice all the good things you do, of course, so it's fine to call attention to them sometimes. If your friend down the street has the flu, talk to your kids about how hard it must be to be sick and what you could do as her friend to help—like bringing her soup or offering to pick up medicine at the store. And don't hesitate to remind your kids what you do to help *them*. When they roll their eyes after you ask them to clean their room, refresh their memory that you did the laundry yesterday so they could wear their favorite shirt today. You can even engage in a more deliberate tit for tat: *Remember how I bought you those new sneakers last week? Can you return the favor by cleaning your room now?* Research has shown that kids prefer helping people who've helped them in the past, but first they have to realize they've been helped—and kids aren't always aware of the seemingly invisible (but endless) things we do for them.

Reality check: I know—oh, goodness, do I know—that it's impossible to be kind all the time. I lose my temper with my kids more than I'd like to admit. But you can use your own mistakes as teaching moments, too. Maybe say, *Shoot, I'm sorry I yelled at you a few minutes ago. I was really stressed out about the fact that we were running late. What do you think I could do next time to calm myself down?* Your kids will be relieved to know that you also struggle with big emotions and that you don't always act as selflessly as you'd like. It's good for kids to recognize that everybody is a work in progress, including you—and that we all deserve compassion and kindness, even in our most imperfect moments.

KEY POINTS

1. Talk about and validate feelings—yours, other people's, and your children's. Tie your kids' actions to their effects on other people.
2. Let your kids help around the house and encourage them to donate time and resources to meaningful causes.
3. Make the expectations you have for your children's behavior explicit. Discuss them as a family; create house rules.
4. Model kindness and generosity yourself.

CHAPTER 2

"This Is Too Hard."

How to Raise Kids Who Are Ambitious, Resilient, and Motivated

WHEN MY SON was five, he asked if he could learn the cello. I was thrilled: I play the piano, and I've always hoped that my kids would find the same joy in music. But a few weeks after he began taking lessons—after the thrill of trying a cool new instrument wore off—the problems started. The first was getting him to practice. Every time I would bring up the topic, he would groan, refuse, and sometimes throw tantrums. Then, if I miraculously *did* get him to practice, he would break down with every tiny mistake. "This is too hard!" he would wail. I would explain that yes, it was difficult but that he would get better with practice. "I don't want to get better, I want to already be good," he would say. If I complimented him and said he sounded great, he would shoot back, "No I don't, I sound terrible!" He was, in fact, pretty good for a five-year-old, and he did improve, but either he didn't see it or the progress wasn't fast enough to sustain his interest. Each twenty-minute-long practice session felt like a three-hour-long battle of wills. Eventually he asked if he could quit, I felt kind of relieved, and neither of us has thought much about the cello since.

Yet I have often revisited the broader questions the experience raised. If my son didn't want to put effort into a challenging task he was naturally drawn to, what would happen when he had to do hard things he had no interest in at all? What if he didn't have enough resilience, enough ambition, enough *grit*? Was there anything I could do as a parent to turn things around and shape him into a self-motivated kid who actually enjoys interesting challenges?

Since then, I have read quite a lot of research on motivation and grit. What I've learned has been surprising and a tad frustrating, because I realized I've been using a widespread tactic to motivate my kids that actually has the long-term effect of *undermining* motivation. Knowing what I know now, of course the cello was a disaster!

Since I started changing my approach, though, my son has come a long way. Recently he learned the recorder in school, and the other day he came home thrilled that he had earned an orange belt from his music teacher for all the practice he had done on "Old MacDonald Had a Farm."

"You know what, I might practice some more right now!" he said.

My head almost exploded.

WHY MOTIVATION MATTERS

On some level, everyone understands the importance of motivation and effort. But research suggests that, deep down, we tend to favor "naturals" and "geniuses" over people who succeed because they work or study hard.

In a 2010 study conducted by psychologists Chia-Jung Tsay and Mahzarin R. Banaji, people were asked to judge the performances of musicians they were told were either "naturals" or "strivers." Although both music clips they heard had been performed by the same musician, the participants judged the "natural" as more talented, more likely to succeed, and more hirable. In a follow-up study, Tsay performed the same experiment, but using the example of entrepreneurs rather than musicians. Again, people judged the business proposal of the purported "natural" to be superior to that of the "striver," even though they were actually evaluating two different parts of the same proposal. This happened even when the judges were accomplished musicians or entrepreneurs themselves.

As parents, we secretly hope our kids will be naturals. We look for early hints, feeling smug if our kids learn to talk or read (or play the cello) earlier than their peers. I remember sitting down to a work dinner a few years ago with parents who spent the entire meal telling me how precocious their three-year-old was. I've noticed that effort and motivation are rarely referenced in these kinds of conversations. If anything, the implication is that effort is a sign of lack of genius. The parents at that dinner told me that their three-year-old had figured out how to read "without even really trying," as if trying were somehow an indication of failure or ineptitude. People who *can't* have to try. People who *can* just do everything effortlessly.

But this parental obsession with precociousness can be counterproductive. After all, we all know exceptionally smart people who went on to do less in life than we expected, and we know people who didn't seem terribly bright or talented but wound up doing amazing things. That's because effort and motivation really matter, and they matter more than signs of early genius. So, no: Your kid doesn't need to know how to play "Für Elise" before the age of eight. As Stanford University psychologist Carol Dweck explained in her book *Mindset*, "Many of the most accomplished people of our era were considered by experts to have no future. Jackson Pollock, Marcel Proust, Elvis Presley, Ray Charles, Lucille Ball, and Charles Darwin were all thought to have little potential for their chosen fields."

Research has pointed to the value of effort and perseverance for a long time. In 1926, for instance, a Stanford psychologist named Catharine Morris Cox published the results of a study in which she analyzed the biographical details of 301 historical figures, including physicist Sir Isaac Newton, philosopher Sir Francis Bacon, astronomer Nicolaus Copernicus, and composer Franz Joseph Haydn. She found that although many eminent individuals did have high IQs, intelligence was not the only thing that predicted how accomplished they became. And there were interesting outliers. Copernicus, she estimated, had an IQ of 105, which is only slightly above average. (Cox estimated their IQs based on detailed developmental histories.)

Cox found that what she called "persistence of motive," which included the propensity to set long-term goals and to not abandon them in the face of challenges or boredom, predicted eminence in her sample more than intelligence. "High but not the highest intelligence, combined with the greatest degree of persistence, will achieve greater eminence than the highest degree of intelligence with somewhat less persistence," she wrote. In other words, motivation and effort—not IQ—were what separated the people who accomplished the most from those who accomplished the least.

Some research even suggests that IQ itself is rooted in effort and motivation, at least in part. In a study published in 1972, California education researcher Calvin Edlund gave IQ tests to low-to-middle-class kids between the ages of five and seven. Then, seven weeks later, the same kids took a slightly different version of the IQ test again, but half were offered an M&M for each answer they got right. The students who were offered the candy did remarkably better on the second test—their IQs went up an average of twelve points—than on the first, whereas the students who didn't get candy did equally well both times, on average.

In a similar study conducted by University of South Florida researchers, kids from various socioeconomic backgrounds were split into three intelligence groups based on their IQ scores on an initial test. Then the kids in each IQ category were split into three more groups before being given a second test. One-third of them were offered an M&M for each correct answer; one-third were offered M&M's from a bowl throughout the test, regardless of their answers; and one-third were offered no M&M's. The researchers found that although the medium- and high-IQ kids didn't improve when candies were given for correct answers, the low-IQ kids did—to the point where their second scores nearly matched those in the IQ group one level up. The low-IQ kids who were given M&M's no matter what, or who didn't get any M&M's at all, did not do any better the second time.

These findings suggest that motivation and intelligence aren't entirely distinct concepts (or at least, the imperfect ways in which we measure intelligence can be influenced by motivation). One could even go so far as to argue that motivation might be one aspect of intelligence—that how hard we try directly shapes how smart we become. Maybe, then, we should focus more on fostering motivation in our kids and obsess a bit less over signs of their brilliance.

MOTIVATION VERSUS GRIT

Before I go on to explain research-backed strategies for motivating your kids, I want to introduce you to one more concept. When you think about people who've gone on to do really amazing things, you'd probably agree that their success was driven by more than just garden-variety effort. People who make a difference in the world also tend to be resilient and persistent in the face of challenges, and they are extremely passionate and single-minded in pursuit of their goals. Passion combined with perseverance is what University of Pennsylvania psychologist Angela Duckworth calls "grit"—it's "committing to challenging projects and working diligently toward their achievement over extremely long stretches of time," as she explained in a 2015 research paper.

The potential of grit isn't just theoretical; there's also interesting research behind it that suggests that grit does foster success. Duckworth and her colleagues have created what they call a "grit scale" to measure a person's propensity for grit, and they have found that how much grit a person has predicts how well they will do in the future, especially in challenging situations. (Their scale is based on how strongly a person agrees or disagrees with statements like "New ideas and projects sometimes distract me from previous ones," "Setbacks don't discourage me," and "I often set a goal but later choose to pursue a different one.")

In one study, Duckworth and her colleagues assessed new cadets at West Point military academy with her grit scale and then tracked their success at the academy, discovering that the cadets' grit scores predicted whether or not they would make it through their initial and extremely rigorous summer training (during which some cadets drop out). In fact, grit scores predicted their perseverance that summer above and beyond a composite score that West Point had created based on the cadets' high school rank, SAT score, participation in extracurricular activities, and performance on physical aptitude tests. Although grit didn't strongly predict a cadet's grades or physical performance during their time at West Point, it predicted whether or not they made it through that first summer and whether or not they eventually graduated.

In other research, Duckworth has found that grit scores predict which students will do well in the finals of the National Spelling Bee, which soldiers will finish the US Army's rigorous Special Operations Forces selection course, and which students in Chicago public schools will graduate. Privilege—benefits afforded to some people and not others, which include things like wealth, whiteness, and being able-bodied—matters, too, of course: If you consider two kids who each have a lot of potential and grit, but one has more privilege, the privileged one is almost certainly going to fare better because he is given more opportunities and has to overcome fewer challenges. This chapter isn't about privilege, but I think that's important to mention.

It's not that gritty people never quit things, or that they'll happily spend years working on anything you ask them to. Usually, they choose to work hard on things they find innately interesting, and they might quit other things on the way to finding that true passion. So if your kid asks to stop taking ballet, that doesn't necessarily mean she's lacking grit. Likewise, my son's decision to quit the cello wasn't necessarily a harbinger of doom. Grit, as Duckworth wrote in her aptly titled book *Grit*, comes into play when a kid does eventually find a real, true passion—if they have grit, they won't give up on it easily or push it aside to make room for a new dream a few months later.

Grit and motivation are good for parents to focus on for another reason, too: They take the focus away from ability, smarts, and achievement. Research suggests that when parents (and teachers) obsess over ability, smarts, and achievement, they actually *undermine* children's motivation in the process. In a classic study, education researcher Deborah Stipek, now at Stanford University, and her colleagues found that kids who attended academic, achievement-oriented preschools rated their own abilities as lower, had stunted expectations of their own success, and were less motivated than kids who went to more relaxed preschools in which they chose their own activities in a play-based atmosphere. Indeed, *how* we motivate our kids to do the things we want them to do matters. So which approaches should you embrace, and which ones should you eschew? Here's what the science suggests.

Motivation Strategy #1
Encourage kids to try new, fun, *hard* things.

Angela Duckworth's research suggests that grit is built from four components: interest, practice, purpose, and hope. People have grit when they enjoy what they do (interest), have the self-control to engage in regular and deliberate practice to improve their skills (practice), believe that their work matters and has a positive impact on society (purpose), and can remain optimistic in the face of challenges (hope).

Duckworth has two daughters, and as you might imagine, people ask her all the time what she does with them to foster grit. One rule she has created is the Hard Thing Rule: Her kids have to do something fun that also requires deliberate practice, and they can't quit it in the middle of the season or school year. Importantly, too, they have to pick the activity themselves; it can't be parent imposed. By encouraging her kids to try hard things and persevere with them, Duckworth hopes that they will learn to handle and overcome challenges and maybe even develop a life-long passion. "The ultimate goal is to develop a calling—a fun thing that is also a hard thing," Duckworth wrote in *Grit*.

One of Duckworth's daughters chose the viola as her "hard thing," but it doesn't have to be a musical instrument or even a solo activity. It can be any structured extracurricular activity, Duckworth said, that involves having an adult in charge who is not the parent and that is designed to foster interest, practice, purpose, and hope. "If I could wave a magic wand," Duckworth wrote, "I'd have all the children in the world engage in at least one extracurricular activity of their choice, and as for those in high school, I'd require that they stick with at least one activity for more than a year." (This is another moment when I can't help thinking about how privilege shapes grit; extracurriculars can be expensive.)

Duckworth also emphasized to me over the phone one day—ever a multitasker, she talked to me while she was grocery shopping—that it's also important for parents to let kids quit activities at the end of the school year or season if they don't love them, and then try something new, because it can take time for kids to find their passion. "I think when kids are young, they must explore," she said.

Ideally, too, the teacher or coach working with your child should be warm and supportive, and make the learning process fun. For his book *Developing Talent in Young People*, University of Chicago psychologist Benjamin Bloom and his colleagues interviewed 120 individuals who had become especially successful in their fields. He and his team found that many of them had been mentored as young kids by coaches or teachers who made learning feel fun and rewarding.

Extracurriculars can also be great because they lead to what psychologists refer to as "success spirals." When kids have opportunity to achieve something that feels good, that accomplishment instills confidence, which then motivates them and leads to more accomplishments. In his book *The Procrastination Equation*, University of Calgary motivation scientist Piers Steel said that Boy Scouts and Girl Scouts, as well as wilderness programs such as Outward Bound, are exceptionally good instigators of success spirals. Kids remember the success of building fires and setting up tents, and those experiences "gradually build into a narrative that helps a child face the next challenge," he wrote.

Really, though, any challenging extracurricular can start a success spiral, Steel said, as long as it provides "a circle of encouragement and a venue for achievement." He tells the story of a boy who grew up with self-confidence and anxiety problems but for whom everything changed after starting to learn a new martial art. Although the boy struggled with it at first, he eventually earned a yellow belt, which became an iconic accomplishment that his parents brought up whenever he faced a new challenge.

I can't help thinking of my son and his desire to practice the recorder; the early affirmation he received seems to have also started a success spiral. Do I wish his passion were for something other than the recorder? Absolutely. But we all have to start somewhere.

Motivation Strategy #2
Praise effort, not skill or smarts.

You may have heard people use the term *growth mindset* before, which is often contrasted with *fixed mindset*. When people have a growth mindset, they believe that ability and intelligence are largely shaped by effort and hard work. When people have a fixed mindset, they think that ability is instead mostly innate—you are born smart or not, end of story. You may already even know that mindset is in part shaped by how you praise your kids. But it's not all as simple as it sounds, and people often misunderstand the research. So let me unpack the findings and their implications in a bit of detail here.

In one of the most famous studies in the mindset field, psychologist Carol Dweck and her colleague Claudia Mueller invited fifth graders from three public elementary schools—one in the Midwest composed mostly of white kids, and two in the Northeast with mainly Black and Hispanic kids—to participate in a series of studies. First, the researchers gave all the students intelligence tests and told them they'd done well. "Wow, you did very well on these problems. You got [number of problems] right. That's a really high score," they said. Then they praised the students in various ways for their success. One-third of the kids were told "You must be smart at these problems," another third were told "You must have worked hard at these problems," and the last third were given no additional feedback after being told they'd done well.

Next, the researchers asked the students what kinds of problems they would like to do next: Ones that were "pretty easy, so I'll do well" or "problems that I'll learn a lot from, even if I won't look so smart." They found that the kids who had been praised as "smart" were much more likely to request the easy problems, whereas those praised for "hard work" were more likely to choose the challenging problems. The control group was evenly split.

When the students were later given harder problems to do—ones that they did indeed struggle on—those who'd been praised for their smarts were less likely to persist on the problems than those who'd been praised for hard work, and they also said they enjoyed the challenge less. When the researchers listened to the students reporting how well they'd done on the problems to other students, they heard 38 percent of the students who had been praised for being smart *lie* about how well they'd done (saying they'd solved more problems than they actually had), whereas only 13 percent of those in the hard-work group, and 14 percent of the control group, lied.

The findings point to a pretty clear conclusion: When you praise kids for smarts or ability, they become less interested in learning and overcoming challenges and they become more interested in safeguarding their reputation. In a nutshell, they lose motivation and launch into self-protective mode. Those who are praised for working hard, on the other hand, are more likely to embrace challenges and stay motivated.

Why does this happen? As Dweck explained, praising for ability and intelligence primes kids to think of ability as a fixed trait. They either have it or they don't. *If succeeding means I'm smart, then failure must mean I'm dumb*—therefore they avoid failure by avoiding challenges.

If, on the other hand, kids believe that success comes from working hard and overcoming failure (which happens to kids who are praised for their effort), then they come to see failure as useful—a brief, but essential, stumble on the road to success. As Dweck explained in *Mindset*, "In one world [the fixed mindset], effort is a bad thing. It, like failure, means you're not smart or talented. If you were, you wouldn't need effort. In the other world [the growth mindset], effort is what makes you smart or talented."

After hearing everything you shouldn't do when praising your kids, you're probably ready to hear what you should do. It's fairly easy: Praise kids for effort. Say things like *You worked so hard on that drawing. I love it!* And when frustration hits—when your kids (like mine) say things like *I'm not good at the cello*—you can gently push back with something like *Well, you're still learning how to play the cello, so you haven't mastered all the hard things yet*. (*Yet* is a great growth mindset word to have in your vocabulary, because it sends the message that ability changes over time.)

Be sure, also, to *tie effort to outcome*. Many parents, Dweck said, emphasize effort without making the link to success or performance. When your child succeeds because of her hard work and perseverance, that's when you want to be praising her for effort, and you want to make the causal chain apparent: *You are playing that song so well now. It must be because of all the careful practice you've been doing! I love how you spent extra time on the passages that really gave you trouble.* (As Duckworth explained in *Grit,* effective deliberate practice involves reflecting on and focusing in on weaknesses, and setting "stretch goals" that zero in on improving specific aspects of performance.)

To foster a growth mindset in our kids, we have to think about more than just praise, though—we need to be thoughtful in the ways we respond to our kids' failures and successes. Recently, my son did well on a math test "because it was easy," he said. A good grade is nice, of course, but how do I praise for effort if he didn't expend any? What I ended up saying to him was that although I was glad he did well, I was sad to hear that he hadn't been challenged—because when he's challenged, his brain grows, and I really want his brain to keep growing.

It's also not effort alone that we want kids to embrace—it's effective, productive effort. If your daughter comes home with a failing grade on a Spanish test, it's probably not going to help to admonish her to "just study harder next time." Instead, ask her why she thinks she didn't do well and help her brainstorm new strategies so that her efforts will be more effective in the future. (Of course, if she didn't study at all, then you can point out that studying is a necessary part of the learning process.)

Finally, we shouldn't admonish our kids, or ourselves, for sometimes falling into fixed mindsets. As I mentioned earlier, the ideas that ability and intelligence are innate, and that success is tied to intelligence, are deeply embedded in our culture. It takes time (and effort, ha!) to cultivate a growth mindset, and we will never fully overcome our tendency to think in more fixed terms. Dweck admits that she, too, struggles to maintain a growth mindset all the time, and she's been studying mindsets for more than thirty years.

Motivation Strategy #3
Teach strategies to minimize procrastination.

If your child is a procrastinator, join the club. Kids are, in a sense, *natural* procrastinators, and for good reason: In order to complete a complex, long-term task, a person needs to have a well-functioning prefrontal cortex, the part of the brain responsible for planning and focusing. That cortex has to beat out the constant distractions provided by the limbic system, the part of the brain that deals with immediate wants and desires. This is a hard enough feat for adults to achieve, but for kids, it's practically impossible, because their prefrontal cortex hasn't even finished growing and maturing (it doesn't stop growing until they're about twenty-five).

At its core, though, procrastination isn't about time management or even self-control—research suggests it's rooted in negative emotions. We (and our kids) procrastinate because we're bored, because we're scared of the task (scared we might fail, for instance), or because we're frustrated because the job feels too hard. So instead, we turn our attention to things that will provide us with solace or joy—or at least a bit of relief. Cat videos on Twitter. Doughnuts. Facebook.

In one of the first studies to suggest that negative emotions fuel procrastination, researchers at Case Western Reserve University in Ohio made people feel sad or happy by having them read different kinds of stories. Participants in the "sad" condition imagined being a hurried car driver who caused an accident that led to the death of a child, while those in the "happy" condition imagined saving a child's life. Then they asked all the subjects to study in preparation for an intelligence test. They found that the subjects who'd been made to feel upset were more likely than those who felt happy to procrastinate—to play video games or do puzzles instead of study for the test.

In other words, when kids (and adults) feel down, they prioritize making themselves feel better. "It's very frustrating when kids procrastinate because we see it as a very irrational behavior," Duckworth told me, "but it's also rational in the sense that they're just trying to make themselves happy in the moment." And who can blame kids for doing that? I don't know about you, but I do it all the time.

One solution to the procrastination problem is to make a daunting or boring task feel more fun or less scary. Let's say your kid is procrastinating because his homework assignment is terribly boring. Steel, the author of *The Procrastination Equation*, suggested turning it into a game or competition. If your kid read twenty pages for his book report last night in an hour, could he read twenty-two in an hour today? My son took the slowest showers until I challenged him one day to finish a shower in under five minutes. I left an egg timer within his view when he stepped in; he was out in two minutes. (OK, maybe the strategy was a little *too* effective.)

If the task at hand is being put off because it's daunting or scary, on the other hand, then a good strategy might be to make it seem less terrifying. If you can, sit down with your child when the project is first assigned to break it up into smaller, more easily doable steps that are "due" at various points. That way, each task feels less overwhelming, and when the individual parts are completed, it feels like an accomplishment—which fuels confidence and motivation (a success spiral).

Even better, have your child set deadlines with a group of

peers so he feels somewhat accountable and because doing so creates an atmosphere of camaraderie (or commiseration). If it's a final paper, perhaps he sets a deadline for choosing the topic, then another deadline for the outline, then one for an initial rough draft. "The trick is taking the time to acknowledge incremental change, perhaps by recording your performance in a daily log," Steel suggested. (It might help for your kid to make the goals painfully specific, too; instead of "choose the topic" it could be "go to the library, thumb through six books, spend forty minutes doing internet research, and then decide on the topic.")

To give a task more positive meaning and relevance, it may also help for your kids to tie it to a goal. If your daughter aspires to become an architect, explain how doing a good job on this assignment could help her down the line—it will teach her skills that might make it easier for her to get into a college with a good architecture school. As Steel wrote, you want "a string of future goals that you find intrinsically motivating to hook your present responsibilities on to."

Finally, help your kids recognize and eliminate their distractions. Does your child work with his cell phone right next to him, lighting up incessantly? Does he have an email tab open that he checks every three minutes? Sit down with him and brainstorm ways to redesign his environment so he is not bombarded every four seconds with Far More Interesting Things Than Homework. One computer program that Steel recommends is RescueTime, which lets you see what you've been doing with your time and assists with goal setting; SelfControl is another, which blocks social media and email for a certain amount of time. It's fine (and good) to take scheduled breaks, but the external world shouldn't be giving our kids 8,423 unscheduled breaks every single hour.

Motivation Strategy #4
Don't rely too much on rewards.

A few years ago, when my son was struggling with some behavioral issues, my husband and I went to see a psychologist, who recommended that we set up a "points system." Every time our son did things we liked—cleaned his room, helped his sister, said thank you—we would give him a few points, which we would announce and write down. Each point translated into one cent and one minute of screen time. It seemed like a positive way to encourage responsible behavior and manage screen time and an allowance: a triple win. We tried it, and lo and behold, it worked. My son really did start taking more initiative and behaving better.

Soon after, though, I stumbled across articles that warned against the hazards of using rewards as motivators. A 2016 article in *The Atlantic*, "Against the Sticker Chart," warned me that rewarding kids for good behavior "can erode children's innate tendency to help others." *Money* magazine ran a story in 2015 titled "The Hidden Downside to Rewarding Your Kids for Good Behavior." Education guru Alfie Kohn has written an entire book on the subject, *Punished by Rewards*. The concern, which can be traced back to research from the 1970s, is that rewarding kids for being polite, doing chores, or finishing their homework extinguishes their innate desire to do those things down the line. Worse, I read that rewards could make kids callous and manipulative. I imagined my son leering at me: *How much will you pay me not to whack my sister with this flip-flop?*

Faced with this conundrum, I dug into the research myself, and eventually wrote an article for *Slate* on the topic. The headline, written by the editors, was rather provocative: "Go Ahead,

Heap Rewards on Your Kid." My argument, though, was more nuanced. As I wrote, "What I've found after digging into the research is that these blanket condemnations are unwarranted. Rewards can be useful in some situations and inappropriate in others, much like every other parenting tool."

In my piece, I unpacked one of the earliest and most famous studies on rewards, published in 1971 by Edward Deci, a psychologist at the University of Rochester. Deci invited twenty-four subjects, all undergraduate students, to participate one by one in a three-day experiment. On the first day, he introduced them to the cube-based puzzle game Soma, in which players arrange pieces into various shapes. Deci provided them with drawings of configurations and asked his subjects to reproduce them within a period of thirteen minutes while he left the room. The second day of the experiment was much like the first, but for one important detail: Deci offered half the participants one dollar for each configuration they could make within the thirteen-minute time limit, while the other half kept doing puzzles without being rewarded. And on the third day, the subjects were given puzzles again, but no one was offered money. Each day, when Deci left the room, he told the subjects that if they didn't want to do the puzzles, they could "do whatever you like while I am gone," including read magazines that he had left for them. Then Deci would watch behind two-way glass to see how much time they spent on the puzzles.

As you probably guessed, on the second day, the subjects who had been offered money devoted more of their time to doing puzzles. Deci noticed, though, that these incentivized subjects then spent *less* time on the puzzles on the third day, when the rewards had been rescinded, compared with the time they spent on them on the first day. And on that third day, the never-rewarded group spent more time on the Soma puzzles than the previously re-warded group did. What was going on? As Deci concluded, there seemed to be a "decrease in intrinsic motivation for the activity following the experience with monetary rewards."

There are two important things to keep in mind about this study. First, the purported drop in intrinsic motivation on the third day was not statistically significant, which means that we can't be sure the difference wasn't due to chance. Second, Deci centered his study on Soma precisely because, as he explained, "it seemed that most college students would be intrinsically moti-vated to do it." In other words, he was studying how rewards change a person's interest in something they *already find enjoyable*.

Yet "who on earth would think about using rewards if a child was interested in an activity?" asked Virginia Shiller, an assistant clinical professor at the Yale University Child Study Center and author of *Rewards for Kids*, when I interviewed her for my article. "You only think of offering incentives if a child is struggling and resisting." In other words, Deci's findings didn't seem applicable to the situations in which parents offer rewards.

I dismissed Deci's findings back when I wrote that *Slate* article— I just didn't think the evidence supported his claims that rewards are ineffective or dangerous. But after reading more of Deci's work, and thinking more about how menial tasks sometimes make *me* feel, I've revised my thinking.

I think that rewards may undermine interest in activities that can be, on some level, intrinsically gratifying. Even tidying one's room or clearing one's plate from the dinner table can be satisfying—they are things you (or your child) can feel good about doing, because they help to maintain a nice home and they are helpful for the family. I am *constantly* tidying my house, and that's because I like the sense of accomplishment I feel when I'm done, and because I enjoy spending time in a tidy room. (And because, with two kids, if I didn't, we would be living in a sty.) So while tidying might not be all that intrinsically fun in the moment, I get joy out of having *done* it, and I am, therefore, intrinsically motivated to do it. I worry, now, that rewarding kids for tasks like this could make them less interested in doing these things in the future.

In a well-known 1973 study, for instance, Stanford University researchers placed drawing paper and markers in preschool classrooms and watched to see whether the kids used the materials to draw. Then, a few weeks later, they individually invited the kids who had been most interested in drawing into another room to draw for a visitor who was coming to see the school. To some invited students, the researchers promised a reward for drawing. Other students were asked to draw and unexpectedly received the reward after they finished their drawings. And a third group was asked to draw but was never promised or given rewards. Then, a few weeks later, the researchers repeated the first phase of the experiment again—they left markers and paper in the preschool rooms and watched to see whether the children drew. They found that the kids who'd been promised and given a reward for drawing a few weeks earlier had since lost interest in drawing; the reward they had received made the activity less intrinsically interesting.

The problem with using rewards as motivators, Deci said, is that the approach feels *controlling.* People get more satisfaction out of doing things they have chosen to do compared with things they feel they have been manipulated to do. So if I give my son points for cleaning his room, then he will associate cleaning his room with feeling controlled, and he also won't feel the satisfaction of having *chosen* to clean his room. Deci worries, too, that the use of rewards can make kids feel that your love for them is contingent upon what they do or how they act, which is bad for their self-esteem (for more on self-esteem, see chapter 6).

So I'm not as keen on rewards as I used to be, and I've eased up on using them with my kids. They seemed to work while we used them, but I found that when I stopped so aggressively providing rewards, my son did stop doing some of the things he'd been rewarded for doing (such as tidying his room). Once, he even reached down to pick up a piece of trash that had fallen on the floor, then stopped and cocked his head and said, "Would I get points for picking this up?" which I suppose was a perfectly reasonable thing for him to ask, but also kind of made me want to crawl into the trash can myself and stay there.

Deci took care to point out that rewards are, however, OK in certain contexts. If you use them sparingly for things that kids really despise, that's fine. They are also perfectly acceptable, he wrote, as an acknowledgment of hard work after the fact—like when you take your kids out for ice cream on the last day of school, to celebrate how much they learned and how hard they worked. But saying *I'll take you out for ice cream if you get all As on your report card* is another story; that, again, is using a reward as a motivator.

If you're reading this after having rewarded your kids for years, don't fret: You have not ruined them for life. Kids are resilient, and it's possible to recalibrate their internal motivation compass at any age. After we stopped using our points system (we slowly fizzled it out without the kids really noticing), my son did not collapse in a pile of sloth. He very quickly learned to adapt, and we found other, noncontingent ways to manage his screen time and allowance. And I do think rewards can sometimes be useful in a way that naysayers rarely acknowledge: Rewards can create good habits, and once a child has good habits, motivation doesn't matter so much anymore, because the behavior becomes automatic. We have seen this with my son: Yes, we initially gave him points to clear his plate, but after a while it just became a habit—something he did every day, no matter what. He still does it today, even though he doesn't get any points.

OK but, some of you may be thinking, *if I stop using rewards, how do I make my kids actually do what I want them to do?*

Deci suggested that instead of pressuring kids or offering rewards, parents should instead encourage kids to do what they need to do, acknowledge their feelings (like *I know you might not want to do this, but I really need your help*), and provide them with explanations and choices (as in, *Would you prefer to clean up the basement, or unload the dishwasher?*). But, Deci wrote, there is no magic wand for getting kids to do what you want them to do. "Motivation must come from within, not from techniques," he wrote in his book *Why We Do What We Do*. "It comes from their deciding they are ready to take responsibility for managing themselves." (Still: To learn some constructive ways to shape behavior, see chapter 8.)

In a classic study published in 1984, Deci's colleague and frequent collaborator Richard Ryan, along with three other colleagues, conducted an experiment with six- and seven-year-old kids who were doing an art project. The researchers wanted to encourage some of these artists to work neatly without inadvertently undermining their motivation to create beautiful art.

In one group of kids, they used controlling language, such as "Be a good boy/girl and don't make a mess with the paints" and "Don't get the colors all mixed up." With a second group of kids, they created expectations by sharing information, saying, "I know that sometimes it's really fun to just slop the paint around, but here, the materials and room need to be kept nice for the other children who will use them." The two approaches had vastly different outcomes: The kids in the latter group spent more time painting, and their paintings were judged by independent judges as being of higher quality than paintings made by the kids who were given controlling instructions. Clearly, how we motivate our kids really matters—and the less controlling our efforts feel, the more creative and motivated our children will become.

So when we are less controlling with our kids, they may be less likely to immediately comply with our requests—but more likely to develop intrinsic motivation. In the long run, we plant important seeds that may grow and flourish over a lifetime.

....

KEY POINTS

....

1. Encourage your kids to try fun, challenging activities. Don't let them immediately quit.
2. Praise for effort, not skill or smarts. Tie kids' successes to their effort, too.
3. Make daunting or boring tasks seem less scary and more fun. Minimize distractions.
4. Use rewards sparingly.

CHAPTER 3

· · · · · · · · · · · · · · · ·

"You're Dumb and Ugly!"

How to Raise Kids Who Don't Bully—and Who Help Those Who Are Bullied

A T THE CHILD Mind Institute's 2019 spring luncheon, a fundraising event held in a swanky space on Park Avenue in Manhattan, hundreds of well-dressed benefactors sipped iced tea as actress and writer Ali Wentworth moderated a panel discussion. "There is a whiff of unkindness and corruption in our society right now—and I feel like my fear is that our children are losing a sense of compassion and empathy and kindness," Wentworth said as she introduced the topic of discussion, "Raising Kinder Kids." The two panelists onstage were Angela Santomero, the creator and executive producer of the shows *Blue's Clues* and *Daniel Tiger's Neighborhood*, and psychologist Rachel Busman, senior director of the Child Mind Institute's Anxiety Disorders Center.

For the better part of an hour, the three women discussed strategies for fostering kindness at home while the audience nodded along. Then, as dessert was served, Wentworth opened the floor to audience questions. Out of the five questions attendees asked, four centered on bullying. "What should I do if other kids aren't nice to my child?" one mother asked. "How should I talk to my kids about other people's lack of kindness?" inquired another. And then: "If my son is being bullied, should I call the bully's parents, and if so, what should I say to them?"

Listening to these questions, I was struck by the fact that although this was supposed to be a discussion about what parents can do to raise kinder kids, the parents in the room were focused on what they should do when *other people's kids* aren't kind. A woman sitting next to me, who worked at the Child Mind Institute, picked up on the dynamic, too: After the fourth question, we exchanged looks. "Why is it that everyone is assuming that their child isn't the one doing the bullying?" she whispered to me.

When I got home and dug into the research, I realized that what I had observed was evidence of a widespread phenomenon. Parents often worry that their kids will be bullied—a 2017 national survey found that US parents rated being bullied as the biggest health concern they had regarding their kids, above drug use and internet safety—but they woefully underestimate the possibility that their kids could do any bullying. When researchers at the University of New Hampshire surveyed kids and parents, they found that 31 percent of fifth graders admitted to teasing or picking on others, but that only 11 percent of their parents thought their kids ever did such things. The parents of kids who bullied were especially unlikely to suspect a problem: When the researchers talked to the subgroup of students who had admitted to picking on peers, they found that only 2 percent of those kids' parents were aware of their children's behavior. Parents of bullies, in other words, are among the least likely to think that their kids are being mean.

Look, I get it: I don't want to entertain the notion that my children could ever bully, either. #Notmykids, right? But our country's bullying statistics suggest that we all need to open our eyes. A 2014 meta-analysis of eighty studies estimated that about one in three twelve-to-eighteen-year-olds engages in traditional bullying—defined as deliberate, repeated harm inflicted onto others who can't defend themselves—while nearly one in six engages in cyberbullying via digital devices.

If this sounds high, consider that there are many ways kids can bully, and that bullies come in all shapes and sizes. "The way we usually talk about bullying to our children is unrealistic," wrote parenting educator Rosalind Wiseman in her book *Queen Bees and Wannabes*, "because most bullying experts talk about it as if one kid is 100 percent evil and the other is 100 percent innocent." In reality, kids can frequently bully, occasionally bully, or bully one day and be bullied the next. Some never instigate bullying but still laugh along with the perpetrators. Put another way, bullying is a continuum, and a child's involvement and role can change from day to day.

Bullying is not, of course, a new phenomenon—there are references to it in centuries-old books including *Jane Eyre*. (I'm not quite that old, but I sure remember being called "four eyes" in elementary school due to my thick glasses.) Over the past two decades, though, bullying has been getting a lot more attention. That's in part because of what happened on April 20, 1999, when two teenage boys opened fire in the cafeteria of Columbine High School in Colorado. Although the boys' actions didn't appear to be a response to bullying, the massacre incited serious concern over the emotional health of American teens, and suddenly everyone was talking about just how common and devastating bullying is.

Yet even though bullying has gotten a lot of attention in recent years, and we think of bullying as an obvious, easily understood concept, research suggests that many kids who bully don't even realize that what they are doing is harmful. They don't always recognize how their behavior affects others; they sometimes think everyone's just having fun. This means that the kinds of conversations parents have with their kids about bullying can help bridge crucial gaps and reduce the chance that their kids will unintentionally hurt their peers.

WHAT BULLYING IS—AND ISN'T

If your kid isn't invited to a birthday party, that's a bummer, but it isn't bullying. If a student in your daughter's class says something mean to her once, that's not bullying, either. And if your child gets a C on a test, or gets sent to the principal for acting out in class, that doesn't mean his teacher is a bully. Bullying has to be repeated, deliberate harassment or abuse—as Wiseman explained, it involves "stripping someone of their dignity and their inherent worth" by attacking them repeatedly based on a perceived inherent trait (which could be something as simple as being too quiet, or it could be rooted in their ethnicity, religion, gender identity, or sexual orientation). Crucially, bullying involves a perceived power dynamic—it's one child in a position of social or physical power picking on another child with less.

Typically, kids bully because they are trying to impress their peers, gain power and attention, and boost their position on the social ladder. (But as I'll explain in a minute, that's not the whole story, because kids who bully often have difficult home lives that make them crave power among their peers in the first place.) In her book *Sticks and Stones*, journalist Emily Bazelon explained the various ways bullying can boost social stature. "Maybe they're after a laugh from another kid they want to impress, or induction into a clique; maybe they want to publicly distance themselves from a friend they sense is now seen as a loser," she wrote. There are plenty of ways in which meanness and aggression can be rewarded in social situations. Have you ever watched kids at recess?

Some bullying, though, isn't overt or physical. Among girls especially, bullying can be entirely social, involving passive-aggressive slights like exclusion and rumor spreading. (Many of you have probably heard of, if not seen, the movie *Mean Girls*, which is all about this kind of bullying and was based on Wiseman's book.) In a 2007 study, former Duke University psychologist and neuroscientist Kristina McDonald and her colleagues videotaped sixty fourth-grade girls as they talked with a close friend. Over a period of just fifteen minutes, the girls engaged in thirty-six episodes of gossip, on average, involving twenty-five different people.

Social bullying often starts early. My friend Celia—you may remember her daughter Ella from chapter 1, who was less than fazed by her great-grandmother's death—told me about a bully who targeted Ella in preschool. This little girl, who was five at the time, policed and controlled Ella's—and other kids'—social interactions. She dictated who could play what, when, and with whom, and often engineered playgroups to exclude specific kids. *In preschool*. "When I was there for my parent observation day, she kicked Ella out of the group that was playing on the playground, and then when Ella found a boy to play with and was happily digging in the dirt with him, this girl came over and took over the game and again pushed Ella out. It was kind of stunning," Celia recalls.

Why are girls so often mean to each other? Again, it's all about power and social status. As Wiseman explained in her book, girls want to be accepted and to have good standing within their group of friends, to the point where they may turn against each other to maintain or boost their position. Girls may also believe that "it's more important to maintain a relationship at all costs, instead of realizing that how they are treated within that relationship should be the basis for whether or not they stay in it," Wiseman wrote.

Kids may also be cruel to one another because they aren't sure how to express their anger in a direct and healthy way, so instead they communicate it passively, through things like revenge and backstabbing. In some situations, too, kids may feel uncomfortable about the social bullying they're observing but be too scared to speak up about it. "When a group decides to exclude one girl, for example, many of the girls in the group are likely to know that it's wrong and even feel uncomfortable about it, but they won't necessarily have the language to express it or the assertiveness skills to put a stop to it," wrote child and adolescent psychotherapist Katie Hurley in her book *No More Mean Girls*.

Cyberbullying is another scary phenomenon these days, especially for parents (like me!) who struggle to keep up with the latest social media and technology trends. The Cyberbullying Research Center defines cyberbullying as willful and repeated harm inflicted through the use of digital media. But instead of thinking about cyberbullying as a terrifying new beast, it's better conceived of as garden-style bullying happening in a different context. Given how common devices are these days, cyberbullying is certainly worrying, but if it's any consolation, it still appears to be less common than traditional bullying: In 2018, more than two-thirds of US teens said that bullying was still more likely to happen in person than online, according to a Pew Research Center survey. Bullying researchers have found that when schools effectively tackle regular bullying and teach emotional regulation skills, cyberbullying tends to decrease, too. And one upshot about cyberbullying is that it is easier to document and prove to school administrators or authorities, because there's usually a built-in digital footprint.

Certainly, though, there are aspects of cyberbullying that make it scarier than the old-school kind. Traditional bullying typically happens at school, which means that it stops once kids walk through their front door at the end of the school day. Cyberbullying, on the other hand, can happen anytime and anywhere, as long as your child has access to a device. And while spoken words are fleeting—they only linger in the air for as long as it takes to say them—cruel texts and Facebook comments can last forever, re-traumatizing a kid every time those words are seen (and shared). The audience for a cyberbully can also be vastly larger than for a face-to-face bully, which can strengthen the impact.

THE LONG-TERM EFFECTS OF BULLYING

If you're tempted to think of bullying as an innocuous rite of passage—something kids should learn to shrug off because "boys will be boys" or some such—please reconsider. Being bullied can be incredibly scarring, increasing a kid's risk for depression, anxiety, and dangerous self-harm later in life. When researchers surveyed young LGBT adults as part of a 2011 study, they found that those who were frequently bullied in middle school and high school were more than five times as likely as other young LGBT adults to have attempted suicide at least once.

Lori, a friend of mine, recently told me about the bullying she suffered throughout elementary and middle school. She was called names, she was spat at, and she was punched. "Most of the bullying happened on the school bus, and the kids who were doing it were popular, so they drew in other people to pile on me. It felt like bullying me was a shortcut to the cool kids' group," she said. When Lori told other adults about it, including teachers and her parents, they essentially ignored it, telling her she was making too big of a deal about it. "In hindsight it felt like gaslighting before gaslighting was a thing—I thought I was the ugliest, least appealing person on the planet, and I must deserve it," she said. Although Lori got through the experience—she is now forty-four and a successful communications manager—she said that the bullying has shaped her life in pernicious ways. "I never realized until recently how much the bullying and lack of support affected me even as an adult—my self-esteem, confidence, staying with someone who treated me really badly for far too long," she said.

Another friend of mine, Claire, now forty-seven, told me she was bullied to the point where she thought she was inherently unlovable. Her bullies spread rumors about her, threw food at her in the cafeteria, and shoved maxi-pads in her face. It created a vicious cycle of self-loathing that has "taken me my whole life to dismantle," Claire said. "Even now I have to consciously make the effort not to frame situations in terms of that whole thing."

This is all terribly depressing, but there's some good news to consider, too. Bullying is often characterized as a school issue, because, yes, it often happens at school. But parents are important, too. Research suggests that what happens at home, and how parents talk to their kids about bullying and anger, can influence whether or not kids act aggressively toward other kids. We can also teach our kids how to respond to bullying in ways that may deter it in the future.

Anti-Bullying Strategy #1
Talk about bullying.

In the powerful 2013 book *Bullying Under Attack*, teenagers and young adults around the country shared their first-person bullying accounts. Some of the writers had engaged in bullying themselves, and many hinted that their home lives had been unhappy. One bullying teen mentioned a father who rarely spoke to him except to scold him.

It makes sense that kids who bully might have less than ideal home lives—bullying is primarily about getting and maintaining power, and if kids don't have power at home, they'll be hungry to acquire it elsewhere. Research suggests, for instance, that when kids don't get the supervision and attention they need at home, they are more likely to bully others. Bullies are also more likely than non-bullies to have seen or been victims of domestic violence. Seeing or experiencing violence starts to normalize it, inciting kids to think of it as an acceptable way to solve problems.

Ultimately, the parents who are least likely to end up with kids who bully others are those who adopt an *authoritative* parenting style—they set boundaries and rules, but they also listen to their kids, negotiate with them, and explain their reasoning rather than barking orders. Research has shown that *authoritarian* parents, on the other hand, who are more distant and treat their children with less respect and independence, are much more likely to wind up with kids who have trouble controlling their aggression. (For more on these parenting styles, see chapter 8.) If you're there for your kids, regularly engage with them (put your phones down when you do!), and respond to them with warmth and compassion, your kids will have a much easier time engaging with their peers respectfully.

Even so, you'll need to talk with your kids about bullying on a regular basis. Bullying is something that seems so obviously bad that parents feel like they don't need to directly address it. But the fact is, some kids really don't "get it" and need extra guidance on this front. Jan Urbanski, a researcher who oversees the Olweus Bullying Prevention Program at Clemson University's Institute on Family and Neighborhood Life, said that when she runs programs in schools, she often interacts with kids who really seem not to recognize that their behavior is bullying. These students may engage in what they think of as harmless teasing and assume everyone's having fun, failing to read the signals to the contrary.

In a 2003 study, researchers in Spain and Italy gave 179 kids between the ages of nine and thirteen a questionnaire that assessed whether they tended to be bullies, victims of bullying, or neither. Then they showed the kids a series of cartoons that depicted bullying and asked them questions about how they would feel if they were the ones doing the bullying and how that bullying might affect the kids being targeted. A whopping 70 percent of the kids who tended to bully, they found, weren't even aware that bullying behavior was hurtful. Other research suggests that 15 to 20 percent of kids actually *admire* bullies and think that kids being bullied deserve what they get.

So explain to your child exactly what bullying is, the various ways it can manifest, and why it's not OK for them to do it. Make sure they understand that it's less about their intention than about the other person's interpretation. If your kid repeatedly teases someone else, even if they don't mean any harm, it's bullying if the other kid feels powerless and is hurt by it. (If you're the type of parent who teases your kids in good fun, then you need to make extra sure to explain this—if you tease, your kids will try it, too, and they may not be as adept at perceiving the boundaries between harmless teasing and harmful taunting.)

Research has also found that some kids who bully are not as skillful as non-bullies at putting themselves in other people's shoes—they struggle with what is called *theory of mind*, or perspective taking. To help teach this skill, ask your kids to imagine how other people are feeling. If you're watching a movie or TV show together, pause it every so often and say, "How do you think that character feels right now? What just happened to her and what do you think that feels like?" If you stumble upon a sibling argument or a fight that erupts during a playdate, do the same thing. "I know you're upset right now, but let's think for a minute: Why do you think your friend might be sad?"

It's also helpful to give your kids a framework for how to respond when they see bullying happen. Many parents advise their children to do nothing—to stay out of it as much as possible. This is well-intentioned, but it's actually bad advice. As part of the Youth Voice Research Project, researchers surveyed nearly twelve thousand fifth through twelfth graders about the kinds of interventions that did and did not stop bullying from happening. In a preliminary analysis, 87 percent of students said that doing nothing either did not help or actively made the bullying worse. Of course, your kid doesn't have to swoop in on a white horse and challenge a bully, which can be hard (not to mention dangerous) to do. Reporting the incident to a teacher afterward can be helpful, but depending on the school climate and how responsive teachers are, a child might not always want to do this, either.

So what should you tell your child to do? One productive approach is for kids to reach out to and be kind to victims after a bullying incident—to sit with them at lunch, for instance. When I was in high school, one popular girl in my class went out of her way to reach out to other kids who were socially ostracized and bullied. I noticed and remembered her kindness, and I know it helped. In the Youth Voice Research Project, kids who had been bullied said that the two most helpful things their peers had done to support them were to listen to them and spend time with them. Being kind to the person being bullied may also deter future bullying: When a bully sees other kids being nice to their target, they sometimes stop, because they realize their behavior might get pushback and is not having the intended ostracizing effect.

As a parent, then, talk to your kids about being good bystanders—if they aren't comfortable speaking up in the moment, explain that they can still make a difference by supporting bullying victims at other times and in other ways. Having these conversations can really help: In a 2018 study, researchers watched as parents advised their fourth- and fifth-grade kids about what they should do when they see bullying happen. Later, the researchers observed these kids at school during bullying situations to see what they actually did. The kids of parents who'd advised them to reach out and support bullying victims were much more likely than other kids to do just that.

Anti-Bullying Strategy #2
Teach your kid about anger.

Society constantly pressures girls to suppress anger and other so-called masculine emotions. "Boys will be boys," we hear when boys get upset, yet girls who raise a stink are labeled as "dramatic," "aggressive," or even "hysterical." Girls are taught to be seen but not heard, to keep big feelings inside, and to shake aggressive emotions off without expressing them—which is one reason why so much girl-on-girl conflict is unhealthy, indirect, and passive-aggressive.

To push back against these expectations, we as parents need to talk to our kids about feelings, including anger—label them, discuss them, allow them, as I explained in chapter 1. This may sound silly—aren't kids going to learn about feelings even if we don't talk about them constantly?—but as Katie Hurley explained in *No More Mean Girls*, "Many school-age and middle school girls struggle to name more than two or three feelings." We do need to talk about feelings, and we need to do it regularly, both with boys and with girls.

We also need to allow our kids to experience their feelings, no matter how big they are, without shaming them. Telling them to "calm down" or "buck up" does the opposite: It teaches kids that expressing their feelings is unacceptable and that they should bury them instead. This doesn't mean that you can't set rules about how and where your kids express their emotions and what kind of expression is appropriate. When my daughter is upset, her go-to response is to scream as loud as possible on the kitchen floor for fifteen minutes; when she starts down that path, I acknowledge and label her feelings—*wow, it sounds like you are really frustrated!*—and then, if she continues, I tell her that her screams are hurting my ears, and if she needs to keep doing it, she has to take it up to her room or step outside.

When kids are angry at their friends and don't know how to handle it, they sometimes also make choices that look a bit like bullying. They may talk about their friends behind their back and do passive-aggressive things to hurt them, like posting mean things about them on social media. To help kids manage their anger appropriately, Wiseman recommends teaching kids an approach she calls SEAL, which they can use whenever they are upset with another person and want a framework for expressing those feelings directly. SEAL has four parts, which I will quote verbatim here:

Stop and Strategize. Breathe, listen, and think about when and where you want to talk to this person. Do you want to do it now or later—or maybe a little bit of both?

Explain. What happened that you didn't like and what do you want?

Affirm. Admit (recognize) anything you did that contributed to the conflict, but affirm your right to be treated with dignity by the other person and vice versa.

Lock. Lock in the friendship, take a vacation, or lock the friendship out.

Anti-Bullying Strategy #3
Know what to do if *your* kid is bullying.

It's never, ever fun when the school principal calls. Last year, our principal phoned to report that my eight-year-old had called another boy a name on the school bus. Although the principal said my son was not the instigator, he nevertheless joined in on the bullying. I was devastated.

The first thing I did when my son got home was to ask him what had happened. This is a good first step, said Amanda Nickerson, director of the Dr. Jean M. Alberti Center for the Prevention of Bullying Abuse and School Violence at the University at Buffalo, because it's important to hear your child's perspective. This doesn't mean you need to accept his or her story at face value—and if you find yourself doing that, do a self-check. Parents desperately want to believe their kids can do no wrong, so we're often too inclined to believe their pleas of "I'm innocent!"

In response to my question, my son first said that he was there when the bullying happened but that he hadn't joined in. (In other words, yep, "I'm innocent.") When I calmly pressed him, though, he admitted he had called the boy names a couple of times.

No matter where you feel blame lies—maybe you decide your kid didn't actually do anything wrong—these conversations are still very important, as they're opportunities to discuss bullying and why it's unacceptable and to explain your expectations as a parent. I told my son that day that I expect him to *always* treat others with dignity and respect. I also went on to explain that even if he is not *trying* to be mean, he needs to be aware that name-calling and teasing can really hurt, and therefore it's not OK. It can be helpful to remind your kids of a time when they were treated this way. *Remember how sad you felt when that boy at camp called you names?*

If your child does engage in bullying, it's also important to consider an appropriate punishment. Nickerson recommends linking the consequences to the situation: If your child was bullying online, perhaps you restrict their internet access for a while. If they bullied during a soccer game, have them sit out the next two games. Consider, too, having them make reparations for their behavior. Nickerson said that when her kids do something bad, she makes them write apology notes in which they take ownership for their behavior and explain what they'll do to make up for it. In my case, I had my son apologize to the bus driver and the boy he bullied, but next time I might have him write a letter, too. And talk to your child about what a true apology is—that it needs to reflect a genuine understanding of what was done that was harmful, and that it doesn't blame the victim or make excuses.

Anti-Bullying Strategy #4
Take action if your kid is being bullied.

If your child tells you he or she is being bullied, first, ask for details. The more specifics you can get about what's going on, the better. (And if there's documentation or evidence you can collect and keep, do that too.) "Understand the context a little bit before you just go in with 'Say no more, I'm flying into the school,'" said psychologist Rachel Busman at that Child Mind Institute luncheon. Sometimes, you'll learn that the situation is more innocuous than it seems—that your kid is just fighting with an old friend, say. Resist the temptation to admonish your child or interject their explanation with advice; the goal is to collect as much information as you can without giving your kid reasons to hold back.

After you hear your child's side of the story, your immediate inclination may be to call the parents of the kid doing the bullying and yell at them. Try not to. Instead, take some deep breaths and think about whether a call like that would be productive. If you don't know the other child's parents, they may be quick to defend their kid and even accuse you or your child of lying, which will only make you more upset. If you do know the parents and you think they would be reasonable, consider talking to them if you think it may help, but wait until you've calmed down.

Sometimes kids feel afraid or ashamed about being bullied and might not open up about what they're going through. Studies suggest that as many as 40 percent of kids who are bullied don't tell any adults about it and that 25 percent don't tell anyone—not even other kids. But you can look for warning signs, which include losing interest in school or sudden grade drops, trouble sleeping or nightmares, and saying they feel sick on school days when they seem healthy. If you see these signs, make time to talk with your child one-on-one in a warm and sympathetic way, and try to do it at a time when you think they'll be receptive. Tell them that you know they may feel scared but that you need to know what's going on so you can work together to identify solutions.

When advising your kid on what to do—and not to do—in response to bullying, my main suggestion is this: Don't tell your child to fight back. There's something so satisfying about the idea of a victim getting his or her revenge on a deserving bully, but real life rarely plays out like *The Karate Kid*. Victims who fight back tend to lose—kids who bully often pick their targets specifically because they are smaller or less physically inclined—and research suggests that many victims who attempt to fight end up getting bullied *more* afterward.

If your child is being cyberbullied, take a screenshot of the evidence (and make sure your kids know how to do this, too). Then advise your child to block and report the bully on the social media platform they are using. Encourage your child to tell you or another trusted adult about any cyberbullying they experience. The organization STOMP Out Bullying (stompoutbullying.org) has a free and confidential live HelpChat Line for young people between the ages of thirteen and twenty-four. The Cyberbullying Research Center (cyberbullying.org) has additional information about cyberbullying and how to handle it.

If your child is in elementary school, and the bullying or cyberbullying seems serious, consider talking to your child's teacher or a school psychologist. (Kids sometimes ask their parents not to get involved, but it's important that you do, Urbanski said—explain to your child that the school can keep the report anonymous if you ask them to and that things could get worse if the school doesn't know.) If your kid is in middle or high school, you might want to go to a trusted teacher or the school psychologist. If you don't get a suitable response, loop in other members of the administration, such as the principal.

When talking to school staff, tell them in detail what has been happening and ask them what steps they can take to resolve the bullying. Together, make a safety plan and put it in writing. A safety plan should include a list of actions that the school staff will take to address the issue—for instance, monitoring specific locations where the bullying tends to occur—as well as a list of actions your child should take if bullying continues. And if your child is really struggling, consider finding him or her a therapist, too.

Anti-Bullying Strategy #5
Encourage your kid's school to fight bullying effectively.

If you're concerned about bullying at your child's school, what can you do to advocate for change? First, make sure the administration knows there's an issue and suggest that they conduct a schoolwide survey to get a handle on the scope of the problem.

If your child's school is responding to bullying in a way that you find counterproductive, talk to teachers or administrators. One thing schools should not do, for instance, is bullying "mediation," which involves sitting bullies and their victims down together to try to work out their conflicts. Mediation can work when people of equal stature are having problems; it doesn't work with kids whose relationship is strained by a power imbalance. Researchers also suggest that schools move away from zero-tolerance punishments like "three strikes and you're out" suspensions and expulsions and respond to bullying with more restorative approaches that attempt to make amends for harm done to the victims.

Unfortunately, if there's a systemic problem, schools really have to dedicate themselves to the issue to fix it. While a handful of school anti-bullying programs are available for schools to implement, research suggests that most of them are only marginally effective, especially in middle and high school. That's because schools all too often implement these programs in a slipshod fashion—they treat them as quick fixes, rather than vehicles for systemic transformation of school culture. (Teachers are often among those who need to change the most: They need to learn to respond to bullying immediately and in the right ways, or else students will assume they don't care.) The challenges here are understandable, though. Teachers are stretched extremely thin, so these programs end up being taught to students piecemeal, without much thought or investment. And those once-a-year bullying assemblies? They're almost certainly useless on their own.

Some research suggests, however, that broader social-emotional learning (SEL) programs—which teach kids about communication, empathy, and social problem-solving, and which can be easier for teachers to implement than anti-bullying programs—can help with certain forms of bullying. In a two-year clinical trial involving thirty-six schools, researchers tested how the SEL program known as Second Step affected bullying. They found that students in Illinois schools who used the program were 56 percent less likely to say they'd experienced homophobic name-calling and 39 percent less likely to say they'd experienced sexual harassment compared with kids in schools that didn't use the program. A 2011 meta-analysis also found that kids who participated in SEL programs scored 11 percent higher on standardized tests, which suggests that when kids feel safe and supported at school, they learn better, too. A handful of evidence-based SEL programs are available for schools; the nonprofit Collaborative for Academic, Social, and Emotional Learning maintains lists of these programs on their website, CASEL.org, and you can point school administrators to the site for inspiration. If cyberbullying is a problem at your kid's school, you might also want to talk to administrators about weaving some instruction on digital citizenship into the curriculum.

Bullying rarely goes away on its own, but when schools take the issue seriously and implement evidence-based programs and approaches, they can transform school culture. And in schools where students treat one another with respect and compassion, they learn better, develop stronger bonds, and end up leading happier, healthier lives.

....

KEY POINTS

....

1. Talk to kids about what bullying is, why it's bad, and what they should do when they see it.
2. Give kids tools to manage and communicate their anger effectively.
3. If your child is bullying, talk to them about why it's not OK and instigate appropriate consequences.
4. If your child is being bullied, collect information and, if needed, work with the school to create a safety plan.
5. Talk to your child's school administrators about effective anti-bullying policies and prevention programs.

CHAPTER 4

· · · · · · · · · · · · · · · · ·

"I'm Telling the Truth, Dammit!"

How to Raise Kids Who Won't Lie or Swear—
or At Least, Not When It Matters

I VAGUELY REMEMBER MY son's first crawl, his first steps, and the first time he said "mama." But I really remember the first time he swore.

It was shortly after he had turned three. He was playing with his toys in the other room, and I'm guessing he was getting frustrated, because for the zillionth time, his zoo animals weren't fitting in his zoo truck. Suddenly I heard: "Fuck it chuck it!"

I froze.

My first thought was: *Did I just hear what I think I heard?* Then I wondered: *Is it bad if I laugh? Because that was hilarious.* Finally I got around to musing: *Shit, what do I do now?* I surmised that he didn't really know what he was saying—that he knew from the (of course very few!) times he had heard the f-bomb uttered by me that it was an emotive word and that he was feeling frustrated and had decided to try it out. But I guessed that he didn't know it was a *bad* word and that he certainly didn't know its literal meaning. (I don't know where the "chuck it" came from, but doesn't it perfectly capture how you feel when you're frustrated with an object? Fuck it chuck it indeed!)

When my daughter was around the same age, she began to experiment with lying and deception. More often than not, it involved candy. Our house rule is that the kids can have candies from their Halloween baskets at dessert time but they can't just wolf down Snickers bars whenever they please. Yet on more than one occasion, my daughter has snuck candy from her basket up to her room, and then lied to me when I've asked her about it. Once, when I checked on her in the middle of the night, I found her sleeping happily atop five empty candy wrappers, chocolate smeared all over her face.

When it comes to kids behaving in unsavory ways, there are a few things you should know. "Don't think you can prevent swearing—you're doomed to failure if you think that's going to happen," said Timothy Jay, a psychologist at the Massachusetts College of Liberal Arts and the author of *What to Do When Your Kids Talk Dirty.* "We've recorded *fuck* and *shit* in every age range that we've studied." (Also, despite what your parents may say, people don't swear any more now than they did thirty-five years ago, according to Jay's research.) Likewise, if your kid has been lying, "That's very, very normal," said Kang Lee, a developmental psychologist at the University of Toronto who has been studying lying in children for twenty years.

Kids emulate their parents, and let's face it, we aren't always paragons of politeness and honesty. But even if kids don't hear swear words or lies from you, they'll hear them at school, on TV, or at the recreation center—and then, yes, they'll try them out at home. By the time kids enter school, they know about thirty to forty offensive words. Studies also find that half of all kids start lying around age two or three, and that most kids have told their first lie by the age of four. As one paper concluded, "The emergence of lying as a behavior is a milestone of children's normal development."

So yes, lying and swearing are both typical kid behaviors—and sometimes, they're even requested and rewarded (like when we ask little Annie to pretend to love the ugly sweater Grandma just gave her for her birthday). Of course, we don't want our kids to go overboard, lying left and right and constantly dropping f-bombs. But these bad habits aren't all bad; they're signs that our kids are, well, growing up.

LYING AND SWEARING MEAN YOUR CHILD'S BRAIN IS WORKING

Although we think of lying and swearing as Terrible, Horrible, No Good, Very Bad Things, the fact that kids try them out means that their brains are developing normally. Kids can only curse, after all, if they can successfully learn new words and pick up on social conventions.

And when kids lie, it's not a sign that they're on the road to delinquency—it's a sign that they are developing important psychological skills. One is theory of mind, the ability to recognize that other people can have different beliefs or feelings from you. In order to fib, your child has to realize that although he knows full well that he broke the vase, you do not (at least, not yet). In fact, the ability to deceive is considered one of the chief skills associated with having fully developed theory of mind skills. (One study even found that after initially honest three-year-olds were taught to improve their theory of mind skills, they immediately began lying.) Lying also requires executive function, a complex set of skills that includes working memory, inhibitory control, and planning capabilities. Your kid has to hide the truth, plan up an alternate reality, tell you about it, and answer any follow-up questions in a way that's consistent with his story. Good job, kid!

Researchers say that lie-telling in kids progresses through three levels: The first "primary" lies happen around two or three, when kids are first able to make deliberately untrue statements. These lies tend to be infrequent. But then, around age three or four, kids tend to reach the "secondary" lie stage, where they much more readily lie to cover their butts. Then, between the ages of seven and eight, kids can tell "tertiary" lies, in which they become frightfully adept at maintaining the plausibility of their lies in response to questioning. These tertiary lies require not just theory of mind but also good memory and self-regulation skills (after all, they have to stay calm and poised even when they're worried you're onto them).

So kids who lie are demonstrating important cognitive skills. But paradoxically, they also lie in part because they don't have great cognitive skills. Children are emotional and impulsive—they struggle with inhibitory control, one aspect of executive function—which is why, despite your clear instructions not to, they will continue to use their forks as drumsticks and hit their siblings. Then, to cover up their mistakes, they'll lie to avoid getting punished. In other words, kids lie because they can't help defying you, and they don't want to suffer the consequences. Really, can you blame them?

There are, of course, several types of lies, and research suggests that each kind develops a little differently. The first kind of lie that kids tell is the type that keeps them out of trouble, usually to cover up transgressions. In a classic 1989 study—you'll see this general setup in a handful of studies I mention in this chapter, so pay attention—researchers took individual three-year-olds into a room equipped with a hidden video camera and a one-way mirror and sat them facing away from a table. The researchers told the children they were going to put a surprise toy on the table and instructed the kids not to look at it. Then the researchers left the room. They returned either once the children had peeked at the toy (most did) or after five minutes had gone by, and they then asked the kids whether they had peeked. They found that 38 percent of the kids who had snuck a peek lied, assuring the researchers that they hadn't looked at the toy. In a similarly designed 2002 study coauthored by Lee, 54 percent of three-year-olds lied about peeking, whereas more than three-quarters of kids aged four to seven did. Apparently, kids in early elementary school *really* don't like to get into trouble.

Kids also lie for personal gain, like when they tell their friends they are strong enough to pick up a car or that they always get to eat cookies for dinner. These are called *instrumental* lies, and because they are slightly more sophisticated than the hiding-transgressions lies, they often appear a little later, around kindergarten.

And then there are the "white" lies, which kids tell to be polite or benefit others. Research suggests that self-serving lies tend to become less and less common as kids get older, but that some white lies become more and more common with age. In a 2019 study, Victoria Talwar and her colleagues at McGill University and the City University of New York engaged one-on-one with more than a hundred four-year-olds in ways that set them up to lie. Then they did the same things with the kids two years later. The children, they found, were more likely to lie to cover their butts at age four than they were at six, but they were much more likely to tell certain kinds of white lies when they were six than when they were four. White lies require rather complex thinking skills, because kids have to empathetically understand another person's state of mind and know what they need to do to shape that state of mind. They have to know that although they definitely didn't want wool socks for Christmas, Aunt Meg's feelings would be hurt if they actually told her that.

And, of course, kids learn how to lie (and swear, for that matter) because parents do it all the time—in fact, we often *encourage* white lies. One year during holiday break, my husband and I decided to take the kids to an indoor trampoline park for the day. But when we woke up that morning, our daughter had a fever. My husband told our son that he would still take him, but that it would be best to tell his sister they were just running errands, lest she feel sad for missing out. My son was shocked by the suggestion. "But, Daddy, that's a lie!" he said, mortified. My husband felt sheepish afterward, but I'm pretty sure they still told the fib (or at least, told a lie of omission). The things you'll do to avoid a tantrum.

Still, even though swearing and lying are normal and sometimes socially acceptable, you don't want your kids deceiving and cursing at you all the time. Here are some research-backed strategies you can use to set language limits and encourage your kids to be honest when they need to be.

Lying and Swearing Strategy #1
Identify causes, and model the behavior you want to see.

First, let's talk about swearing. If your kid has developed a nasty potty mouth, you might be wise to try to identify the source of the bad language and limit it. Has he been sneak-watching *The Wire*? Binge-reading Hunter S. Thompson? Perhaps it's more likely that he's been overhearing *you* as you talk about your mother-in-law. Kids have an amazing knack for not listening when you want them to, but the reverse is true, too: They are often keenly paying attention when you think they aren't. And ultimately, "A parent who swears a lot," said Tovah Klein, director of the Barnard College Center for Toddler Development and the author of *How Toddlers Thrive*, "will have a hard time getting her child not to."

The same goes for lying: Kids do as we do, not as we say. You might be thinking to yourself, *I never lie in front of my kids!* But in all honesty (ha), you probably do. Maybe they've seen you fib to a telemarketer that they have the wrong number, or tell your friend that you absolutely loved her woefully under-salted vegan chili. It isn't always bad when kids see you fib, but it's worth having a conversation with your child about different kinds of lies— why it's OK to tell certain kinds of lies (to protect other people's feelings, say), but not other kinds of lies (such as for personal gain). But again, be sure you practice what you preach, because parents often lie for personal gain in front of their kids, too— and even encourage their kids to do the same. If you've ever told your child to fib about his age to get into the museum for free, you're essentially telling him that lying for personal gain is OK.

Interestingly, too, kids are more likely to lie if they have older siblings. Again: They learn by example.

Research confirms that kids—especially school-aged ones—will lie more after they've seen adults lie. In a 2014 study, University of California psychologists Chelsea Hays and Leslie Carver performed an experiment with nearly two hundred kids aged three to seven. First, to half the kids, the experimenter told a lie. She said, "There is a huge bowl of candy in the next room, want to go get some?" Then, once in that room, she confessed she had been lying. The other half of the kids were told there was a fun game in the next room, with no mention of candy and no lie.

Next, the experimenter asked each of the kids to play a guessing game. The kids had their backs to her while she played the sound of a toy, then the kids were asked to guess what the toy was. Right after playing the sound but before the kids were given the chance to guess, the experimenter said she had to run out to grab something and told each child not to peek at the toy while she was gone. When she left, a hidden camera watched to see what the children did, and the experimenter returned ninety seconds later. She asked the children if they had peeked at the toy while she was gone.

The researchers found that school-aged kids in particular—those between the ages of five and seven—who had been lied to at the beginning of the experiment were much more likely to peek, and also much more likely to lie about having peeked, than school-aged kids who had not been deceived. (Preschoolers did not differ in terms of peeking or lying based on whether the adult had lied to them, perhaps because they were too young to understand exactly what was happening.) "Parents and teachers sometimes use lying as a way of controlling children's behavior or emotions," the authors wrote, and "this strategy may have deleterious effects on children's own honesty."

Kids are also more likely to lie if they observe an adult lying and getting away with it, even if that adult wasn't lying to them. In a 2019 study, kids were split into groups and watched researchers do various things. Some of the kids watched researchers tell lies to their friends, while other kids watched them fess up and tell the truth to a friend about something bad that had happened. Then some kids saw the researchers being yelled at for lying or for telling the truth. Other kids saw the researchers get rewarded for lying or for telling the truth.

In the next part of the study, the researchers had the kids play the don't-peek guessing game again. And guess what happened? Those who saw the adult tell the truth and get rewarded for it— and those who saw the adult lie and then get punished for it— were much less likely to lie. The various conditions didn't affect whether or not the kids peeked, but they did affect whether the kids lied about peeking. Clearly, kids notice when other people lie (or tell the truth), and they make important inferences—and modify their own behavior—based on how those people were affected by their dishonesty (or honesty).

These findings have obvious implications for how we should respond to our kids when they tell the truth, even if that truth is unsavory: We should praise them for being honest, even when we are unhappy about every other aspect of the situation. Last year, my son accidentally broke a night-light he had been surreptitiously playing with at a friend's house, and he confessed to it right away. Although I was upset about the broken light, I knew it was an opportunity to reinforce the virtues of honesty, so I thanked him for telling me the truth and told him it was OK. Later on, after he and I had calmed down, I talked with him more about the importance of also respecting other people's property, and that it would have been better if he hadn't played with the light in the first place. But that initial reaction—in which I rewarded his honesty—was important and, hopefully, sent him the message that honesty is the best path forward. Telling the truth can be hard—and it's far harder when we are immediately punished for it.

Lying and Swearing Strategy #2
React calmly, ask questions, and explain how words can hurt.

When you hear your kids curse, by far the best way to respond is *calmly*—if you respond at all. With young kids, "the less attention paid, the better," Klein explained. "When children get a big rise out of the adults, that can solidify the use of the word because the attention was big—*Wow, that really bothers Daddy!*" If you don't react, the words tend to disappear faster.

Still, sometimes the bad words linger even when you ignore them. Then what? "The worst thing is to yell or scream," Jay said—and please don't wash your kids' mouths out with soap, he added. If your child is young—a toddler or preschooler—you could first try to understand why your kid used the word in the first place. "Say, 'Hey, that's an interesting word—where did you hear that? Do you know what it means?'" Jay suggested. Then proceed in one of two ways. One option is to tell him it's not a word he should use at home. But that approach can backfire, because what you've just done is given your kid a weapon that he can fire at you when he's upset or wants your attention.

A potentially better approach is to allow your child to use the swear word within limits. "Tell her, 'Some people don't like that word, but in your room you can say it anytime,'" Klein said. (Of course, different rules can apply to different words, as I'll explain more in a minute; if the word is truly offensive, you can set stricter limits, like *We never say that word anywhere, because of how much it can hurt people.*)

Be sure, too, that you are distinguishing *anger* from *cursing.* It's important for kids to know that the emotions they feel are OK; it's how they express or deal with them that matter. If your kids tend to curse when they're angry, acknowledge their feelings—*You must be so mad!*—but discuss more appropriate ways for them to express their rage. *It's perfectly fine for you to feel upset, but you can only use that word in your room.*

If your kid is old enough (say, over the age of six or seven), you might also try explaining why curse words can be offensive. "Try to get them to think about how that word sounds to somebody else," Jay said. You can point out to your kids that other people will form impressions of them based on the language they use, so if people find their language rude or offensive, they might get judged, and not in a good way.

Ultimately, Jay suggested that parents not necessarily eradicate bad words from a child's vocabulary—that, he said, can be an impossible task—but instead teach a kind of "etiquette" of offensive language, so that your kids understand what kinds of language can be used in what contexts. It's also important, of course, to teach kids what kinds of bad language are *never* acceptable. For instance, if your kids use a word or phrase that is discriminatory or abusive (such as a racial slur), have a (calm) conversation with them about why that word or phrase hurts other people and why it's never OK to say. And try your best not to shame your child in the process—often, kids use language without having any idea of their weight or meaning. (If they *keep* using the words after you've had a serious conversation, though, then you might want to consider appropriate consequences.)

Also, go over your child's school handbook together and discuss their school's language rules. In school settings, federal law prohibits language that constitutes sexual harassment as well as language that constitutes racial or gender discrimination. Have a sit-down conversation with your kids about what these terms mean and why they are illegal.

Lying and Swearing Strategy #3
React calmly and emphasize the importance of honesty.

When you catch your child in a lie, try to stay calm. "Point out what he has just done, and tell him what you expect him to do, which is to tell the truth regardless—and tell him why it's important to tell the truth," Lee said. Talk about how it's important for family members to trust one another, and that honesty is essential for strong, loving relationships.

It's also crucial, as mentioned earlier, not to get mad at your kid when he does tell the truth. Parents very often say things like *I promise I won't get mad if you just say what happened*, and then what do we do? We immediately get mad at them for telling us what happened. This teaches kids that truth-telling gets punished. They'd be better off lying.

When our kids do lie to cover their butts, we should also separate the lie from the misdeed. Address the fact that your kid broke the TV, and address the fact that she lied about it—but don't conflate the two, because they're different. Talk to your child about these two transgressions individually, and perhaps at separate times. And again: If your kid broke the TV but was actually honest about it, you should, hard as it may be, commend her for her truth-telling even though you're ready to kill her about the broken TV.

It may also help to frame your discussions around the concept of honesty rather than the concept of dishonesty. It sounds arbitrary, but hear me out: Lee and his colleagues tested how different kinds of stories could curb kids' tendencies to lie. They used the story of George Washington and the cherry tree, in which Washington confesses to chopping down his father's tree and is commended for confessing, and the boy who cried wolf, which warns against lying by highlighting its negative consequences. They found that kids learn more when they're taught about the benefits of honesty than when they are warned about the downsides of dishonesty.

I learned this one myself, actually. Last winter, my five-year-old discovered that she could get crackers at the school nurse's office if she pretended to feel sick, so she started making regular visits, complaining that various body parts hurt. One morning before school, I told her the story of the boy who cried wolf. Yet that day at school, guess what happened? She marched right back to the nurse's office for more crackers. I should have gone with good old George Washington.

Lee also cautioned against punishing kids—particularly toddlers and young preschoolers—for lying, because they often do not fully understand the concept of honesty. Punishing a kid for lying can also backfire, because kids understand that they only get punished if they are *caught* lying, so they may continue to lie or, in fact, become *more likely to lie* to avoid punishment.

A 2011 study illustrated this phenomenon in an alarming way. Kang and Talwar, the McGill psychologist, recruited eighty-four preschoolers, half of whom attended a school that harshly punished students for misbehavior and half of whom attended a school that did not punish so harshly. In one-on-one sessions, the researchers asked each student to play the same toy-guessing game described earlier, where kids were told not to peek and later were asked if they had peeked. The kids in both schools were equally likely to peek—about 80 percent of them did—but the researchers found stark differences in whether the children then lied about peeking. Only 56 percent of the kids attending the nonpunitive school lied about having peeked, but a shocking 94 percent of the kids attending the punitive school lied.

The kids attending the punitive school were also better liars, in that even though they knew what the toy was since they had peeked at it, they were more likely to guess incorrectly at first so as not to arouse the experimenter's suspicions. Put another way, it seems parents (and teachers) need to be careful that they don't punish lies so harshly that they actually end up encouraging kids to learn how to lie more effectively, and to stick to their lies, to avoid the consequences.

This said, don't be afraid to discuss and even employ *natural* consequences to deter your kids from lying. Tell little Susie that if she keeps lying, you may not always be inclined to believe what she says. And if your kid, like mine, lies about needing to use the bathroom in order to stall bedtime, tell him he gets *one* chance to go potty before bedtime, at whatever time he chooses; if he plays the potty card when he doesn't really need to go, he may end up uncomfortable—or even soil himself—later on, which may be the very lesson he needs. (Unless you are in the middle of potty training—then, well, all bets are off. Good luck and Godspeed.)

When your kids are old enough to understand, you'll also want to color your discussions about honesty a tad, because society values honesty as well as politeness, and the two can contradict. Take, for example, mealtime. Maybe you say to your kids, "Why is it that you don't blurt out, 'This is the most disgusting pie I've ever had' at somebody's house?" asked Angela Crossman, a developmental psychologist at CUNY's John Jay College of Criminal Justice. "What are the ways you can handle these situations where you're still being an honest person as much as possible, but you're also not being a rude or disrespectful or ungrateful person?" She suggested that parents talk about the importance of honesty but caution about saying things that are mean. Maybe instead of saying something bad about the pie, your kid could truthfully compliment the pretty pie dish instead.

And if you're facing a situation in which you *really* need your child to be honest, research suggests that asking your kid to promise to tell the truth might help. In one study, eight-to-sixteen-year-olds who had initially lied about cheating on a test, but were then asked to promise to tell the truth about it, admitted to having cheated. In a similar study, three-to-seven-year-olds who were asked to promise to tell the truth were much more likely to admit they had peeked at a toy when told not to than kids who had not been asked to promise. It sounds corny, but with kids, promises can really work.

Finally: If you think your kids' lies are a sign of a deeper problem, talk to your pediatrician or a child psychologist. Excessive

lying *can* be a symptom of conduct disorder, attention-deficit/
hyperactivity disorder, or oppositional defiant disorder. Generally speaking, Lee said, kids who have behavioral problems tend
to be not only frequent liars but also poor liars, even when they
should be old enough to lie well (around the age of seven or eight).

Lying and Swearing Strategy #4
Be open with your kids about your life.

I often wonder how much of my adult life I should be sharing
with my kids. Should I tell them I had a bad day at work? Share
that the PTA meeting was a disaster? And more relevant to the
topic at hand, should I confess to my kids when I have told a lie or
broken a rule?

Research suggests yes—the more we share with our kids, the
more open they'll be with us. In a 2018 study, psychologist Joan
Grusec and her colleagues surveyed mothers and their twelve-to-
fourteen-year-olds about how likely they were to share their concerns with one another and to confess to breaking minor rules.
The more open the moms were about their concerns, they found,
the more open their kids were, too—and the more generous and
kind the kids' teachers thought they were, too.

It makes sense: When kids feel as though it's OK, even welcome, for them to talk about their problems, and when parents
respond to those admissions with warmth and support, kids
are then much more likely to open up again. Research has also
found that when parents frequently reminisce about their past
emotional experiences with their kids, their children develop
better emotional understanding skills, which are important for
perspective-taking and the development of empathy. Openness

between parents and kids is believed to improve kids' coping skills, too, because during these conversations parents often discuss ways to handle emotions and solve difficult problems.

This, I know, is not a natural thing for parents to do. We complain to our spouses and friends that we had a tough day, but we don't necessarily do it with our kids. And for good reason—we don't want to burden or scare them. But every so often, it really is good to tell kids how we feel, and to share what we're dealing with (maybe with the help of a euphemism or two if it's really not kid appropriate). That way, they learn that problems are things families share with one another—and help each other resolve.

··

KEY POINTS

··

1. Lying and swearing are normal, but it helps to model the behavior you want to see.
2. React calmly when your kids lie or swear. Allow kids to swear in private (or other situations you consider appropriate).
3. Stress the importance of honesty.
4. Be open with your kids about your own struggles and feelings.

CHAPTER 5

"Girls Can't Do That."

How to Raise Kids Who Aren't Sexist

ONE MONDAY A few summers ago, after coming home from a family camping trip, my friend Laurie sat down to answer work emails. Her husband was out, so she was home with her seven-year-old son, Luke. Luke was annoyed that she was working rather than paying attention to him, and he kept coming in and interrupting her. Laurie is an engineer and science writer; her husband is also an engineer.

"Why are you taking so long? Can't you stop now?" Luke said to her after barging in (again).

"You don't complain about Daddy when he's at the computer," Laurie replied.

"Well, he's working."

"I'm working, too!"

"But," Luke said, "*his* work is more important."

If I had a penny for every sexist thing I've heard kids say, I would be lounging on a beach in Bermuda rather than writing this book. My jaw has practically become unhinged from dropping to the floor so many times. Many comments I hear center on the notion that girls or boys can't do or wear certain things; Luke's comment suggests that some kids have already internalized the idea that a man's contributions to society are more valuable than those of a woman. (Laurie said that her husband does earn more than she does, but that Luke doesn't know that. And, by the way, she has a PhD, and her husband doesn't.)

Sexism fuels so many of our country's ills. It's why men become CEOs—and US presidents—when women are often more qualified; it's why mothers still do the lion's share of child-rearing and housework even when they work as many hours as fathers (a discrepancy that became especially salient during the coronavirus pandemic); it's why millions of women each year are sexually assaulted yet few ever see justice. Although we're slowly making progress toward building an egalitarian society, we have a long, long way to go—and we won't realize this goal if we don't fundamentally change, as a culture, how we see, talk to, and engage with children.

This is because sexism takes root early. Kids begin making inferences about gender from the time they can distinguish it—typically before their first birthday—and the signals we send them as parents often unintentionally tell them all the wrong things. Most of the time, we don't even realize what we're doing. I wish I could say I'm a 100 percent gender-egalitarian parent, but I've noticed I'm much more likely to comment on my daughter's appearance than I am on my son's. This sends the message that her looks are more important than his—that a larger proportion of her self-worth is defined by her appearance than it is for him. That's . . . not good. Yet studies have shown that many progressive, gender-egalitarian parents reinforce age-old, sexist gender stereotypes. As one peer-reviewed paper I read concluded, "Despite the fact that the majority of mothers could be classified as having egalitarian beliefs, they appear to do little to inculcate such beliefs in their children."

To be fair, this isn't entirely our fault. We have all been conditioned over the course of a lifetime to notice and adhere to gender stereotypes. We are products of a sexist society, and as much as we may, on an intellectual level, desperately want to reject these outdated ideas, old habits often get the best of us. But we can, bit by bit, break out of our habits for the sake of our kids. No, really, we can! When I began paying attention to how I was engaging with my kids, I got way better at catching myself *before* I said things I shouldn't say. And in a way, the fact that sexism is learned at such a young age is a good thing, because it means parents have more power to intercept the world's sexist messages than they would if, say, sexism were learned during the more autonomous teen years.

Of course, kids don't grow up in a bubble, nor would we want them to (well, most of the time). But we can temper the messages they receive by being more careful at home. We can be thoughtful about the ways in which we refer to gender in conversations and be mindful of the toys, activities, clothes, and habits we encourage our kids to embrace so as not to feed harmful stereotypes. We can also help our kids recognize gender bias and the ways in which it shapes the world so that they can more effectively push against it.

But before I get into these approaches, a quick note. In this chapter, some of the research I describe, and some of the anecdotes and advice I share, imply that there are two genders. In fact, gender is not binary. As many as 2 percent of babies are born intersex, which means they are biologically neither boys nor girls.

Many children also do not identify with their assigned gender. So although I refer to "boys" and "girls" throughout, I recognize and respect that many kids do not fit into these simplified categories.

BLUE, PINK, TRUCKS, DOLLS: WHAT'S THE BIG DEAL?

Now I want to step back and explain why the messages we typically send our kids about gender are harmful—because the reason is not intuitive or obvious. When I was pregnant with my daughter, I received tons of girly gifts from friends and relatives: lace bonnets, hair bows, more pink dresses than I knew what to do with. And you know what? After having a boy, I was *excited* to dress my little girl in ruffly concoctions, and I didn't see why it would be a problem. The differences in the way we treat little boys and girls don't scream "boys are better than girls"; we're not giving boys gilded trophies and girls pieces of coal, after all. So why is it bad to acknowledge and highlight the gender differences we see in our society every day?

Recently I drove to Bethlehem, Pennsylvania, to visit with developmental psychologist Rebecca Bigler and find out. Bigler had just retired as a professor of psychology and women's and gender studies at the University of Texas at Austin, where she had served on the faculty since 1991. Bigler has spent her life studying the development of prejudice in children, and she is well known among psychologists for creating, with Penn State University developmental psychologist Lynn Liben, a theory known as the Developmental Intergroup Theory. It's a framework that explains how and why kids develop sexism, racism, and other prejudices.

Bigler is a pretty big deal, so I was nervous when I pulled into her driveway. But Bigler's demeanor is the opposite of intimidating. She's like your cool aunt—a little zany, a lot feminist, and very, very smart. She has a broad smile and long gray hair, which she refuses to dye brown, much to her hairstylist's chagrin. (I'm telling you this because I think the expectation for women to dye their hair is a sexist one, and Bigler's choice not to embodies exactly who she is: a woman who refuses to be told who to be or how to look, and who desperately wants to remold our society into one in which hairdressers stop telling women to dye the gray out of their hair.)

Sitting in Bigler's living room, which had floor-to-ceiling bookshelves stuffed with books on every topic you can imagine, we talked about why it's a problem when parents make a big deal out of gender. In a nutshell, she said, the trouble is rooted in how kids' brains work—what their brains do with this information and why.

Little kids may seem carefree and devoid of responsibility— case in point, I just heard my daughter loudly singing a song about porpoises—but they actually have a tough job: to figure out the strange world they've been born into as quickly as possible. To do this, they pay close attention to what everyone around them is doing and saying and then try to parse out what's important.

For just a minute, let's forget about all the ways in which gender matters in our world and just focus on language. Kids are, of course, tuned into what we say from a very young age. And we are *constantly* sending them messages that gender matters. "We use gendered nouns all the time: 'Good morning, boys and girls,' 'What a good girl,' 'The man is at the corner,' 'Ask that lady,'"

Bigler said. "That tells kids that gender is really important—because otherwise, why do you label it hundreds of times a day?"

There are so many visual characteristics that distinguish individuals from one another: hair color, hair length, eye color, skin color, handedness, height, and weight, to name but a few. But which of these do we communicate *almost all the time* when we talk about other people? Every time we use "he" or "she" pronouns, we indirectly indicate gender—but we don't indicate any of these other details. "We turn their gender into their personhood," Bigler said. If we did live in a world in which a person's hair color was mentioned every single time we talked about them, you can be damned sure that kids would quickly discern that hair color matters. And I might start dyeing the gray out of *my* hair.

Now think about all the other ways—beyond language—that we signify and differentiate gender. Girls and boys have different bathrooms, different sports teams, different aisles at the toy store, sometimes even different schools. Even at my kids' co-ed public school, teachers ask students to line up separately by gender all the time. Over and over and over again, we bombard kids with the notion that gender is one of the most important social categories we have. And that's where the problems begin.

THE STEREOTYPE PROBLEM

Once kids realize that gender is a big deal, they try their best to understand its meaning. "What we think happens in kids' minds is the kids say, 'You are labeling me a girl hundreds of times a day. It must mean *something*. Girls must be different in important ways from boys. Why else would you be doing this?'"

Bigler explained. So kids start making inferences—often problematic ones.

When trying to understand categories, kids often overgeneralize and create rigid rules that are sort of, but not exactly, accurate—crude stereotypes, if you will. With gender, this might manifest as a belief that "all girls" and "no boys" like pink, or that "all boys" and "no girls" like football—more broadly, the idea that boys and girls are fundamentally different from one another, and that boys should never do "girl things" and vice versa.

As you probably know if you're a parent, kids themselves are often the strictest gender police. In a 2003 experiment, researchers asked kindergarten teachers to record comments their students made about gender over the course of three months. When the researchers analyzed the recordings, they found that a whopping 97 percent of the comments the students made about gender enforced crude stereotypes. One boy playing with a butterfly puppet was admonished by a peer who told him, "You need to have a boy puppet and give that girl puppet to a girl."

Research has shown that boys, more than girls, tend to focus on what genders *can't* or *shouldn't* do, perhaps because they feel so much pressure to adhere to masculine norms themselves. Girls don't feel this pressure to conform to feminine ideals to quite the same degree: So-called tomboy girls are much more socially acceptable than are so-called effeminate boys because of the status difference in our culture between women and men. Males are the high-status group, so they lose standing when they adopt stereotypically feminine, and lower-status, characteristics.

In one study, University of Oregon developmental psychologist Beverly Fagot observed preschoolers at school over a six-year period and found that peers criticized non-gender-conforming boys five to six times more frequently than their more gender-conforming peers, and that these boys also received only a quarter as much positive peer feedback. Since masculine traits are linked with power in most scenarios, boys sacrifice power when they "act like girls," whereas girls can sometimes gain power when they "act like boys."

When children build group stereotypes, they often also invent differences that don't reflect reality. In her book *Parenting Beyond Pink and Blue*, developmental psychologist Christia Spears Brown, who studied under Bigler, explained that even though her husband is by far the neatest person in the house, her five-year-old daughter, Maya, announced one day that she needed to clean her room because "boys are messy and girls are neat."

As kids create these rules about gender, they also look around and take stock of what girls and boys and men and women tend to do in the world. They might decide, based on examples they see, that women cook and are teachers, and that men play football and are firefighters—but that men never cook and women never fight fires. If they watch TV, they'll probably glean that boys tend to be more heroic and physically strong and that girls tend to be demure and wear a lot of lipstick.

They'll also start to discern the power discrepancy between the genders when they notice that all US presidents have been men and that most superheroes are still boys. They might even draw causal inferences from it: *If the most powerful positions are always held by men, then I guess men must inherently be more capable than women.* Bigler's research has shown this: Just before the 2008 presidential election, she and three colleagues interviewed more than two hundred five-to-ten-year-olds about who they thought should be president of the United States and how they felt when they found out there had been no women presidents. The results were, in a word, depressing: One-fifth of the kids said they thought only men should be president, and more than one-third of kids under the age of nine believed it was *actually illegal* for a woman to be president. One nine-year-old boy said, "Men have courage and responsibility. Who knows what women would do?"

At first, when they are young, girls don't think of themselves as inferior to boys. In a 2017 study published in the journal *Science*, developmental psychologists Lin Bian, Sarah-Jane Leslie, and Andrei Cimpian told five-, six-, and seven-year-old kids a brief story about a person who was "really, really smart." The kids were then asked to guess which of four strangers they saw in photos—two men and two women—was the protagonist. The five-year-olds tended to believe the "really, really smart" character was someone of their own gender—boys picked men, and girls picked women. This is classic in-group versus out-group psychology: Whatever group you belong to, you like better.

But the study found that the hierarchies start to shift in girls' minds around the age of six. This is when girls begin to internalize the idea that they're not as smart or as capable as boys. When the researchers in the study asked six- and seven-year-old girls which of the four strangers was the "really, really smart" protagonist, the girls were more likely to pick a man. (The boys picked men no matter how old they were.)

Just after she turned six, my daughter illustrated to me the depth of her own internalized sexism. She turned to me and asked whether she could one day change into a boy. I wasn't sure what she was getting at, so I asked: "Well, do you want to turn into a boy? And if so, why?" She replied—and this absolutely shattered me—that she wanted to change into a boy so that she could one day become president. Believe me, she and I have regularly talked over the years about how women *can* be president; we've discussed the fact that Hillary Clinton ran for president and almost won, and I've explained to her that women lead plenty of other countries, including Germany and New Zealand. But despite our many conversations about this, she still, somehow, had inferred from the cues she gets from our culture that girls simply cannot be president.

As kids get older—eight, nine, ten—they develop more cognitive flexibility, and many realize that gender norms are largely based on social conventions. It might dawn on them that girls are expected to look pretty and boys are expected to act tough, but that society itself largely fuels this pressure. But at around the same time, children also start to develop moral reasoning, and in some kids, these gender stereotypes get moralized instead of relaxed—kids start to think that girls are expected to be demure and boys are expected to be assertive simply because they believe "this is the right thing to do," said Campbell Leaper, a developmental and social psychologist at the University of California, Santa Cruz.

OK, but, some of you might be thinking, *my son has been obsessed with trucks since he was practically a newborn. Aren't some gender stereotypes driven by biology rather than culture?* Researchers concede this is a very difficult question to answer, in part because we can never really separate out nature from nurture, even in babies. "Boys and girls have different biological experiences prenatally, and different biological and social experiences from the time they are born, and these influences interact with one another, so disentangling them is difficult," said Carol Martin, a child development researcher at Arizona State University.

Still, it's likely that peer and parental influences still shape even early gendered behavior; biology does not have to be the cause. "Most of it is [that] kids are playing with what their parents buy them," Brown said. Or they're mimicking what other toddlers of their gender do—toddlers who might gravitate toward what are considered gender-appropriate toys because of what they have been offered or encouraged to play with before.

Plus, adults respond to and interact with boys in very different ways than they do girls, even from the time they are infants—and these interactions shape kids' behavior down the line. In a classic study, researchers at Cornell University showed college students a video of a nine-month-old baby being surprised by a jack-in-the-box. The students were more likely to describe the baby's response as "angry" if they were told the baby was a boy, and they were more likely to describe the response as "fear" if they were told it was a girl.

In another study, three- and five-year-olds watched videos of one-year-olds playing and were told one was a boy and one was a girl (they varied which baby they said was which gender). Even the three-year-olds were much more likely to describe the baby they thought was a boy with stereotypically masculine adjectives—mad, strong, loud, and smart. If they were describing the girl, the kids were more likely to choose stereotypically feminine adjectives—scared, weak, nice, and dumb (yes, dumb). Research has also found that parents use broader emotional language and explanations when they talk to daughters than to sons (with sons, they tend to emphasize only anger). These discrepancies could have meaningful effects in terms of how comfortable kids become with feelings and how well they learn to handle them.

Ultimately, the gender stereotypes children latch on to do nothing good. Research has shown that boys who adopt masculine "toughness" behaviors have less interest in school, lower self-esteem, lower math standardized test scores, and more symptoms of depression compared with boys who don't. (One theory is that boys who feel like they have to be tough are less likely to ask for help when they need it—just like that old cliché that men never ask for directions.) Girls who internalize the idea that their value stems from how they look get lower grades (perhaps because they believe they're less intelligent) and have more symptoms of depression compared with girls who do not hold these beliefs.

And here's the crux of the problem: The more ingrained kids' gender stereotypes become, the more likely they are to conclude that girls are inferior to boys—that boys have higher status because they biologically deserve it. In other words, gender stereotypes directly fuel sexism. Making matters worse, as kids transition into adolescence, these gender stereotypes and sexist beliefs shift in an important way: They become sexualized, fueling sexual harassment and sexual assault.

Starting as early as age ten, male gender stereotypes start to incorporate ideals of male dominance, aggression, and sexual callousness, while female ideals start to center on sexuality and attractiveness. Studies find that the more strongly boys believe these stereotypes, the more likely they are to make sexual comments, to tell sexual jokes in front of girls, and to grab girls. In a 2018 survey of more than one thousand US adolescents conducted by researchers with the nonprofit organization Plan International, researchers found that boys who grew up mostly playing with "boy" toys, such as trucks and guns, thought more about girls' bodies than they did about girls' thoughts and personalities—and they were less likely to believe that there should be equal numbers of men and women as leaders in work, politics, and life. This isn't to say the toys themselves fueled sexism, but it's likely that growing up in a home in which gender stereotypes are emphasized in various ways (including through the toys parents offer or buy) increases the chance that boys will grow into teens with sexist beliefs.

As the survey authors explain, "Boys are clearly under pressure to behave in certain ways that are deemed 'appropriate' for their gender: being physically and emotionally strong, not exhibiting weakness, and showing interest in sex. They are also receiving the same messages as girls do—that girls should be valued for their physical traits and sexuality rather than their abilities or intelligence." Fifty-five percent of girls surveyed said they heard boys making sexual comments or sexual jokes about girls at least several times a week.

These trends continue into adulthood. Men who adhere strongly to norms of masculinity are more likely than other men to sexually harass and sexually assault women, possibly because, as psychologists theorized in a 2015 paper, they "feel compelled to be sexually aggressive and/or coercive toward an intimate partner to maintain their need for dominance."

And just like that, we find ourselves where we are today: in a gender-lopsided, discriminatory society. But research is starting to suggest a way out—and parents, it turns out, can lead the charge.

Anti-Sexism Strategy #1
Watch your language.

After sharing a pizza at a local restaurant, Bigler and I returned to her living room to chat more. Bigler opened up her computer and began showing me photos. Most were of kids smiling in brightly colored T-shirts.

Bigler, as you'll recall, has always been interested in understanding what causes kids to develop prejudice. She asks: What has to happen for a child to learn to dislike groups of people? Why is it that people often harbor gender- and race-based prejudices, but no discernible prejudice regarding eye or hair color (other than blonde jokes, which, to be clear, are also pernicious)?

To answer these questions, in 1992, Bigler began running a series of experiments in partnership with various schools, summer school programs, and day care centers. Every day for several weeks, some kids arrived at school and were told to put on blue shirts, while others were told to wear red ones. The T-shirts essentially created a new social category that was very easy for kids to see. (Bigler knew from earlier work that one requirement for the development of prejudice is "perceptual discriminability," a fancy way of saying that kids need to easily be able to tell which group a person fits into in order to develop strong feelings about it.)

Bigler and her colleagues then began tweaking the kids' classroom environments as they wore their T-shirts. In one experiment, Bigler had teachers in some classrooms completely ignore the shirt colors—they never mentioned them or separated the kids by color in any way. In other classrooms, teachers were told to regularly highlight the colors, but in a neutral way. They would say, "Good morning, blues and reds!" at the start of the school day, and they would line the kids up by color and refer to individual students by color. (Importantly, the teachers never allowed the groups to compete against each other—they weren't allowed to play games against each other at recess, for instance. Competition is a surefire way to breed prejudice, and Bigler wanted to see what happens when categories are made salient but in a neutral way.)

After weeks of teachers doing this on a daily basis, Bigler and her colleagues surveyed the students. In classrooms in which teachers didn't call attention to T-shirt colors, the students developed very little prejudice against kids wearing the other color. In classrooms in which teachers regularly called attention to the shirts in a neutral way, however, the students became quite prejudiced—blues believed that they were smarter than reds, and vice versa, even though they'd been given no evidence to suggest there were group differences in intelligence.

What does all this have to do with sexism and gender? Well, you can think of the T-shirts as proxy for gender—they're a social category that's easy to see and effectively splits classrooms into two groups, just as gender often does. What Bigler's studies suggest, then, is that when adults draw verbal attention to social categories like gender, it incites kids to develop prejudices against, and stereotypes about, those in the other group. In a follow-up study published in 2001, Bigler and Brown confirmed just how important verbal labeling is: Even when students saw posters in their classrooms suggesting that blues really *were* smarter than reds (because, say, the blues had earned more spots on the school's competitive math team last year), students didn't develop strong prejudices unless their teachers *also* called attention to the T-shirt colors during class. The studies point to one key conclusion: "Gender labeling is very, very important for developing gender bias," Bigler said.

It helps to understand how language fits into the broader

framework Bigler has developed regarding the development of prejudice. In order for children to develop prejudices about a social group, Bigler has found that several conditions need to be met. The first one—and this one is required—is that the social group needs to be recognizable. Kids easily have to be able to discern what people are members of which group (which typically happens with gender; we can usually tell boys apart from girls). Then at least one of these next three conditions has to be met, and the more that are, the more likely it is that prejudice will develop:

1. The groups are disproportional in size. Minority groups are distinctive and more likely to become targets of prejudice. Generally, this characteristic doesn't contribute to sexism, but it can in specific environments, such as when there are only four girls in a twenty-person chess camp.
2. The groups tend to self-segregate, often without explanation. This happens mostly with race, but it can happen with gender in certain situations, too, such as when boys and girls play separately during recess.
3. The groups have been made "psychologically salient," in that people label the groups or group members verbally or assign different groups of kids to different tasks. This happens *all the time* with gender, which is why Bigler considers language to be one of sexism's main drivers.

What this means for parents is that we should ease up on gender labels ourselves. It takes intention, but do your best to refer to people as "kids," "students," and "people" rather than "boys," "girls," "men," and "women." So instead of saying *Those girls are playing soccer,* say *Those kids are playing soccer.* "When I read to my kids, it's, 'The kid was standing on the corner,' as opposed to what the author really wrote, which was 'The boy was standing on the corner,'" Brown said.

It's hard, though: As soon as I started paying attention to gendered language, I realized that I'm constantly using the word "girl" or "boy" when I really don't need to be.

It's not that you can't or shouldn't talk about gender with your kids—in fact, as I'll discuss later, it's important to talk to your kids about sexism. What we shouldn't do is highlight gender *unnecessarily* in conversations that aren't about gender. That's counterproductive, because it reinforces the idea to our kids that gender matters and that genders are different in meaningful ways.

If you feel comfortable doing so, you might also want to request that your kids' teachers stop using gender labels or gendered categories. Some preschools in Sweden have started doing this, and a recent study found that students in these schools developed less pronounced gender stereotypes over time compared with students at other schools.

Finally, avoid making generic statements that lump all boys or all girls into a single category, like *Boys sure are energetic!* or *Girls are so affectionate.* A while back, I picked my son up from horseback riding camp—he was the only boy there that day—and the woman in charge spent five minutes telling me (and him, unfortunately) how refreshing it was to have a "calm" boy like him at camp because "boys are never calm, and they're always such terrible listeners." It was all I could do not to interrupt her to point out that clearly, given my son's behavior, not *all* boys are hyperactive and terrible listeners.

Anti-Sexism Strategy #2
Encourage cross-gender friendships and interactions.

The next time you walk onto a school playground during recess, survey the landscape. Chances are, you'll see two distinct clusters of kids: boys on one side, girls on the other. Kids often segregate by gender, and it's a vicious self-perpetuating cycle: The more girls play with girls, the stronger their bonds get and the closer their interests align; same goes with boys, until all of a sudden the two groups really are quite different and they don't know how to talk to each other anymore. (A friend recently told me that her child's PE teacher lines students up boy, girl, boy, girl specifically because, in this arrangement, the kids don't talk to each other.) One study found that by the time kids are six and a half, they interact with same-gender peers eleven times more often than with opposite-gender peers. Research has also shown that the more girls and boys play with same-gender partners, the more their play becomes gender stereotypical.

To bridge these gaps—and help your kids realize that they might have more in common than they realize with kids who don't share their gender—arrange cross-gender hangouts and playdates (virtually, if needed, because of the pandemic). Ask your daughter what boys she sometimes likes to play with and invite them over; do the same for your son. I still vividly remember the after-school playdates I had during elementary school with a boy named Alex. At first, we struggled to find common ground. I didn't know how to play with Transformers, and he wasn't into my toy musical instruments. But soon enough, I discovered that playing with Transformers was actually really fun—and that Alex wasn't as different from me as I thought.

"Encouraging co-ed friendships is one of the most important things parents (and teachers) can do," Martin said. "When they interact with each other like this, both girls and boys learn about each other and their similarities, become more comfortable with one another, and we believe that it may provide a kind of social resiliency, allowing them to deal with a range of social experiences."

When kids are still in elementary school, consider signing them up for mixed-gender activities, too, such as mixed sports teams. (After puberty, Bigler said, these can get trickier because of strength and size differences, but for younger kids, there's really no reason to separate them.) If your daughter only wants to invite girls to her birthday party, encourage her to invite a few boys. As for gender-segregated schools, researchers are largely in agreement that these are more harmful than helpful—they typically don't boost academic performance, and studies have shown that kids who attend them adhere more strongly to gender stereotypes than do kids at co-ed schools.

Encourage your kids to try non-stereotypical activities as well. Even at a young age, kids intuit which activities are "appropriate" for their gender and which aren't, and if you leave the decision entirely up to them, they'll often veer traditional—boys will want to play soccer and girls will ask to take ballet. (I'm speaking from experience here, believe me.) Because of this, Leaper, the UCSC psychologist, cautions parents against simply following their kids' leads—parents should go further, he said, and urge their kids to try the activities they might not instinctively lean toward. You have to be subtle, though, or your kids might feel you're butting in and resist you as a form of rebellion. Parenting is never easy, is it?

Anti-Sexism Strategy #3
Rid your home of stereotypes—as best you can.

One sunny day in September 2019, I took the train to Brooklyn to meet a twenty-one-month-old toddler named Wildfire and Wildfire's father, Bobby McCullough. When I arrived at their apartment, Wildfire was napping, so Bobby and I sat down in their living room to talk. This wasn't your typical New York family, and not just because Wildfire's mother works full-time while Bobby stays home as the primary caregiver. What really distinguishes them is that they have decided that Wildfire has no assigned gender.

Before Wildfire was born, Bobby and Lesley, Bobby's partner, stumbled upon a newspaper article about a Canadian family who had fought to have their baby's health card printed without a gender designation. Bobby is deeply committed to social justice issues, especially surrounding transgender rights and gender equality—so the idea of not throwing their baby into a "boy" or "girl" box, where the child would immediately be inundated with stereotypical toys and clothes and pressures, was extremely appealing. Bobby and Lesley decided that when Wildfire was born, they would use they/them pronouns and not reveal anything about Wildfire's anatomy to other people. This approach, known as *gender-open* or *gender-creative* parenting, is a small but growing trend among progressive parents around the country.

As we sat talking and listening for sounds on the baby monitor, Bobby explained to me that the goal was to hold space for whatever gender expression Wildfire might want to identify with or explore. "We're not assigning them a nonbinary identity," Bobby said. "In a way, we're doing literally the opposite, which is exposing them to a wide range of opportunities and options and then allowing them to find themselves." In other words, Wildfire may well be a boy or a girl; the point is, it's up to Wildfire to decide. And until Wildfire does, they will have the opportunity to wear "girl" clothes and "boy" clothes, and try out every kind of activity and identity they want. Bobby points out that one in sixty individuals are born intersex—with sex characteristics that don't conform to binary notions of male or female—so there's a chance that Wildfire is, in fact, neither a biological "boy" nor a biological "girl" in the most traditional sense, anyway.

Raising a child in this way—even in progressive Brooklyn—isn't easy. Strangers frequently ask Bobby "what Wildfire is," and Bobby has to explain that they're letting Wildfire decide, which, as you can imagine, incites mixed responses. Some people think it's awesome; others, not so much. One person responded by saying that what they were doing was "against God." And, of course, there's the concern that Wildfire could get picked on for not adhering to traditional gender norms. But as Bobby sees it, telling a child to behave a certain way just to protect them from bullying is misguided—it's essentially victim-blaming, because you're putting all the responsibility on the victim rather than on the bully (or the bullying culture). Still, I absolutely understand the instinct: I remember once, when my son was a toddler and was begging us for pink sneakers (before he had learned pink was "not OK" for a boy), my husband and I had a long discussion about what to do. The desire to protect our kids from pain and stigma is strong.

When Wildfire woke up, we walked to a local playground in Prospect Park. Wildfire has a shock of black curly hair, huge dark eyes, and an adorable giggle. As Wildfire toddled around the playground and played with pink chalk, I was struck by the fact that my brain was having a very hard time processing the experience. Much to my dismay, I kept finding myself trying to figure out Wildfire's sex, as if it were somehow crucial to understanding their identity. Wildfire was wearing a leopard-print shirt and peach-colored pants, so I found myself assuming that they were "really a girl." Once I even slipped up and used the pronoun *she*, after which I'm pretty sure I went sheet-white. Bobby was unfazed and said, "Don't worry about it. It's not conscious. That's just your brain giving you signals." It reminded me of something Bobby had said to me earlier: "I have had to work really hard at unlearning things that I even know are blatantly wrong. They're just ingrained."

I'm forty-one years old, so yeah, these stereotypes have become *really* ingrained in me. You couldn't extract them with major surgery. But with intention, I've found that I can at least limit the stereotypes I expose my kids to—and you can, too. Again, you won't be perfect at it, and you won't be able to shield your kids from the rest of the world's stereotypical thinking, but you can make a dent if you try. Even if you're not ready to embrace gender-open parenting, you can still check yourself when you find yourself putting your child into a "boy" or "girl" box, and in this way you can help reduce the risk that these stereotypes will become ingrained in your kids.

My first piece of advice: Parents of babies and young kids, don't overdo it with gendered clothes. Girls don't have to wear pink and purple, and boys don't have to wear blue and red. In fact, before the 1950s, there was no set gender-color symbolism. Girls often wore blue, while boys were commonly seen in pink. The current expectations are based on nothing but recent tradition and marketing.

Resist the temptation to buy toys that "fit" their gender, too. (Lest you think that things have recently improved on the toy front, research by sociologist Elizabeth Sweet has shown that toys have actually become more gender-stratified over the past fifty years.) When my daughter was a toddler, she loved playing with my son's trucks and trains. Populate your home with a range of kinds of toys and books and clothes, at least until your kids are old enough to make requests themselves. To keep grandparents in line, create gift wish lists that skew counter-stereotypical.

We also need to be careful not to subtly steer our kids toward the "right" kind of behavior. Research suggests that some parents (especially dads) become *very* uncomfortable when their boys play with dolls, and they often admonish them for doing so. Teachers too: One study found that boys were criticized much more frequently by teachers when they were engaging in "feminine" behaviors like playing kitchen or dress-up. In another study, researchers observed preschool and kindergarten kids during recess and took note of when teachers encouraged or reprimanded them. They found that 90 percent of the time when teachers were encouraging, it was when students were engaging in gender-stereotypical activities. On the other hand, 91 percent of the time when teachers reprimanded kids, it was when the students were engaging in counter-stereotypical activities—boys playing in the kitchen and girls playing with construction materials, for instance.

Kids notice this kind of feedback, and it shapes their choices and beliefs. In one well-known study, University of Oregon researchers Beverly Fagot and Mary Leinbach observed eighteen-month-olds at home with their parents and continued to do so regularly until the children were four. When parents strongly pushed gender-stereotypical toys on their kids, those children began labeling gender (calling girls "girls" and boys "boys") at a younger age. By twenty-seven months, the early labelers also engaged in more gender-stereotypical behaviors. By the age of four, these early labelers also knew more about what each gender "should" and "should not" do.

Be aware, too, of the ways in which stereotypes might be shaping your interactions with and perceptions of your kids. One study observed families at a museum science exhibit and found that parents were three times more likely to explain scientific concepts to boys than to girls. And in a 2014 *New York Times* op-ed, former Google data scientist Seth Stephens-Davidowitz pointed out that parents search online for information on whether their sons might be "gifted" 2.5 times more often than they do for their daughters.

We do harmful things to our sons, though, too: We're often quick to admonish them when they show fear, sadness, or pain. We tell them *buck up* or even (cringe) to *stop acting like a girl.* Yet casting boys as stoic and physical and girls as weak and emotional sends the message that one gender has power and competence and the other does not, and it can be alienating for boys who don't espouse these ideals. It also primes boys to act out in ways that "prove" they are traditionally male. Research suggests that boys who are made to feel emasculated are more likely than others to sexually harass and perpetrate sexual violence. Instead of telling boys to toughen up, then, we should do the opposite: Acknowledge their feelings and try to get them to talk about and understand them. Say things like *It sounds like you're angry right now*, or *Let's talk about why you don't want to go to school today.*

Ideally, if you have a son, find a time every day where you sit down with and check in with him about his feelings and struggles; I often do this right before bedtime. Discussing emotions with a boy—especially a tween or teen—might seem awkward at first, but you might be surprised at how hungry he is to make an emotional connection. Compared with girls the same age, research shows that adolescent boys often maintain superficial friendships because of the pressure they feel to be "macho." But, as child psychologists Dan Kindlon and Michael Thompson explained in their book *Raising Cain*, when parents give boys permission to feel and connect, they can then bring that openness to their friendships. "What boys need, first and foremost, is to be seen through a different lens than tradition prescribes," they wrote. "Individually, and as a culture, we must discard the distorted view of boys that ignores or denies their capacity for feeling, the view that colors even boys' perceptions of themselves as above or outside a life of emotions."

Be mindful of the messages you send your kids by what you do and don't talk about, too. If you're a father, share your feelings rather than bottling them up and encourage your son to do the same. If you're a mother, don't fret about your appearance or your weight, especially not in front of your daughter. Bigler was once asked to appear on TV to comment on a new controversial breastfeeding doll that had just come to market. Her daughter was with her, and she pondered whether to put on makeup and do her hair for the filming. In the end, she didn't. "There are these moments where you're like 'Holy shit, I've got to model the right thing here.' That was my moment. So I went on TV looking totally wonky and terrible," Bigler said. She wanted to show her daughter that her expertise was what mattered, not her appearance. (And for anyone who's curious, she thought the breastfeeding doll was fine. "It does not ever harm a child to know that what breasts do is feed babies," Bigler said.)

What if you suspect your child might not identify with their assigned gender? Bottom line: Be supportive and understanding. Ask them what they want and need and adopt their preferred gender pronouns. Research has shown that transgender and gender-expansive kids have higher self-esteem and fewer symptoms of depression when their parents support and affirm their identities. This means you shouldn't encourage your child to hide who they are in order to fit in with peers or avoid being bullied. Books that might be helpful include *The Transgender Child* by Stephanie A. Brill and Rachel Pepper and *The Gender Creative Child* by Diane Ehrensaft and Norman Spack. Your family might also want to work with a gender therapist.

Anti-Sexism Strategy #4
Discuss gender discrimination.

A few years ago, a family friend bought my daughter the book *Good Night Stories for Rebel Girls*. It's an impressive collection of short biographies of women who've done amazing things. Nearly every story includes a nod to the fact that the women had to push against discrimination to achieve what they did, though, and I remember feeling vaguely uneasy about it. I wondered: *Is it really a good idea to be hitting my daughter over the head with the idea that girls are told by society that they aren't good enough?*

Although we need more research on the effects of these kinds of messages, studies suggest that talking with kids about sexism is a good thing, particularly with kids over the age of five or six (which is when, if you remember, many girls start to internalize the idea that they're not as smart as boys). By this age, girls are already noticing the signals society is sending them about their relative worth—they can see quite clearly that women hold less powerful positions than men do. Yet without any knowledge of gender discrimination, kids are likely to attribute these hierarchical differences to innate differences between the sexes, which is not what we want them to do. "Every kid is left to figure out this alone: Why are the chemists men, why are the nurses females? Without enough explanation by adults, they make one up, and they don't make up gender discrimination," Bigler explained. (They infer it's because boys are better.) One of Bigler's studies, which she coauthored with psychologist Erica Weisgram, found that when girls were taught about gender discrimination in science, they became more interested in science than before—perhaps because, Bigler and Weisgram wrote, the knowledge quashed their belief that they wouldn't be capable scientists.

It's also important, of course, to talk to boys about sexism. Patricia Devine, a psychologist at the University of Wisconsin-Madison, has spent her career studying implicit biases—attitudes and prejudices that unconsciously affect our beliefs and actions—and has evaluated interventions that help to reduce them. Boys are inevitably going to have sexist thoughts, given the society we live in, and Devine's research suggests that they'll only stop having them once they learn to recognize these thoughts and understand that they are unfair. To get to that point, we have to teach boys that sexism exists and why it is wrong. Bigler agreed: "You would never fight an injustice that you don't know exists," she said.

There are plenty of ways to bring the issue of sexism into conversations with your kids. One is to use the media as a conduit.

When a sexist scenario unfolds on a TV show your kid is watching (because—surprise!—skewed gender ratios and stereotypes are a big problem in children's television and commercials), bring it up right then and there, Bigler said: *Why do you think they're only showing boys going on these adventures? Do you think that's fair?*

Use everyday experiences as conversation starters, too. If you're at a store and a stranger tells your daughter, "Oh what a pretty dress," build on it. "You could reply with 'Thank you, yes, her dress is pretty, and she's very smart, too,'" Bigler said. Or, if you'd prefer to avoid confrontation, discuss the comment's implications with your daughter afterward. "You can say, 'Why did she say your dress was pretty? I think that has something to do with how she thinks girls should look. I wonder if she says boys look pretty. I'm kind of offended—I think your dress *is* pretty, but I don't think that's what's important about you.'"

Crucially, too, engage with your kids when *they* make sexist comments. You'll get plenty of opportunities, but you'll have to pay attention: In a series of studies published in 2004, psychologists Susan Gelman, Marianne Taylor, and Simone Nguyen observed mothers and their children as they read and discussed picture books. They found that even gender-egalitarian mothers regularly ignored or even subtly affirmed gender stereotypical comments their children made. It's like we don't notice sexism when our adorable kids are the perpetrators.

I do remember one particularly egregious example involving my son, though. When he was six, he told me that he and his friends don't let girls play soccer with them during recess because girls aren't as good and cry too much. I was mortified, and I can't really remember what I said in response. Probably the wrong thing. But after speaking with experts, I have learned that parents should not immediately admonish kids for sexist comments in a *shame on you* kind of way—rather, it's better to ask questions and get a conversation going. (You don't want your kids to feel immediately defensive and upset, because then, they may stop listening; plus, you want to get more information so you can understand their misconceptions and engage with your kids more constructively.)

In this situation, I could have asked my son why he thinks girls cry more than boys and then talked to him about social norms. I could also have pushed back on the idea that girls aren't good at soccer by pointing out counterexamples, such as that his female friend Charlie is an excellent soccer player. In general, when kids make comments like *Only girls like to dance*, it can help to point out similarities that exist across the sexes (*Don't you know a couple of boys who do like to dance?*) and differences within the sexes (*Some girls don't like to dance, right?*). These kinds of discussions call attention to gender but in a potentially constructive way. They help kids recognize and push against the stereotypes and discrimination they will inevitably see and hear outside the home instead of merely tacitly affirming them, as in Bigler's T-shirt experiments.

I'm happy to report that my son has since reformed his sexist soccer opinions. In fact, one night when he was nine, he began talking with my husband about World Cup scores and said, offhand, "And then there was the time I watched the US win!" My husband was baffled until he realized our son was referring to the Women's World Cup, not the Men's.

Finally—and although this might sound obvious, it is worth pointing out because many parents don't actually do it—tell your kids exactly what your beliefs are on sexism and gender. Explain what feminism is—and what it's not, because wow, misperceptions on this one abound. (A good place to start is that feminists believe that everyone, regardless of gender, should have equal rights and opportunities.) Tell them how you feel about gender discrimination and why you think it's important to fight against it. Tell them, for instance, that you think it's unfair that society expects women to look a certain way and that women don't get paid as much as men do for the same work.

"Your job and your privilege is to share your values," Bigler said. "Futures depend on it."

· ·

KEY POINTS

· ·

1. Don't point out and label gender. It's "kids" and "students," not "boys" and "girls."
2. Encourage cross-gender friendships and counter-stereotypical activities.
3. Avoid steering your kids toward gendered toys, clothes, and behaviors, and be a good role model. Let your son cry; discuss science with your daughter; don't obsess over your appearance if you're a woman or avoid talking about feelings if you're a man.
4. Challenge kids' sexist comments and discuss gender discrimination.

CHAPTER 6

"I'm Perfect."

How to Raise Kids Who Have Healthy Self-Esteem—but Aren't Narcissistic

FOR KIDS WHO share so much of their DNA, mine couldn't be more different in their outward displays of self-confidence. My six-year-old recently got toothpaste on her dress while brushing her teeth, and in response she burst into tears, dropped to the floor, and rolled around screaming, "I'm the *worst person ever!*" My nine-year-old, on the other hand, acts as though his knowledge already surpasses that of Albert Einstein. Whenever we point out that he's wrong about something, he disagrees, as if the number of moons orbiting Jupiter is a matter of opinion.

So sometimes I wonder: Is my daughter's self-esteem too low? Is my son's too high? Do their declarations truly reflect how much they value themselves? What, if anything, should I be doing to make sure they have the right amount of self-esteem—not too little, not too much—or does a "right amount" even exist?

Self-esteem is one of those psychology buzzwords we all kind of understand, but not really. To put a strict definition on it, it is a measure of how much confidence and value people feel they have, akin to their sense of self-worth. We've all heard of self-esteem because, since the 1980s, Americans have been a little, shall we say, *obsessed* with the concept. In 1986, the governor of California, George Deukmejian, signed legislation that created the Task Force to Promote Self-Esteem and Personal and Social Responsibility, which concluded that boosting Californians' collective levels of self-esteem would lower rates of crime, teen pregnancy, drug abuse, welfare dependency, and school underachievement. The final report published by the task force declared that "self-esteem is central to most of the personal and social problems that plague human life in today's world."

That's a bold statement, and it is based on a bold assumption— one that has fueled the larger self-confidence movement and given rise to organizations such as the National Association for Self Esteem. The assumption is that the United States is suffering from an ongoing epidemic of low self-esteem, and that this deficiency is outright dangerous. You've probably heard that teens with low self-esteem are more likely than other kids to be depressed, to be anxious, to drink, to do drugs, and to commit crimes. This is all true. But what might come as a surprise is that the inverse of this statement is *not* also true. High self-esteem is not a panacea against all things bad, and kids with high self-esteem often make bad choices, too. Many kids who bully have high self-esteem, as do plenty of kids who admit to cheating. In an exhaustive review of the research literature, social psychologist Roy F. Baumeister and his colleagues concluded that "raising self-esteem will not by itself make young people perform better in school, obey the law, stay out of trouble, get along better with their fellows, or respect the rights of others."

If I'm honest, this news came as a bit of a shock to me. I had considered high self-esteem as a be-all and end-all parenting goal, and I'm not alone: A close friend advised me to make my very first chapter about self-esteem, because isn't it the most important thing? If your child has high self-esteem, the thinking goes, everything else will just kind of fall into place.

Yet the idea that your kids will get straight As and say no to drugs if you teach them to value themselves is just, well, wishful thinking. (In fact, the pressure parents put on kids to get those straight As is part of the problem; more on that in a minute.) Making matters worse, it can be hard to tell just how much self-esteem a child actually has. Some kids with low self-esteem act as if they're confident and happy because they are desperately trying to *look* confident and happy. Also, research has shown that the strategies parents typically use to boost their kids' self-esteem often backfire. Some actually undermine a child's confidence. Others send kids down the path to narcissism, fostering in them the unhealthy notion that they are better than everyone else, deserve a gilded life, and should blame others for their failures.

This doesn't mean that self-esteem has no value, nor does it mean that parents shouldn't ever think about it. When I interviewed Eddie Brummelman, a psychologist at the University of Amsterdam who studies self-esteem, he said that while the benefits of self-esteem may not be as world-changing as people think, they're still important. Among other things, healthy self-esteem reduces the risk for many mental health problems. When we nurture in our children a sense that they are inherently good, lovable, and worthy, they can get out of their own heads, stop worrying about what everyone thinks of them, and lead meaningful lives. But how do we nurture healthy self-esteem in our kids without, you know, accidentally screwing them up instead? It's easier than you think.

SELF-ESTEEM VERSUS NARCISSISM

First, I want to correct a misconception that many parents have about self-esteem. There's a widespread worry that if you foster healthy self-esteem in your kids, you could inadvertently turn them into self-loving narcissists. I have good news on this front: Narcissism is a very different beast from healthy self-esteem, and it develops differently, too. You can't just fill a child's self-esteem bucket "too high" and turn him into a narcissist. (Also, you may have heard of well-publicized research suggesting that we are experiencing a new "epidemic of narcissism" in the United States, in that teens today are much more narcissistic than teens from decades past, but recent studies have challenged these claims.)

As it turns out, there's a big difference between self-content kids and narcissists. Kids with healthy self-esteem accept and love themselves for who they are and don't base their sense of self-worth on others. Narcissists, on the other hand, are constantly in comparison mode, believing that they're better than everyone else—but also consumed by the need to prove their superiority.

How do kids become narcissistic? Brummelman has been studying this question for years, and he's found that narcissists usually have parents who put their kids on pedestals—who believe their children are smarter and better than everyone else and treat them that way. (Interestingly, these parents also tend to give their kids unusual first names.) We have all met parents like this, who would probably look adoringly at their children even as those children were throwing dog poop at them. *He just has so much spunk, doesn't he?* the parent might say, just before getting smacked in the face with poodle feces.

Unfortunately, though, kids with narcissistic traits often *are* quite troubled. They can bully (because bullying makes them feel superior to their peers), and they can respond to criticism or rejection with anger and aggression. Their lives are also often pretty sad: Narcissists boast and brag and criticize others to get others to like and admire them, but their strategies ultimately backfire, alienating the very people they want to win over. To make matters worse, they rarely seek help for their problems, perhaps because they cannot recognize they need it. (Note, though, that narcissism doesn't develop until the age of seven or eight. Before that, kids can certainly *act* like narcissists, but their declarations that they are the Most Exceptional Humans Ever are, in fact, developmentally appropriate and *not* a sign that a kid is growing up to be Donald Trump.)

Again, if you're not the kind of parent who smiles lovingly at your child while he does obnoxious things, you probably don't have much to worry about with regard to narcissism. But as I'll explain next, parents often *do* make mistakes—albeit well-intentioned ones, ones I've made myself—that can have lasting effects on kids' self-esteem.

WHAT TODAY'S PARENTS GET WRONG

Raising a kid is not easy these days. In addition to all the age-old child-rearing challenges, we also have to contend with the fact that our children's success feels more elusive to us than it did to our parents and grandparents (not to mention that we've recently weathered a pandemic that has kept our kids out of school). Every year, elite colleges receive more and more applicants for the same number of spots. At the ten most competitive US universities, the admissions rate dropped by nearly 60 percent between 2006 and 2018, from an average of 16 percent in 2006 to 6.4 percent in 2018; at the top fifty universities, the rate dropped by nearly 40 percent. No wonder admissions scandals have been rampant.

The issues parents face today encompass a lot more than just college admissions. When the Organisation for Economic Co-operation and Development (OECD) asked parents in 2019 to rank their top three long-term economic and social fears, 60 percent said that they worried that their children would not achieve the level of status and comfort that they have. That's in part because kids will have to earn a lot more money than their parents did in order to maintain the same standard of living. We're all terrified on behalf of our kids, and for good reason.

So it probably comes as no surprise to most of you that American parents—especially those from the middle- and upper-middle classes—now put a ton of pressure on their kids to be exceptional. It starts young: Kids who haven't yet turned two are being professionally coached for preschool interviews; three-year-olds are taking Mandarin and coding classes to "get ahead"; kindergarteners are being required to learn chess; fourth graders are taking SAT prep classes and working with private sports coaches. There's even a national chain of preschools called Crème de la Crème that teaches toddlers Mandarin, theater, and robotics in facilities that feature on-site STEM labs, baseball diamonds, art studios, basketball courts, and computer labs. (Important note: Research suggests that kids who attend play-based schools learn just as much as, if not more than, kids who attend more academically focused schools.) It's no longer good enough for our kids to be nurtured and well-rounded, and to enjoy learning; they now have to win competitions, make All-American sports teams, and get leads in the musicals while also, of course, getting straight As and acing the SATs.

In his 2015 book *Our Kids: The American Dream in Crisis*, Harvard emeritus political scientist Robert D. Putnam explained that in the 1980s, middle- and upper-class American parents—especially highly educated ones—began to shift their ideas about what it meant to be a good parent. They began moving away from Benjamin Spock's "permissive parenting" approach and toward a new kind of "intensive parenting," fueled in part by the idea that children will be more successful if we push them harder at a young age. So now, forty years later, toddler STEM labs.

Don't get me wrong; I'm one of these parents, too. I haven't enrolled my kids in Mandarin classes, but I worry perhaps too much about whether they will succeed and what I need to do to ensure they will. When my son brings home his report card, it's all I can do not to analyze every grade and ponder what his poor marks for handwriting mean for his future. If competition is much fiercer than it used to be, how can we not feel the pressure and, intentionally or not, shift some of that pressure onto our kids? Who can blame us for feeling scared and wanting to do everything we can to give our kids a leg up?

Here's the thing, though: This pressure is not good for our kids' self-esteem. Research suggests that when parents overemphasize achievement, kids start to infer that achievement defines who they are and how much value they have. And sometimes, our disappointment and anger over their failures is so palpable that they feel like our love for them is contingent upon their success—reinforcing the idea that their value, and lovability, is defined by what they do, not who they are.

I'm not saying any of us outright say that we won't love our kids if they get Cs, but kids make these inferences based on how we act. In a survey published in 2014, Harvard University Graduate School of Education researchers interviewed more than ten thousand middle and high school students from thirty-three schools across the country about what they thought their parents wanted most for them. Two-thirds of the students said they believed their parents would rank achievement over caring for others. The students were also three times more likely to agree than to disagree with the statement "My parents are prouder if I get good grades in my classes than if I'm a caring community member in class and school." In her book *Kid Confidence*, psychologist Eileen Kennedy-Moore argued that healthy self-esteem is essentially the ability to let go of the question "Am I good enough?"—and when parents pressure their kids to achieve, they never give kids the chance to stop asking that question.

Psychologist Suniya S. Luthar has been studying this phenomenon for decades. Starting in the late 1990s, she and her colleagues studied affluent suburban high school students in the Northeast. They found that relative to inner-city kids from low-income families, affluent kids were more likely to use substances including alcohol, marijuana, and other illicit drugs and to suffer from anxiety. The affluent girls, they found, were also two to three times more likely to have symptoms of depression compared with national averages for teenage girls. It's counterintuitive, considering all the advantages that these kids are afforded over the course of their lives.

Since then, Luthar has expanded her research to study more geographically diverse samples of kids and has shifted her focus away from affluent kids to kids who specifically attend high-achieving schools—that is, schools with high test scores and lots of extracurricular offerings, whose students often go on to attend elite colleges. These students typically, but not always, come from middle-to-upper-middle-class households with high-achieving, two-income families.

Luthar's research suggests that the problems afflicting these students have only been getting worse. They are still more likely than other kids to be depressed and anxious, to smoke cigarettes and marijuana, to drink, and to dabble in hard drugs. They are also just as likely to engage in delinquent behavior as less affluent kids are, although the kinds of delinquencies differ (low-income kids are more likely to carry weapons, while high-income kids are more likely to cheat or steal).

In research conducted in 2019 that involved nine cohorts of kids attending high-achieving private and public schools around the country—more than 7,500 kids in total—Luthar and her colleagues found that kids from elite schools were more than *six times as likely* as average American kids to experience symptoms of anxiety and depression. These trends continue after high school, too: Luthar and her team found that women from high-achieving high schools are, at age twenty-six, three times more likely than women of the same age in the general population to be diagnosed with drug or alcohol dependence, while young men from high-achieving schools are twice as likely as other men to be diagnosed.

So what is it about these schools that is so dangerous? In a 2019 paper, Luthar and her colleagues framed the cause this way: "At the core of all these problems is one overarching cause, and that is *unrelenting pressures to accomplish* ever more and distinguish oneself as among the best" (emphasis hers).

This pressure is not just coming from schools and teachers; a lot of it comes directly from parents. In a 2017 study, Luthar and her colleagues interviewed more than five hundred middle school students attending elite schools. They asked the students to rank the three most important things they believed their parents valued in them out of a list of six items: being respectful to others; attending a good college; trying to help others in need; excelling academically; being kind to others; and having a successful career in the future. They also asked the students how critical their parents were of them. They then gave the students tests that evaluated their self-esteem and psychological health, obtained their school grades, and asked the students' teachers to rate their classroom competence.

They found that the students who perceived that their parents were primarily concerned with their achievements rather than their kindness and generosity had lower self-esteem, had more psychological problems, and actually did *worse* in school compared with the kids who felt their parents didn't put these academic pressures on them. "If your self-esteem is tied to whether or not you'll make it on all of those very high bars that you've set for yourself—or others have set for you—and you don't make any one or more of them, well then that makes for disappointment and depression," Luthar explained to me. Other research has found that when parents accentuate the importance of good grades over the importance of learning itself, kids are more likely to doubt themselves.

Again, this is about kids' *perceptions*—it's unlikely that the parents of these kids ever said anything like *Honey, just so you know, it's more important to get good grades than to learn or to be a kind person.* But when parents obsess over report cards and shower their children with praise when they accomplish feats rather than when they're generous and kind, this is the obvious inference kids make.

In 2019, the National Academies of Sciences, Engineering, and Medicine published a report that highlighted all these concerns. "Studies using varied samples and methods have converged in indicating relatively high levels of adjustment problems, likely linked with long-standing, ubiquitous pressures to excel at academics and extracurriculars (among) students attending high-achieving schools," the report said. And in 2018, the Robert Wood Johnson Foundation published a report on adolescent well-being based on interviews with twenty-five thought leaders in the field. It argued that "a family and/or school environment characterized by extreme pressure to succeed or to outdo everyone else—often, but not exclusively, occurring in especially affluent communities—can affect youth in significantly deleterious ways."

If this is making you feel panicky, like *Oh shit I've totally screwed up my kids*, take heart. Most (if not all) of us have put pressure on our kids to succeed; this doesn't mean they're all doomed to live in a cloud of self-shame for the rest of their lives. And again, who can blame us for wanting the best for our children? When we push our kids to excel, we're doing it out of love, and we're doing it because there are real changes taking place in society that terrify us.

So it's unrealistic and, frankly, kind of silly for me to argue that you should stop having high hopes and expectations for your kids. That's not going to happen, and it wouldn't be good for anyone if it did. But the research suggests that we should try, as parents, to find a bit of balance between the expectations we have for our kids and the love and affection we show them. What hurts kids is pervasive, persistent pressure to achieve, combined with criticism or a withdrawal of our affection when they fail.

"What we need to do, which we are not doing, is pay every bit as much attention to the psychological well-being of our kids as we do to their achievement," Luthar explained. Here are some strategies for finding the right balance and nurturing your kid's self-esteem.

Self-Esteem Strategy #1
Tell your kids you love them for who they are—
not what they do.

I know I'm being repetitive, but far too many kids think their parents value their achievements and prowess over and above everything else. "I see it all the time with these really bright, really capable kids, who just feel worthless," Kennedy-Moore said. They've come to believe that "to have worth, I need to be impressive." Likewise, clinical psychologist Laura Markham told me that when she was a tutor before she got her PhD, kids frequently told her that they thought their parents cared more about their SAT scores than they cared about them.

We need to actively challenge these notions with what we say and do. This doesn't mean you need to be constantly doting on your kid or telling her she's amazing. But every so often, stop and think about your interactions and whether they communicate your unconditional love.

When I interviewed University of Pennsylvania psychologist Angela Duckworth about motivation and grit, I asked her about this complicated push and pull: On the one hand, we want to have high expectations of our kids, but on the other, we don't want them to think that achievement is the most important thing. How do we do both?

She thinks that it all rests upon the notion of contingency: It's OK to want your kids to do well, but it's bad when kids feel that your love for them is *dependent* upon their actions and achievements.

"I think that's the contingency that kids are really worried about—that there [will be] a withdrawal of affection and care," she explained. She said it might help to regularly tell your kids you'll love them no matter what. "I do think just saying it, like, 'Hey, I love you unconditionally'—it's like the Runaway Bunny, you can't get away. 'I'm just going to love you no matter what. And I could be disappointed and love you at the same time; these things are not exclusive.'"

So if you do things like pay your kids for good grades or threaten them with punishment if they get bad grades, you might want to reconsider. These are well-meaning—and totally understandable—approaches designed to ensure that our children succeed, but they inadvertently also send our kids the message that their value is contingent upon their grades.

Parents sometimes communicate these contingencies in more passive-aggressive ways, too, through what are called *conditional positive regard* and *conditional negative regard*. A parent using conditional positive regard might be nicer and more generous with kids when they are doing well in school or win the chess tournament; a parent using conditional negative regard might be less patient and kind when their kids get Bs or a participation trophy. Although parents using these approaches don't explicitly say *I'm being mean today because you got a C on your math test,* kids nevertheless notice the patterns and get the message.

Research has shown that these strategies are harmful for kids' self-esteem and emotional health. In a 2009 study, researchers interviewed ninth graders and their teachers and found that the students whose parents sometimes treated them with conditional positive regard had more problems with emotional regulation and were more obsessed with their grades, while those whose parents used conditional negative regard were more resentful of their parents, also had emotional regulation problems, and were less engaged with school. The kids who fared the best were those whose parents provided them not with conditional positive or negative regard but with *autonomy support,* which means they regularly discussed their values with their kids and respected their adolescents' perspectives. Those kids were well adjusted and academically engaged.

Think, too, about all the well-meaning ways you might criticize your kids that could be counterproductive for their self-esteem. Take sports. We say that we want our kids to play sports so that they learn teamwork and sportsmanship, but then we evaluate their playing and nitpick all the reasons they didn't score—essentially sending the opposite message, framing the sport as being all about winning. When college students were asked in an informal survey what their worst memory was from playing youth or high school sports, the most common response was "the ride home with my parents." We often can't help analyzing the game afterward and peppering our kids with suggestions and critiques. When these college students were asked what their parents did that made them feel good, on the other hand, the overwhelming response was hearing their parents say "I love to watch you play."

These kinds of affirming messages are especially important if you suspect your child may be struggling with low self-esteem. It can be hard to tell, but here are some red flags you can look out for: Kids with low self-esteem might call themselves "stupid" or "bad," believe that everyone hates them, withdraw socially, avoid challenging tasks, cut themselves, or start using substances. Alternatively, they might compensate for their low self-esteem by putting other people down, bullying (see chapter 3), becoming controlling or bossy, or making excuses for their failures.

If you regularly see your child doing these things, it may be that they are struggling with self-worth, so think about how you could communicate that you love them no matter what. And consider getting your child professional help. Kids with low self-esteem often also struggle with depression or anxiety, and according to the Pew Research Center, the number of teens who experienced depression went up by 59 percent between 2007 and 2017. Yet among teen girls who experienced episodes of depression in 2018, only 45 percent received treatment; among teen boys who experienced depression, only 33 percent did.

If your kids are really young, you're probably not obsessing over grades yet, but you still might want to think about how you react to the little behavioral blips that disappoint you, because our responses to those shape their self-esteem, too. In her book *Kid Confidence*, Kennedy-Moore refers to the all-too-common example in which a young child behaves questionably when it's time to leave a playdate. In her example, a little boy and his friend are goofing around while the parents talk, and then he accidentally breaks a picture frame. Getting into the car, his mom is understandably exasperated, as well as embarrassed by her child's behavior in front of the other parent, so she yells at him—something I'm quite sure I've done before after an embarrassing playdate exodus. For kids with low self-esteem, though, this kind of parental anger can feel devastating if it's not contextualized. It can serve as a signal that the child is "bad" or worthless rather than that he just made a mistake that he can fix and perhaps even learn from.

So how do we turn our moments of disappointment with kids into opportunities for growth? Kennedy-Moore suggested doing three things in the moment:

1. Cool Down, Then Connect. Take a few deep breaths and wait until you can imagine the situation from your child's perspective. Then acknowledge your child's view of things. *You're probably feeling pretty bad about how things went in there, huh.*

2. Offer Soft Criticism. Start by providing a reason why your child might have done what he did. *I know you didn't mean to . . .* or *You probably didn't realize . . .* or *I get that you were trying to . . .* are all good ways to start. Then describe the problem: *but when you knocked the picture off the wall, Marco's mother looked very upset.* Remember, too, that it was your kid's behavior that was bad. Don't characterize your *child* as being bad.

3. Move Forward. Help your child identify ways to fix the problem. Maybe say, *What can you do to help Marco's mom feel better?* Brainstorm some ideas, like writing an apology letter, or offering to help out in some way.

Kennedy-Moore recommended, too, that parents try to prepare their kids in advance for situations that often end in strife. If your child struggles each time you leave a playdate, then on the way to each playdate, go over what you'll expect when it's time to leave. Then, if your child handles it well, praise him (more on how to do that next).

Self-Esteem Strategy #2
Praise your kids, but be mindful of how.

What we say to our kids can have a direct impact on their self-esteem, and research suggests that this is especially true of how we praise them. Brummelman, the Amsterdam psychologist, has conducted a handful of studies that suggest that when parents give what he calls "inflated" praise to kids with low self-esteem, their self-esteem drops even more.

Inflated praise is, essentially, praise that is over the top—when your daughter shows you a stick figure drawing and you say, *Oh, that is incredibly gorgeous!* In a 2014 study, Brummelman and his colleagues found that parents are more likely to give inflated praise to kids with low self-esteem than to kids with high self-esteem, probably because they think this kind of praise will give them a needed boost. Indeed, many self-help books argue that one of the best ways to boost self-esteem in kids is to praise them; one survey found that 87 percent of parents believe that children need praise in order to feel good about themselves.

To the contrary. Brummelman has shown that inflated praise actually causes kids with low self-esteem to further doubt themselves and avoid challenging tasks. In a follow-up to the 2014 experiment, he and his colleagues had eight-to-twelve-year-olds make a drawing that was evaluated by a professional painter. The painter gave the kids either normal praise ("You made a beautiful drawing!") or inflated praise ("You made an *incredibly* beautiful drawing!"). Then the researchers told the kids that they were going to draw more pictures but could choose which kind of picture to draw. Some pictures were described as more difficult ("You might make many mistakes, but you'll definitely learn a lot, too"), while others were portrayed as easier ("You won't make many mistakes, but you won't learn much, either"). They found that kids who had low self-esteem and who'd been given inflated praise were more likely to choose easy pictures. Kids with low self-esteem who'd been given normal praise, on the other hand, were more likely to attempt the harder pictures.

Why might this be? Brummelman theorizes that when kids with low self-esteem hear inflated praise, they interpret it as pressure to continue performing exceptionally. They think, *Wow, Mom really liked this drawing, and it seems super important to her that I make good drawings—what if she doesn't like my next one, though?* These kids then launch into self-protection mode, and they end up doubting their ability more. In a 2005 study, Joanne V. Wood, a psychologist at the University of Waterloo in Canada, and her colleagues found that young adults with low self-esteem feel more anxious after victories than they do after neutral outcomes, possibly because their successes could "expose their weaknesses."

As I discussed in chapter 2, research by Stanford University psychologist Carol Dweck and her colleagues has shown that it's preferable to praise a child for effort than for skills or ability. More *You worked so hard!* and less *You're so smart!* But praise doesn't just shape motivation—it can also affect self-esteem. Dweck's research has shown that when kids are praised for smarts or skills, they are more likely to buckle in the face of setbacks than when they receive praise for effort: They give up sooner, perform more poorly when challenged, and have deflated feelings of self-worth. That's probably because when kids are praised for being smart or skilled and then they fail, they begin to question the ability they were told they had.

Praise based on ability also primes kids to focus on themselves, rather than on their actions, inciting them to blame themselves, rather than their actions, when they mess up. In one study, Dweck and her colleagues found that if kids were told *You are a good drawer*, and then they made a mistake on a future drawing, they felt more helpless than kids who had instead been told *You did a good job drawing*. Other studies have found that praising kids for being "smart" increases the chance that they will cheat in order to uphold their reputation. As Dweck and her colleagues have written, when kids "believe their intellectual ability is a limited entity, they tend to worry about *proving* it rather than *improving* it."

Over time, too, kids praised for being smart or good at something come to think of ability as a fixed trait—not something that can be grown or cultivated with practice. So when they fail, they assume that they didn't have as much ability or skill as they thought they had, and that there's nothing they can do about it. In another 2014 study, Brummelman and his team measured self-esteem in more than three hundred eight-to-thirteen-year-olds and then gave them either skill-based praise ("Wow, you're great!") or effort-based praise ("Wow, you did a great job!") after practicing a competitive game. The kids then played the game again and were randomly assigned to succeed or fail. Those who had been praised for skill—and especially those who already had low self-esteem—felt ashamed when they failed, saying that losing had made them feel worthless. The kids who had been praised for effort, on the other hand, did not feel this way. Dweck and her colleagues argue that praising for ability gives kids a sense of contingent self-worth: that their goodness and value are determined by, and contingent upon, their performance.

An aside: You may have heard through the grapevine that *all* praise is dangerous for kids—that it reduces intrinsic motivation, thereby making kids lazy, and that it undermines the quality of the parent-child relationship. I don't agree, and neither do the psychologists I've talked to. "I have never had a kid or adult come in my practice and say, 'You know, the problem was my parents offered too much genuine praise,'" Kennedy-Moore said. Plus, she adds, even if you don't verbally praise your kids, they are still going to see reactions on your face and in your body language. Kids naturally want to please their parents, and it's not *dangerous* to let them know when we feel happy with them.

So yes, praise your kids—just try not to be over-the-top, and praise for effort rather than ability. And be kind to yourself. No parent can remember to do everything "right" all the time. Have I recently praised my children for ability because I wasn't paying attention to what I was doing? Absolutely. Have I given ridiculously inflated praise sometimes, too? You bet. Brummelman reassured me that well-intentioned but imperfect praise every so often is not going to harm your kid—it's when the praise you give is *consistently* inflated, and you're *regularly* giving praise for ability rather than for effort, that problems can develop. So don't worry! You're still doing a good job! (See what I did there? Yup.)

Self-Esteem Strategy #3
Let your kids fail, then reframe their failures.

One of our most important jobs as parents is to protect our children and keep them safe. But when this instinct is too well honed, it can be counterproductive. When we start protecting our kids not just from serious harm but also from challenge and failure, we hold them back and can even make them feel worse about themselves.

A child with healthy self-esteem is a child who feels capable—who feels adept at handling different kinds of situations but who also knows that if he messes up, he'll still be loved and accepted. To truly believe that, a child has to have had the chance to mess up and then realize everything's still OK.

You might be thinking, *Duh, of course.* But researchers and educators argue that parents today are far too quick to protect their kids from failure. As part of her research, Indiana University Bloomington sociologist Jessica Calarco has interviewed dozens of elementary and middle school teachers, and many have voiced this worry. Teachers say they have concerns about their privileged students "not having any problem-solving skills and being too dependent on their parents to do everything for them," Calarco explained to me.

Young people today are certainly facing new difficulties, but parents and teachers tend to respond to them the wrong way: They protect kids from experiencing the struggles rather than helping them learn how to handle them. When I spoke over the phone with psychologist Madeline Levine, the author of *The Price of Privilege*, she stressed that learning how to navigate challenges is a key aspect of self-growth and self-esteem. "Don't get in the way of your kids learning something, because learning builds competence," she said. "That's where self-esteem comes from—it comes from being capable of doing things."

Some of our overprotectiveness stems from understandable concerns over our kids' physical safety. Parents today are, for instance, much less likely to let their kids walk to school alone or ride their bikes to a friend's house than our parents were. But in taking these protective steps, we may also prevent our kids from gaining experience. This isn't entirely our fault; society today puts much more pressure on parents to protect their kids than it used to. In 2015, two parents were charged with felony child neglect when they were late getting home from work and their eleven-year-old played with a basketball in their yard for ninety minutes while he waited for them. I daresay these parents wouldn't have been arrested if this had happened in 1985.

For me, the instinct to protect can be fierce, and I certainly swoop in to protect my kids when I shouldn't. I also underestimate their abilities in ways that hold them back. If you'd asked me earlier this year if I would let my nine-year-old chop wood with an ax and then cut it up with a saw, I would have laughed in your face, thinking he'd surely lose a finger within the first three minutes. But the other day he came home from school and proudly announced that he'd done exactly those things that afternoon, and he still had all ten fingers. The pride he felt stemmed directly from overcoming the challenges of the experience.

Similarly, when kids are struggling with homework, we

shouldn't immediately jump in to their rescue; doing so gives kids the message that they can't do things on their own. Researchers at the University of Illinois surveyed more than two hundred students from second through fifth grade, asking them how they felt when their parents helped them and made decisions for them. The older the kids were, the more they considered their parents' help to be a sign that their parents considered them incompetent. As educator Jessica Lahey explained in her book *The Gift of Failure*, "Every time we rescue, hover, or otherwise save our children from a challenge, we send a very clear message: that we believe they are incompetent, incapable, and unworthy of our trust." (And by the way, college admissions officers say that one key thing they look for in applicants is evidence that they have had to overcome obstacles.)

It might seem counterintuitive that the same parents who push their kids too hard also swoop in to rescue them from challenges. But I think these actions are related, and that they are rooted in the same belief, which I discussed in chapter 2—that effort and failure are signs of ineptitude, and that effortlessness indicates brilliance. If we believe this deep down on some level, it's no wonder that we will do all we can to ensure that our kids lead pristine, failure-free lives.

But we need to push hard against this impulse. Instead of protecting our kids from failure, we need to let them experience it— and frame it as normal, even helpful, and certainly not a character flaw. "What we need to make sure that they understand is that it's not about who they are as a person," said Kali Trzesniewski, a psychologist at the University of California, Davis. If anything, we should convey that their struggles will actually help them *grow* as a person. When your kid is upset over a low grade on a math test or the fact that he didn't get the coveted part in the school play, use the moment as an opportunity to reframe the experience. Maybe you say, *I know you feel terrible right now, and that's OK. When you're feeling better, let's talk—some good can come from thinking through why and how this happened.* This reframing is important, but it can be hard for kids to grasp, because we have taught our kids that when they do good things they should feel good about themselves. Yet we don't want them to think that when bad things happen, they deserve to feel bad about themselves.

As I briefly mentioned in chapter 2, another word that helps to communicate to kids that frustration and failure are a normal part of learning is *yet*. It's not that your kid can't tie his shoes; it's that he can't tie his shoes *yet*. Levine told me that this word is one of her favorites to use with struggling kids. "I love it because it carries optimism with it and reality with it," she said.

When kids successfully handle and navigate challenges, it gives them a sense of self-competency that is crucial for healthy self-esteem. We want our kids to understand that their screw-ups and disappointments are momentary blips they can learn and grow from—and that these blips have no bearing on how worthy they are of our love and affection.

KEY POINTS

1. Kids with healthy self-esteem accept and love themselves for who they are. Narcissists believe they're superior to others and feel the need to prove their superiority.

2. Tell your kids you love them unconditionally, and don't put too much pressure on them to achieve.
3. Praise your kids for effort (not ability), but don't inflate your praise.
4. Let your kids fail, and frame failure as an essential part of the learning and growing process.

CHAPTER 7

"Her Skin Looks Dirty."

How to Raise Kids Who Aren't Racist

In the spring of 2020, after news broke of the murder of George Floyd, my then five-year-old pointed to the photo on the front page of the newspaper and asked me what it meant. It was a picture of a Black Lives Matter protest, and at first, I wasn't sure how to respond. A million things went through my head: Should I give her a superficial answer? Should I explain to her what protesting means? Should I use this moment to back all the way up and talk to her about systemic racism, George Floyd's murder, the Black Lives Matter movement, and white privilege?

I know what I wanted to do: I wanted to take the easy way out. I wanted to give her a quick and simple answer. I wanted to gloss over the terrible incidents that had led to that photograph. Because, let's face it, it's *really hard* to talk about race and racism, especially if you're white (I'll discuss why in a minute). It's also hard to talk with kids about murder and injustice; the parental instinct to protect kids from the harsh realities of the world is fierce. And it's tough to know how much a young child can even process and handle. Would I scar her if I told her what had really happened to George Floyd? Would I perpetuate racism if I didn't?

Before I get into what I did and why, I want to mention something that is probably already quite obvious: I'm white. I have a tremendous amount of privilege, including racial privilege, and a lifetime of experiences as a white person that are extremely different from the experiences (and concerns) of parents of color. Although I have included a bit of information in this chapter about the kinds of conversations that can help parents of color navigate racial issues with their kids, most of this chapter's advice pertains to white parents, both because white parents have the most to learn, and because I don't have the lived experience to advise parents of color on how to navigate these issues. Also, I have adopted the recommendations of the National Association of Black Journalists in using the word *Black* rather than *African American*. I also broadly refer to non-white individuals as "people of color" or "BIPOC" (which stands for Black, Indigenous, people of color).

In that moment with my daughter as I pondered what to do, I also enjoyed another privilege: the privilege of having read dozens of studies, and conducted dozens of interviews, on how and why racism develops in kids so that I could write this chapter. So even though it would be hard, deep down I knew what to do. I took a deep breath and explained to my daughter all the things that led to that picture in the newspaper. I talked to her about what racism is (which we'd discussed before); how racism led to George Floyd's murder; why many Americans were angry and heartbroken and protesting for change; what Black Lives Matter means; and what she and the rest of our family could do to fight for change, too. It wasn't an easy conversation, and I fumbled around hunting for the right words. But that's the thing about trying to raise anti-racist kids: You're going to have to do things that make you uncomfortable.

THE MYTH OF COLORBLIND PARENTING

My decision to tell my daughter as much as I did that day may not make immediate sense. A few years ago, before I dug into the research, I would've questioned it, too. After all, if you bring up the issue of skin color, won't that just *make* kids racist? Isn't it better to raise children to be colorblind, to act like race doesn't exist so kids don't make a big deal about it themselves?

The idea that white kids will be colorblind if you don't talk to them about race is a common one. As part of my research for this book, I surveyed more than eighty parents, asking them whether their kids had ever said or done racist things. A number of parents said no and went on to explain that, in their opinion, their kids were essentially oblivious to skin color. "The kids seem not to mention or notice differences," one parent said. Another explained that her son "seems not to notice race" at all.

Here's the thing, though: Research strongly contradicts this widespread assumption. Perhaps the most important thing I can convey to you is that kids do see race, even if you don't think they do. In a study published in 2005, University of Kent psychologist David J. Kelly and his colleagues showed that babies as young as three months old can and do discern racial differences, and that they prefer looking at faces that share their skin color. Racial awareness and prejudice (meaning preconceived judgments or opinions about people of different races) continue to develop during the preschool years and increase throughout early grade school.

In a seminal 2003 study, developmental psychologist Phyllis Katz, former president of the Institute for Research on Social Problems in Colorado, followed about two hundred infants and their families—half Black and half white—over the course of five and a half years, observing their behavior and conversations. "It is fair to say that at no point in the study did the children exhibit the Rousseau type of color-blindness that many adults expect," Katz wrote when summarizing her findings. When three-year-olds in her study were shown photos of children of different races and asked to choose whom they might like to be friends with, one-third of the Black kids chose only photos of other Black kids, but 86 percent of the white kids chose photos only of other white kids.

In another well-known experiment, sociologists Debra Van Ausdale and Joe R. Feagin observed students in a diverse urban preschool for just under a year. Some of what they saw was, honestly, sickening. They heard three- and four-year-olds say "Black people are not allowed on the swing," "Only white Americans can pull this wagon," and "You're the same color as rabbit poop." One of the examples is so awful I can't bring myself to share it here, but suffice it to say it involved the N-word. (If your assumption is that that this kind of thing doesn't happen anymore, six of the eighty parents I surveyed mentioned having recently heard kids use the N-word.) When the teachers in the study talked to a child's parents about some of the more egregious conversations they heard, the parents were mortified, saying that their child had never spoken about race this way at home.

More recently, in 2012, researchers asked white mothers of preschoolers—mothers who were well educated and did not show any overt racial bias themselves—how racially prejudiced they thought their kids were. Most, like the parents I surveyed, believed that their kids weren't prejudiced at all. When the researchers tested their kids, though, they discovered otherwise: Many of the kids said they wouldn't want Black friends. When the researchers later told the parents what their kids had said, the parents were shocked, distressed, and embarrassed.

I recently interviewed two Black women who are mothers and primary school educators. One was Naomi O'Brien, the founder of the organization Read Like a Rock Star, and the other was LaNesha Tabb, the founder of Education with an Apron. They, too, said they hear white preschoolers saying racist things all the time. Their students say, "'Well, because their skin is black, or their skin is like mud, or their skin looks dirty, I don't want to sit next to them,'" O'Brien said. "And then their parents come to you wondering why you brought up race to their child who 'doesn't see color,' even though they just made somebody feel less than or hurt their friend's feelings strictly based on race."

So yeah: Even if your kids aren't mentioning race in front of you (possibly because they already recognize it as a taboo subject— more on that later), they are certainly noticing it, and they may well be quietly forming biased opinions and sharing them with their peers. This isn't because you're a terrible parent or your child is a terrible kid. It's because of how children's brains work—how they interpret what they see and hear and how they use those interpretations to build social frameworks. And unfortunately, research shows that white parents' instincts on addressing racial issues with their kids—or shall I say *not* addressing racial issues with their kids?—end up making kids more biased, not less.

If you're reading this and thinking, *I'm off the hook here because I do talk to my kids about race*, I also implore you to make sure you're doing what you think you're doing. Given the choice, most white parents avoid explicitly talking about race, even when they're asked to or given the perfect opportunity. In a 2011 study, Brigitte Vittrup, a developmental psychologist now at Texas Woman's University, and George Holden, a psychologist at Southern Methodist University, asked white parents to discuss race with their five-to-seven-year-old kids as part of an experimental intervention. Only 10 percent of the parents complied.

In the same 2012 study in which white mothers said they didn't think their kids were racist and then later found out that they were, researchers also videotaped the mothers as they read two race-themed books to their four- and five-year-olds. One book was *David's Drawings*, a book about a Black boy who creates a picture with the help of a diverse group of friends. The other was *What If the Zebras Lost Their Stripes?*, which asks questions about what would happen if some zebras were all white and some all black, including "Could black and white friends still hold hands?"

Although these books were designed to incite conversations about race, none of the mothers talked about race while reading *David's Drawings*, and only 11 percent mentioned interracial interactions while reading *What If the Zebras Lost Their Stripes?* When the kids asked their mothers specific questions about race, the moms avoided answering or changed the subject. Some *alluded* to race, saying vague things like "We should treat everyone equally" or "Even if we look different, we're all the same on the inside," but rarely did the moms explicitly discuss racial differences and what they mean. That's a problem, because young kids may not interpret vague references to race as being about race.

Why do white parents shy away from talking about race? In 2018, Vittrup interviewed white mothers and found that they avoid the topic for a few reasons. Some say they worry that talking about race might make their kids racist; others believe race isn't a relevant topic to discuss with white kids; some assume that their kids are colorblind and don't want to change that. "They have this attitude of 'I wouldn't want to talk about it because it would make [race] real to my kids,'" said Kristina Olson, a psychologist at Princeton University.

I think there's another big reason, too: White parents don't know *how* to talk to their kids about race, and they're afraid they'll make mistakes. I was terribly apprehensive when I interviewed experts about these issues; I was worried I would use insensitive words or ask offensive questions. And the first few times I talked to my kids about race, including after George Floyd's murder, I was a nervous wreck.

Clearly, for white parents, avoiding the topic of race feels like the simplest approach—so why not keep doing it? Because it backfires, big-time. Research suggests that this colorblind approach has the opposite-than-intended effect and causes children to become *more* racially prejudiced than they would be if their parents talked to them about skin color. In her 2011 study, Vittrup found that kids whose parents did actually engage with them about race became less prejudiced at the end of the study than kids whose parents didn't.

There's another big problem with colorblind parenting, too: It is founded on the idea that if we could all just stop noticing skin color, racism would magically go away. But racism isn't just about individual prejudice; it's a system of inequity fueled by racist laws and policies. We can't end racism unless we—and our children—see racism, recognize its perniciousness, and unravel the system that fuels it. As Ibram X. Kendi, the founding director of the Boston University Center for Antiracist Research, explained in his book *How to Be an Antiracist*, "To be antiracist is to recognize that there is no such thing as White blood or Black diseases or natural Latinx athleticism. To be antiracist is to also recognize the living, breathing reality of this racial mirage, which makes our skin colors more meaningful than our individuality. To be antiracist is to focus on ending the racism that shapes the mirages, not to ignore the mirages that shape people's lives."

SMOG IN THE AIR

Why does colorblind parenting backfire? And how and why do kids become racist all on their own? As I explained in chapter 5, one of kids' most important jobs is figuring out how the world works. As they wander around with their detective hats on, they try to work out which social categories matter and why. Kids observe how different attributes play out in society and whether or not they seem to be meaningful.

They'll notice, for instance, that hair color doesn't really seem to matter when it comes to where people live, what kind of jobs they end up having, or how wealthy they become. But race? Kids quickly infer that race is a biggie, because it seems related to all sorts of important outcomes. Kids see that all but one US president has been white, that the students at school with the nicest houses are white, and that the heroes and doctors portrayed in TV shows and movies tend to be white. They also tend to notice de facto segregation—that people of different races and ethnicities often live in separate neighborhoods, and that schools are often majority white or majority Black. Yet at the same time, they'll also notice that their parents and teachers rarely talk about race, which makes the topic even more titillating: Clearly race matters, but it's also a secret, which must mean it's *extra-super important.*

In her landmark book *Why Are All the Black Kids Sitting Together in the Cafeteria?*, psychologist Beverly Daniel Tatum explained that "cultural racism—the cultural images and messages that affirm the assumed superiority of Whites and the assumed inferiority of people of color—is like smog in the air. Sometimes it is so thick it is visible, other times it is less apparent, but always, day in and day out, we are breathing it in."

Kids inevitably notice all these things about race, and then they make inferences about them in part because their parents and teachers aren't filling in the gaps. "They think there has to be a reason and no one explains it, so then they make up reasons—and a lot of kids make up biased racist reasons," said developmental psychologist Rebecca Bigler, whom we met in chapter 5. Bigler is now a professor emeritus at the University of Texas at Austin, and she has spent her career studying the development of prejudice in kids.

Children also engage in essentialist thinking, which means that they assume that superficial differences (such as skin color) reflect deeper innate biological differences. In the same vein, kids also use transductive reasoning—they see false connections between unrelated things—which means they assume that when people are alike in one way (such as skin color) they are alike in other ways as well (e.g., they are all equally smart or capable). The problem, of course, is that these psychological tendencies fuel stereotypes—ideas that all Black people are one way, and all white people are the other.

When you combine these ways of thinking with the hierarchical differences that kids can readily see, they start to make dangerous assumptions. They start to believe that whites are more privileged because they're smarter, more powerful, or just, well, better.

Other aspects of psychology come into play to promote racial biases, too. Children (as well as adults) exhibit a type of bias known as *in-group* bias, which means that we tend to prefer people who are members of groups we also belong to. In-group bias helps to explain patriotism and school pride. But it can also foster racism, as children may subconsciously think, *This kid looks like me, therefore I like him more*, and conversely, *This kid doesn't look like me, so I'll keep my distance*. Adults and kids also often exhibit what's called *high-status bias*, which means they show preferences for groups of people in society that are powerful.

White kids aren't the only ones who develop these biases. In a study published in 2003, Bigler and her colleagues interviewed ninety-two first- and sixth-grade Black children of varying socioeconomic backgrounds about their opinions of various jobs. The kids ranked jobs typically held by Black adults as lower in status than jobs typically held by white adults, which isn't all that surprising given that this hierarchy does play out in society. But when the researchers made up fake jobs and illustrated that the jobs tended to be held by Black adults, the kids *still* ranked them as inherently lower in status than made-up jobs supposedly held by whites. In other words, these Black kids believed jobs were inherently less prestigious solely because they were held by Black people rather than by white people. High-status bias turned these kids against their own race.

Other studies that have evaluated kids' racial biases have also been disheartening. Some of these studies have measured explicit biases—biases that people openly admit to having—and others have measured implicit biases, which are attitudes or associations thought to reflect people's beliefs on a more unconscious level. Researchers have found that both Black and white kids prefer their own races on explicit bias tests, and that white children show implicit pro-white biases. But Black children often do not show an implicit pro-Black bias. In some studies, Black kids even show an implicit pro-white bias.

To sum up: Kids notice race, they see it's important, and then they invent ways to explain what they see. And what they come up with is usually racist. It's far better, then, if they learn about race from you. Here are four research-backed strategies you can use to undo your kids' burgeoning racial prejudices—and raise them instead as anti-racists.

Anti-Racism Strategy #1
Educate yourself and reflect on your privilege and biases.

A few months ago, Marjorie Rhodes, a developmental psychologist at NYU, told me about an experiment she was running that my kids could participate in on their iPads. The study was called "Neighborhoods and Friendships," and my then five-year-old was especially excited to participate and get some extra screen time. When she started the experiment—I watched quietly from behind her—it quickly became clear to me that the study was investigating the development of racial prejudice.

In one part of the experiment, my daughter was shown side-by-side photos of kids of different races and asked with whom she would like to play the most. I held my breath each time she was asked, wondering if she would choose the white kid. To my relief (and surprise, given everything I have learned), she didn't—sometimes she chose the white kids, yes, but other times she chose the children of color as preferred playmates. I felt a tad smug, as if her answers reflected on me and my parenting: Hooray, my kid hadn't made the "racist" choices.

Then the iPad asked her a new question: When you're at school and it's time to play outside, which of these kids would your *parents* want you to play with the most? My daughter was again shown photos of kids of different races. I was confident she wouldn't choose only white kids, because after all, my husband and I haven't said or done anything racist in front of her. But guess what? She chose the white kids. Every time.

I was horrified, and as I put away the iPad, I wondered what the hell had just happened. I didn't want to press her on it—I felt like that might not be fair, given that I'd encouraged her to do the experiment and be honest—but I couldn't help wondering: Did my daughter think I was racist? If not, why did she think I wanted her to play only with white kids? What had she seen me say or do that translated into *My mom must prefer white people*?

What I realized in that moment was that I needed to educate myself and examine my own patterns of thinking. I needed to know what I was subconsciously doing or saying, what vibe I was giving off to my kids, that made them think I preferred white people. I started reading books to help me reflect on these issues, and I strongly encourage other white parents to do the same, because I believe they have made me a better person and a better parent. Some of my favorites include *How to Be An Antiracist* by Ibram X. Kendi, *So You Want to Talk About Race* by Ijeoma Oluo, and *Me and White Supremacy* by Layla F. Saad.

One thing I learned from reading these books is that my rather un-diverse set of friends sent clear signals to my kids about the kinds of people I valued (or, more important, the kinds of people I didn't value), and that I needed to reflect on why I had such a monochromatic group of friends. I also realized I wasn't talking enough about race and racism; I often avoided the topic because, as mentioned earlier, it's such a hard issue for white people to discuss. In doing so, I was skirting opportunities to normalize the issue of race for my kids, instead sending them the message that race makes me uncomfortable—which they may well have interpreted as that people of color make me uncomfortable.

Because of these books and the work they inspired me to do, I've also become more comfortable recognizing and examining racial issues that crop up in my life. I have come to learn that I, like many other white people who think of themselves as unbiased, absolutely harbor implicit racist biases. One day, for instance, I noticed that my pulse quickened when I realized I was being followed by a Black man, in a way that wouldn't have happened if the man had been white. I'm guessing this has happened before, but this time, I noticed it—and then immediately felt ashamed. That's a step in the right direction, because recognizing our biases is the first step to unraveling them. But obviously, I've still got work to do. White supremacy, I now realize, is not just a social hierarchy but a state of mind, even among white people like me who don't think of themselves as racists—and that we all need to identify, study, and dismantle our own white supremacist patterns of thinking. These lessons can carry over to other spheres of our lives and can absolutely influence our children. How can we teach our children to be anti-racist if we don't confront our own uncomfortable racial issues first?

I've also learned—and am trying to pass on to my kids—that anti-racism isn't an identity but a commitment to practice. A person can only be anti-racist by regularly taking anti-racist actions, whether by reflecting on and undoing their own biases, sharing what they have learned with others, or taking other concrete steps to dismantle systemic racism. I am learning, and I know I'm making mistakes, and that's OK because mistakes are part of the process. The biggest mistake is not making the effort, and letting our white apathy perpetuate the racist status quo.

Anti-Racism Strategy #2
Explicitly discuss race—without shaming your kids.

You're in the supermarket and your three-year-old points to a Black woman who's walking by. "Whoa! Her skin is sooooo dark!" he says. Do you:

(A) Whisper, "Shhhh! We don't say things like that!" to your child and apologize profusely to the woman.

(B) Say to your child, "Skin color doesn't matter. We're all the same on the inside."

(C) Walk away from your cart nonchalantly, pretending he's not actually your child.

(D) Say to your child, "Yes, her skin is darker than ours, isn't it? Skin comes in all sorts of colors," and then explain why.

Let's be honest: Most white parents do some variation of (A), (B), or (C), and we have very good reasons for doing them. Our culture has taught us that race is a taboo subject, one that we—and our kids—absolutely shouldn't talk about in the middle of the grocery store. (Chances are, if you are white, you were also raised by parents who felt the same way.)

"We've been socialized that race is almost a dirty word—something you shouldn't say, you shouldn't notice, and that you should avoid at all costs," said Amanda Williams, a social psychologist at the University of Bristol in the United Kingdom. All too often, because of this, we'll pretend we don't hear our kids' question or comment (C), we'll shame them for it (A), or we'll deny their question or comment as irrelevant or unimportant (B). Again, these are understandable approaches given how we have been socialized, but ultimately, each of these approaches is counterproductive.

We should be especially careful about (A)—snapping at or shushing our kids when they say inappropriate things about race, Williams said. "They're just noticing something in the world, and by shushing them, you're teaching them that that thing is bad," she said. Plus, if you instill in your kids the idea that they can't come to you with questions or ideas, they'll stop coming to you—and they'll fill in the missing information themselves.

The best approach, as you've inevitably figured out by now, is along the lines of (D). After taking a deep breath, try to respond to your child in a non-shaming, non-angry way. You don't have to launch into a ten-minute-long discussion about race right then and there, but you should at least address and either affirm or (gently) contradict his comment, perhaps also adding some context. In this particular instance, you might explain a bit about the science of skin color—that everyone has a chemical in their skin called melanin, which protects against the negative effects of UV radiation. If you have a lot of melanin, your skin is dark, but if you have only a little, your skin is light. How much melanin you have depends on how much your parents have and on where your ancestors lived.

What if your kid says something blatantly racist? Again, resist the temptation to lose your mind, and try to gather more information. "Rather than challenge them on the words, get a sense of what they understand it to mean from their perspective. How do they hear it? Where did they hear it from? How is it being used in the social context they're in? Then you have a better angle to how you can speak to it," explained Howard C. Stevenson, a University of Pennsylvania professor of urban education and Africana studies and the author of *Promoting Racial Literacy in Schools*. In a way, you can see their prejudiced comments as an opportunity— an opportunity to see where they are and what you need to address with them.

Once you understand why they said what they said, though, do help them understand why it was not OK. Tabb and O'Brien suggested saying something like "Thank you for being honest. I've felt that way before, too, but here's why that's racist and wrong." Intention doesn't matter; even if your child didn't mean to say or do something racist, it nevertheless did harm, and they need to know that. In *Me and White Supremacy*, Saad explained that "a common reaction by people with white privilege is to focus on their intention rather than their impact," which "prioritizes how a person of privilege feels about being called out/in versus the actual pain that BIPOC experience as a result of that person's actions."

Another common mistake that parents make is that they *think* they talk to their kids about race, but they actually don't—they instead fall back on vague metaphors like *We need to be nice to people who look different from us.* Unfortunately, kids often don't get the hidden message—they don't realize you're referring to race and skin color unless you actually use the words *race* and *skin color.*

So if you're reading a book with your child that brings up issues of race, pause to connect the dots. Maybe you can even directly connect the story with experiences your child has had. You might say something like *This story reminds me of when you first started taking karate and you noticed that a lot of the other kids had darker skin. When you got to know them, you realized they're a lot like you, right?* As I mentioned in chapter 5, one constructive approach is to highlight within-group differences—*You and Lizzie both have light skin, but you have very different interests*—and between-group similarities—*You and Tom have different-color skin, but you both love karate.*

And when your kids give you an obvious opportunity to mention race, jump on it. I once overheard a white school-aged child ask his father what was causing ongoing riots in their city. The father explained that the riots were in response to police violence. What he omitted to say, however, was that the riots were specifically in response to white-on-Black police violence; he didn't mention anything about race at all, which I felt was a missed opportunity and yet another example of well-intentioned but counterproductive colorblind parenting.

It can also be helpful to bring race up yourself. If you're watching a movie together, pause it to say, *I wonder why the villains in these movies often have dark skin and a foreign accent.* Or *Why do you think we never see a Black Santa Claus?* If you're like me, you'll struggle with these conversations at first, but they do get easier. And even when they feel awkward, remember that whatever your kids don't learn about race from you, they'll learn from their friends or come up with themselves. However bungled or awkward your explanations might feel, they'll certainly be better than the alternative.

It's OK, too, when you make mistakes. Don't beat yourself up if something comes out wrong or if your child makes the wrong inference—you can (and should!) revisit these issues regularly and work through them. Bigler once told me about a young white boy who, after learning about slavery at school, went home and said, "Boy, am I glad I'm not Black!" I'm sure the comment made his parents cringe, but in a way, that child was recognizing his own white privilege, which his parents could have used to spark a constructive conversation. And don't shy away from the work after you get called out by BIPOC for your mistakes. As Saad wrote, being called out "is not a deterrent to the work. It is part of the work." I make mistakes all the time (and have almost certainly made some here in my book!), but whenever someone enlightens me as to why what I said or did was harmful, I learn something important.

If you're a parent of color, or if you are white and have a child of color, you'll also want to talk to your kids about race, of course—but you'll do it in a different way. Many non-white parents talk to their kids about their racial-ethnic heritage and history to foster racial pride, and research has shown that kids of color who have these kinds of discussions with their parents develop a more positive sense of self than kids who don't. Some parents may also want to explicitly prepare their children for the possibility of discrimination, teaching them how to cope with and respond to it when it happens. There's no single right way to do it—it's having the ongoing dialogue that seems to make a difference.

One final note: If you've read chapter 5, you learned that sexism is fueled in part by how frequently we label gender in front of our kids. So you might understandably be questioning the wisdom of bringing up race. Won't that do the same thing? Actually, no. It's true that if you constantly highlight a social category (as we do with our labeling of gender), it makes the category extremely salient in kids' minds and can lead to the development of stereotypes. But if you *never* talk about a social category that is clearly meaningful in the world (as whites tend to do with race), that's counterproductive, too, because our extreme avoidance of the issue sends a strong message along the lines of *Ooh, this topic must be important AND taboo.* Gender and race sit on opposite ends of this spectrum: We talk way too much about gender, and we talk way too little about race.

Anti-Racism Strategy #3
Let your kids experience and enjoy diversity.

When I surveyed those eighty parents about race, a handful responded that their children had never said or done anything racist precisely *because* they live in a predominantly white community. In other words, they seemed to be saying, their kids didn't care about race because they didn't see it. Yet research suggests that kids who live in predominantly white communities, or who go to mostly white schools, are *more* likely than other white kids to develop racial prejudices. Even when they don't see it daily, these kids still learn that race exists—it's on TV and in books and movies, after all—yet they don't have meaningful interactions with people of color to counter their burgeoning assumptions and stereotypes. In a 2005 study, Adam Rutland, a social psychologist in the United Kingdom, and his colleagues gave racial bias tests to preschool-aged kids, some of whom lived in racially mixed areas and some of whom lived in predominantly white areas. The ones who lived in white communities were significantly more prejudiced.

If your child's life isn't all that diverse, what can you do? For one, you can read books and watch TV shows and movies with diverse characters. In a 2017 study, Jennifer Steele, a psychologist at York University in Toronto, and her colleagues read aloud short vignettes that portrayed Black individuals in a positive light to white and Asian children between the ages of five and twelve. A second group of kids heard vignettes that portrayed white individuals in a positive light, and a third group heard stories about flowers. Afterward, the kids were given implicit bias tests. They found that kids over eight who were exposed to the positive vignettes about Black individuals had less pro-white implicit bias than kids who heard the other vignettes. "If you have more diversity represented in the materials you're sharing with your kids, that becomes more familiar to them, and we know that children tend to like things that are familiar," Steele said. In another study, five-to-seven-year-old white kids who watched short videos that portrayed positive interracial friendships (one was *Sesame Street* and another was the show *Little Bill*) developed more positive racial attitudes than kids who didn't.

Some research also suggests that celebrating diversity is better than minimizing its importance. In a 2010 study, researchers at Northwestern University and other institutions had elementary school students read a book about a teacher's efforts to promote racial equality. For half of the students, the teacher in the book emphasized minimizing racial differences. She said things like "We need to focus on how similar we are to our neighbors rather than how we are different" and "We want to show everyone that race is not important and that we're all the same."

The other half of the students read a story in which the teacher highlighted racial differences as something to appreciate and celebrate. She said things like "We want to show everyone that race is important because our racial differences make each of us special."

After the students read the book they were assigned, they were tested to see how well they could recognize racism portrayed in short vignettes. The kids who had read about importance of celebrating diversity were better at identifying bias than the kids who had read about the value of ignoring differences. As the authors concluded, "Our findings raise distressing practical implications including the possibility that well-intentioned efforts to promote egalitarianism via color blindness sometimes promote precisely the opposite outcome."

When you can, you'll want your kids to experience real-life diversity, too. If you're in the position to choose where you live or where your kids go to school, consider diverse options (and if you don't want to, turn the lens inward and ask yourself why—you may have some unresolved race issues yourself). Steer your family toward diverse locales when you leave the house. Are some local playgrounds, parks, public swimming pools, or restaurants more diverse than others? The summer before the coronavirus pandemic hit, my son went to an overnight camp that was only half white, and it was wonderful—he even highlighted its diversity as one of the things he loved about it. He enjoyed making friends with different backgrounds, life experiences, and skin colors.

Indeed, cross-racial friendships can make a huge difference. "Friendships are a major mechanism for promoting acceptance and reducing prejudice," explained Deborah Rivas-Drake, a psychologist and educational researcher at the University of Michigan and coauthor of the book *Below the Surface*. When your kids become close with kids (or adults) of other races, they may start to realize that their biased cultural stereotypes and assumptions are inaccurate.

If your kids are young and you're still organizing their playdates, then think about who you're inviting over and why. You don't want to "tokenize" people of color—don't encourage your kids to befriend Black children *just because they are Black* or because you want to prove to yourself, or to others, that you're not racist. But if you find that you're primarily encouraging your children to hang out with other white children, think hard about why, and see if you can do better.

A quick note about schools: In general, the more diverse your child's school is, the better. But diversity itself isn't the only relevant factor. Diverse schools can (and often are) heavily segregated on the inside (for instance, the white kids end up in honors or gifted classes, and Black kids don't) and these kinds of school environments also foster prejudice. Ideally, you want your child in a diverse school that is highly integrated (including on a class level), where students of different races have meaningful shared experiences together on equal standing. Obviously, this isn't always possible. But if it is—some New York City schools, for instance, have recently taken steps to integrate more fully—it's a factor that's worth weighing along with everything else.

Anti-Racism Strategy #4
Talk to kids about racism and show them how to fight it.

Beyond talking with our kids about race and skin color, we should also talk with them about racism, how it affects people, and what we can do to challenge it. In a 2007 study, Bigler and her colleagues presented short biographies of famous white and Black individuals to white elementary-aged children for six days. Half the kids heard biographies that discussed the discrimination experienced by the Black individuals; the other half heard identical biographies but without the details about discrimination. Afterward, Bigler and her team gave the children tests to evaluate their racial prejudice and discovered that the kids who had learned about discrimination had more positive attitudes toward Black people than the kids who hadn't. (Their attitudes toward whites were the same.) In a follow-up study, they performed the same experiment but with Black kids, to assess whether learning about discrimination would be difficult for them. To the contrary, Bigler and her team found that the Black kids who were taught about discrimination were much more satisfied with the lessons than those who weren't.

If you're struggling with how to talk to your kids about these issues, I get it. It's hard! You don't want to scare your children, but you also don't want to sugarcoat or lie. What you say, and how you say it, will depend on how old and mature your children are and what you feel they're ready to hear. Two things to keep in mind, though: First, your kids aren't too young to learn about racism in some form, given that kids of color *experience* racism from a very young age. White parents get to choose when, where, and how they have these conversations, but parents who are BIPOC don't—and to eschew the subject entirely to protect our kids' innocence is to use our privilege to perpetuate systemic racism. Second: When discussing racism, don't frame it as something that happened a long time ago and is now "fixed" or "gone." Certainly you can mention that things have gotten better in recent decades, but it's important to also acknowledge the ways in which racism still affects people's lives so that kids will know to look out for it and challenge it.

Last year, I asked my kids what they had been taught at school about Columbus Day. After hearing what they learned (and didn't), I talked to them about indigenous Americans and how terribly they have been treated. My eight-year-old then said, "Back then, we weren't nice to Native Americans," which I then used as a jumping-off point to explain that Native Americans and other people of color are *still* not treated well by many Americans, that the very structure of our society reinforces this racism on many levels, and that we need to continue to fight for justice and equality. For ideas on how to broach and frame some of these difficult topics with kids, check out Tolerance.org, a project of the Southern Poverty Law Center. The website is designed for teachers and school administrators, but it has free resources that parents can use, too, broken down by age group. Another resource to check out is Little Justice Leaders, a monthly subscription box for kids in kindergarten through sixth grade that includes a children's book, a craft, and discussion materials for parents on issues related to social justice and racism.

We, as parents, can also lead by example and help kids understand the importance of being anti-racist—actively fighting against racist norms, behaviors, and policies. If you witness someone saying something racist, challenge them (ideally in front of your kids). If you feel like you can't—maybe your mother-in-law said something racist at Thanksgiving and you don't want to ruin the entire meal by making it a thing—talk to her about it afterward, ideally in front of your kids. Or, at the very least, discuss what she said with your kids later. *I love Grandma very much, but I disagree with what she said at dinner last night. What did you think? Let's talk about it.* Brainstorm ways together to get involved in anti-racism movements like Black Lives Matter. Bring your kids to protests (unless you have legitimate reasons not to, like social distancing concerns during the pandemic). Make signs for your yard or your front window.

In her book *So You Want to Talk About Race*, Ijeoma Oluo outlined a number of steps Americans can take to challenge racism, and I think, ideally, we should be taking these steps with our kids in tow. These include bearing witness when you see people of color being treated unfairly in public; supporting local candidates who fight for racial justice; telling school administrators that you value an inclusive education; supporting businesses owned by people of color; and writing letters to your mayor and city council in support of police reform and other anti-racist policies. "Systemic racism is a machine that runs whether we pull the levers or not, and by just letting it be, we are responsible for what it produces," Oluo wrote. "We have to actually dismantle the machine if we want to make change." By taking concrete steps to fight racism, we are sending the message to our kids that they have the power, in their privilege, to truly make a difference.

· ·

KEY POINTS

· ·

1. Kids see race, and then they make inferences about it based on the power structures they see in society.
2. Educate yourself about race and racism, and reflect upon your own biases.
3. Explicitly talk to your kids about race and racism. Don't be vague; make sure they understand you're discussing skin color.
4. Expose kids and yourself to diverse people and ideas.
5. Teach your kids why and how to fight racism.

PART II

....

Strategies

CHAPTER 8

"You Can't Make Me!"

Shaping Behavior and Values

THE ONE SPHERE of parenting that has most drastically changed since I was a kid is discipline. I was spanked a few times growing up, but I haven't spanked either of my two children; the approach has transformed within a generation from a common, seemingly harmless disciplinary tactic to something akin to child abuse. Time-outs, too, have recently become a hot-button topic, with some parenting experts now arguing that time-outs can erode the parent-child relationship and even incite harmful brain changes.

Slowly, it seems, many parents have been moving away from traditional forms of discipline and toward what is called *positive parenting* or *positive discipline*. I see it every day on Instagram—memes warn me that punishments and even praise "are potentially damaging" and that I should "focus more on connection than instruction." Positive discipline rejects the notion of punishment and control in favor of gentle guidance, reasoning, and negotiation. The rationale is that we can make more headway shaping our children's values and behavior when we emotionally connect with them, understand their perspective, and calmly share our beliefs and expectations with them. When we punish, the argument goes, we only make it harder for our kids to listen, understand, and internalize our values.

As the parent of two relatively unchallenging kids (of course they have their moments), this idea makes sense to me. When parents are emotionally supportive, and when they do their best to connect with their kids and gently guide them, their children will be more willing to listen and conform to their ideals. It's a reciprocal relationship: When we give more, they give more, too. When we parent too harshly, on the other hand, we might inadvertently spark an ongoing spiral of punishment, anger, and rejection, which could cause kids to act out more, rather than less.

Generally, my husband and I default to positive parenting (although a couple of times a year, we do use time-outs), and our kids respond well to it. But I also believe that, when it comes to parenting, one size does not fit all—and shaming (or even just worrying) parents for not being able to adhere to a theoretical ideal is not constructive. Warning parents that they're "doing it wrong" because they occasionally punish their kids by taking away privileges or using time-outs feels unfair—especially because, after digging into the research, I think the fears driving these admonitions aren't well founded.

Let me be clear: There are ways of handling challenging behavior that the science tells us aren't constructive (I'll get to those in a minute). But I was surprised to learn that some methods that have been cast aside as harmful don't deserve this bad. With some kids, these methods may not work, but with others, they may be useful in some situations, *if you want to use them*. I stress this last part because I also think that our disciplinary choices are highly personal, and that, armed with an awareness of what the research says, we should do what feels right for us and our families.

Put another way, the dichotomy I so often see characterized on social media between "positive" and "harsh" parenting is, to some degree, a false one—there is a large middle ground, known as *authoritative parenting*, that has impressive science behind it. Moreover, I worry that some parents may misinterpret the positive parenting approach and become *too* permissive, eschewing boundaries and expectations in favor of acceptance in ways that could be detrimental for kids' development.

THE IMPORTANCE OF PARENTING STYLE

First, I want to unpack a concept that directly relates to the science of discipline. *Parenting style* is a phrase that sounds vague but actually has a precise meaning. It is the emotional climate that parents create that shapes their attitudes toward, expectations of, and interactions with their children. The notion was born out of research conducted by German-American psychologist Kurt Lewin just prior to World War II, when he and his colleagues wanted to understand why young people respond differently to different kinds of social climates.

In his most famous experiment, Lewin and his colleagues split ten-year-old boys into two groups that were tasked with making crafts over the course of three months. One group had a "democratic" leader, who was rational and supportive. This leader encouraged the boys to make their own decisions and offered feedback if asked. The second group had an "authoritarian" leader, who was aloof, told the boys what to do, didn't let them participate in decision-making, and praised and blamed them without explanation or reasoning.

When the researchers analyzed the behavior of the boys in the two groups over time, they found a clear pattern. Although the boys in both groups worked equally well on their crafts, those under the authoritarian leader became either apathetic or aggressive, eager to blame others for their problems. The boys with the democratic leader did not develop these worrying behaviors. In fact, among the boys with the authoritarian leader, hostile behaviors were *thirty times more frequent* than they were among the boys with the democratic leader.

In a follow-up experiment, boys were split into four groups, and each group encountered three different types of leaders that switched over time: a democratic leader, an authoritarian leader, and a laissez-faire leader, who was friendly and explained what materials were available but did little else. In this experiment, the boys again became more hostile or apathetic under authoritarian leadership than under democratic leadership. Aggression was high under the laissez-faire leader, too.

These findings suggest that kids do and behave well when they're led by an adult who is respectful and supportive. On the other hand, they become aggressive or apathetic when led by an adult who bosses them around and shows them little respect, or one who provides no guidance or rules at all.

Years later, Harvard researcher Alfred Baldwin translated Lewin's findings into the idea of parenting styles—and then Diana Baumrind, a clinical and developmental psychologist at the University of California, Berkeley, revised these ideas again and began a deep, decades-long study of parenting styles herself.

Baumrind's observations of parents led her to characterize

parents as one of three types: *Authoritarian* parents believe in a clear family hierarchy and expect their kids to adhere to strict rules. They aren't particularly warm or supportive, they discourage negotiations, and they punish frequently (and sometimes inconsistently and without explanation). These are the parents who, when their kids ask *But why?* bark back *Because I said so!*

Permissive (or indulgent) parents are the opposite: They are accepting of their children's behavior, consider kids and parents as essentially equals, don't use punishment, and often give in to their kids' demands and whines.

In between these two extremes are the *authoritative* parents, who are neither coercive nor indulgent. They are responsive but demanding, affectionate but also willing to assert their power. In authoritative parenting, Baumrind stressed, love and control aren't two ends of a spectrum, but two separate dimensions—parents can be both loving and warm as well as highly demanding. Authoritative parents encourage a child's individuality and are willing to explain their reasoning and negotiate with their kids, but they also provide clear structure and boundaries.

Years later, researchers Eleanor Maccoby and John Martin added a fourth parenting style to the mix: *Neglecting* parents. Whereas permissive (or indulgent) parents are not demanding but quite responsive, neglecting parents are uninvolved in their kids' lives entirely, providing little more than basic needs and expecting kids to otherwise fare for themselves.

Children do very differently depending on what style their parents espouse. As research has shown over the years, children of neglectful parents fare the worst. They are often aggressive and disruptive and develop psychiatric problems. Kids of authoritarian parents do second-to-worst. They can have low self-esteem and are more at risk for anxiety and depression. Kids of permissive parents fall next in the hierarchy. They do OK, but they tend to be self-centered and less engaged in school and may have poor impulse control.

The kids who thrive the most, by far, are those with authoritative parents. They are more likely than their peers to perform well in school, are the most independent and honest with their parents, exhibit the fewest risky behaviors, and are also kind and generous. Put another way, the kids with parents who set clear boundaries and hold kids accountable when they violate them are the most well-adjusted—*not* the kids with parents who eschew rules entirely. When I learned this, I couldn't help wondering: How can boundaries and rules and mild disciplinary consequences like time-outs be "dangerous" if the most well-adjusted kids are raised by parents who use them?

IT'S THE KIND OF CONTROL THAT MATTERS

As I dug into the various disciplinary strategies used by authoritarian and authoritative parents, I found some answers. It turns out that certain kinds of controlling tactics are indeed harmful— but not the ones commonly demonized on social media.

As Baumrind discovered in her years of parent observations, authoritative parents use specific strategies to respond to and shape behavior in their kids. They often begin by talking with their kids about their misbehavior—collecting information, reasoning with them, and making requests. If an authoritative parent walked into the kitchen and saw her five-year-old taking money out of her wallet, she might say, *Jody, that's my wallet.*

What are you doing? Then Jody might explain that her teacher announced that their class was collecting donations for a local charity and she wanted to bring some money to school to contribute. Her mom might then say, *I am happy for us to contribute, but I need you to always ask me before taking money from my wallet. Taking money without someone's permission is called stealing, and when you steal from me, it makes me feel bad and trust you less.* Then the mom might follow up with something like *If you do this again in the future without asking, there will be consequences.*

So authoritative parents typically start with clarification and reasoning, and they are flexible and willing to listen to and negotiate with their kids. Punishment is a last resort for these parents, used only when kids continue to exhibit off-limits behavior even after it has been discussed and understood. Authoritative parents want their children to adhere to social conventions and moral codes, but they also want to preserve their kids' free will and independence. They respond specifically to misbehavior and keep their explanations and admonishments centered on *that specific behavior*; in this case, Jody's mom wanted to teach Jody that stealing is not OK.

If Jody's mother were authoritarian, on the other hand, the exchange probably would have gone quite differently. Perhaps the mom would have said: *Jody, that's my wallet. You're stealing! Timeout! You're such a bad girl.* Jody isn't given the opportunity to explain, and Jody's mother doesn't consider her reasoning or the circumstances before responding to the behavior, often invoking immediate consequences. This is why punishments are more common in authoritarian households—both kinds of parents respond to misbehaviors, but they respond very differently.

The most important distinction between the two exchanges, though, is rooted in the last phrase the authoritarian mother used: *You're such a bad girl.* Baumrind found that authoritarian parents often use what's called *psychological control* to get their kids to comply with their demands. Psychological control involves parents manipulating children's feelings or self-identities in order to control their behavior. They withdraw affection when their kids aren't obedient; they guilt-trip them; they manipulate them; they denigrate them. They make kids feel that they are categorically bad or naughty because of the mistakes they make.

Ultimately, the use of psychological control coerces children into feeling that they need to change themselves, which undermines their sense of autonomy and self-worth. As sociologists Brian K. Barber and Elizabeth Lovelady Harmon summarized in a review paper of 108 studies on the topic, "psychological control, as traditionally and contemporaneously defined, is not concerned with behavioral regulation, but with control—and violation—of the child's psychological self."

Indeed, it's psychological control that accounts for many of the negative effects of authoritarian parenting (and importantly, authoritative parents rarely use these tactics). Studies have linked parental psychological control with lower self-esteem in kids; shyness; poor academic performance; self-harm; and more symptoms of depression, anxiety, antisocial behavior, delinquency, aggression, and disordered eating.

So how does all this relate to the positive parenting movement and to discipline more generally? I've found that some positive parenting advocates conflate authoritarian and authoritative parenting. They also conflate psychological control with what's called *behavioral control.* This is when parents respond to particular *behaviors* with conversations or consequences that center on the behavior itself and why it is unacceptable. We should absolutely avoid using psychological control with our kids, but behavioral control—by which I mean converations about expectations, time-outs, and other mild consequences in response to misbehaviors—is an entirely different approach. Children of authoritative parents, who use behavioral control but not psychological control, actually fare best.

To be clear: I'm not saying that you need to punish your kids. Punishments aren't always effective, in part because kids often don't act out intentionally, but rather because they lack certain skills. And I definitely think that parents should avoid using physical punishments, including spanking. What I *am* saying is that if you've been afraid to use time-outs or privilege withdrawals with your kids because you think they're harmful, you can relax a little. So: What's the best way to engage with your kid when he does something you don't like? What kinds of consequences actually work—and won't end up harming your kids? And what should you do if *your* behavior around your kids needs some work? Read on while I tackle some real-life discipline questions.

Behavior-Shaping Strategy #1
Respond to misbehavior with empathy, then guidance.

What does authoritative parenting actually look like, and what should you do when your child does something you consider "bad"? First, let's start with some basics. Positive parenting advocates get a lot of things right when it comes to how parents should respond to bad behavior. Many of their approaches are, in fact, strongly rooted in authoritative parenting.

In their book *No-Drama Discipline*, UCLA psychiatrist Daniel J. Siegel and psychotherapist Tina Payne Bryson explained that "effective discipline means that we're not only stopping a bad behavior or promoting a good one, but also teaching skills and nurturing the connections in our children's brains that will help them make better decisions and handle themselves well in the future." I agree: I think that when our kids misbehave or break rules, these moments become opportunities—opportunities for us to see what skills our kids need to work on, and opportunities for us to share our values.

Because bad behavior is often preceded by big emotions—your son probably hit his sister because he was angry—we should begin by acknowledging and validating our kids' feelings, which helps them feel calm and listen to what we're going to say next. If your daughter has thrown her book across the bedroom in rage, connect with her feelings and say, *Oh, wow, you look so angry!* before you move on to the issue of the thrown book. Give your daughter some space to share why she's mad. *What happened here?* is a good prompt, especially if you say it calmly and without judgment. Then, if she shares, reflect her thoughts back to her to show that you've heard her. *Oh, I totally get that; you feel really mad because you weren't invited to Leah's birthday party.* You might even give her some time and space to calm down before you say anything more. When kids are calm, they are better able to listen and process what we're saying.

In these moments, Siegel and Bryson recommend that parents consider three key questions: (1) Why did my child act this way?

(2) What lesson do I want to teach in this moment? and (3) How can I best teach this lesson? In the thrown-book example, you know, because you asked, that your daughter is angry and feels left out for not being invited to a birthday party.

The next thing to consider is what you want to convey to your child in this moment—what lesson do you want to teach? Perhaps in this scenario you would want to convey that even when your daughter is really mad, it's not acceptable for her to throw things, because someone (or the book, or the house) might be harmed. Perhaps you'd also want to talk to her about more acceptable things she could do when she's angry to make herself feel better.

You'll also want to think about how (and when) to provide this guidance in the most effective way. Do you need to wait a few minutes for her to calm down? Or maybe wait until tomorrow, when you'll have more time and energy? What would be a good way to connect with her on this issue?

What you say to your child, and how you handle the situation, really depends on the kid. If you have caught your son breaking a rule and you can see in his eyes that he feels terrible about it, then you don't need to hammer him over the head with how guilty he should feel; he's already there. Instead, you might have a conversation about why it happened, what he could do next time to avoid breaking the rule, and what he might be able to do now to make the situation better.

For straightforward situations involving minor transgressions, you might also want your guidance to include *induction*, which I introduced in chapter 1. You want to directly connect your child's actions to the reasons they are unacceptable as well as to how those actions affect others. If you are angry because your son left his marbles all over the kitchen floor, tell him that stepping on marbles could cause someone to fall. If your daughter eats candy when you told her no more candy, explain how her defiance feels like a breach of family trust and could make it hard for you to trust her in the future. And if the transgression directly hurts someone else in the family, focus *first* on the victim's feelings. If you catch your son smacking his sister, for instance, respond to the situation by first checking in on her. "Ignore the kid as the perpetrator, and go straight to the kid who's hurt and say, 'Oh, ouch, ouch. That really hurts,'" suggested clinical psychologist Laura Markham, to drive home that the reason their behavior was unacceptable is because it directly harmed someone else.

These steps may be enough to help your child learn from the situation and make better decisions in the future. But I am not convinced that these are the *only* disciplinary tools every parent will ever need. Robert Larzelere, a psychologist at Oklahoma State University and a coeditor of the textbook *Authoritative Parenting*, who used to collaborate with Baumrind (she died in 2018), put it to me this way: Parenting experts "ought to be trying to help parents use the most positive techniques that will accomplish the goals, and try to minimize the severity of negative consequences." But, he added, approaches like time-outs are entirely appropriate to try when these techniques don't work, and they can, with some kids, make a difference. "There's a lot of evidence to back that up," he said.

Behavior-Shaping Strategy #2
If you use time-outs, do them right.

Research suggests that time-outs can be safe and useful when parents employ them properly and in the right situations. In a systematic review of forty-one studies published in 2012, psychologist Daniela Owen and her colleagues evaluated how well various types of nonphysical interventions improved kids' behavior. These methods included forms of "positive" discipline like praise, encouragement, and hugs, as well as "negative" feedback like time-outs, ignoring, reprimands, and stern looks. They found that time-outs and other negative responses were associated with increased compliance in every study they reviewed.

In addition, evidence-based parenting programs, including the internationally implemented Triple P, Positive Parenting Program, recommend occasional time-outs—and these programs successfully reduce misbehaviors. Both the American Academy of Pediatrics (AAP) and the Society for Clinical Child and Adolescent Psychology also condone the use of time-outs when necessary. As the AAP wrote, "Ignoring, removing, or withholding parent attention to decrease the frequency or intensity of undesirable behaviors" is "especially important in promoting positive child behavior."

So why do many positive parenting advocates bristle at the notion of the time-out? One problem, they argue, is that when parents use time-outs, they use them frequently and often in anger. Another reason—one cited by the Natural Child Project, an organization that advocates empathy, responsiveness, and physical touch between parents and children—is that time-outs create "the feeling of being rejected by one's parents." But is this always true? Time-outs are a tool, and like any tool they can be misused, overused, or both. Is it possible to use time-outs well—in a way that helps, rather than harms, our kids?

I think so. But first, let me provide a little context. The term *time-out* is actually an abbreviation for *time-out from positive reinforcement*. Time-outs are based on the premise that kids should be raised in environments that are rich with "time-ins": loving, positive interactions like "reading a story, laughing with them, making popcorn with them, or playing a game with them," said Edward Christophersen, a psychologist and pediatrician at Children's Mercy Hospital in Kansas City, Missouri, and the author of *Beyond Discipline*. When children in nurturing environments do something dangerous or defiant, the idea is to briefly take away positive reinforcement so that they learn to associate the good things—the time-ins—with good, safe behavior.

Time-outs don't work very well, then, if you haven't created a richly positive environment for your child. In other words, "it's the effort parents put into time-in that determines whether or not time-out works," Christophersen said. So when parents and teachers categorically state that time-outs don't work with their kids, it can be a warning sign of more serious problems in the home or school environment. If you rarely praise, hug, or interact positively with your kids, then acting up may be the *only* way they can get your attention. And for kids, negative attention (such as when parents get mad) is better than none.

In addition, time-outs generally only work in positive contexts because the time-out needs to serve as a deterrent, something that *takes away fun*. If your daughter hits another child at a birthday party where she is generally having a blast, a brief time-out will probably keep her from hitting again, because she really wants to keep eating cake and having fun with her friends. If, on the other hand, Max acts up during a long church service and you attempt to give him a time-out for doing so, it's probably not going to work because "he is happy as a clam at getting out of something so dull to him," explained professor emeritus John Lutzker, former director of the Mark Chaffin Center for Healthy Development at Georgia State University. In this case, the attempted time-out is actually more fun than the alternative, so you've reinforced Max's bad behavior by offering him an escape.

This raises another point, which is that parents always need to be aware of what's developmentally appropriate for their children. Your eighteen-month-old won't deserve a time-out for not knowing how to share; sharing is a learned skill, and she probably hasn't mastered it yet. Likewise, few three-year-olds can entertain themselves quietly during long church sermons or while Mom talks for ages on the phone. (Although if Mom keeps giving him brief reinforcements during the conversation—shoulder squeezes, winks, reassuring words—she might occasionally get away with it.) And if your four-year-old doesn't clean up her room when you ask her to, it could be that she doesn't know where to begin, so it may help to break down your instructions into more manageable bits. Always ask yourself whether your child's behavior is truly defiant or just a consequence of the fact that she doesn't have the skills you think she has.

Consider, too, when might be an appropriate situation to use a time-out. If your child is doing something unsavory, start with the steps outlined in strategy #1. If it's a situation in which you can use empathy and guidance, do so—and hopefully she will learn and grow from the situation. If, on the other hand, she continues to break the rules you have gone over several times, then a time-out might be warranted. When the kid "knows better and understands why this is bad, that's when you need discipline, reasoning, and explanation and talking about it—but you also need consequences," explained psychologist Joan Grusec. Or if your child is in an unsafe situation and she does not correct her behavior after a warning, then, again, a time-out might be war-ranted so she understands the gravity of the situation.

What's the proper way to initiate a time-out if your child has thrown her book across the room again? Calmly and simply. "We recommend stating the behavior clearly in terms of what the vio-lation was: 'Now you're going to have to go to time-out because you threw your book,' rather than saying, 'You're being bad' or 'That's awful,'" Lutzker said. "It's not supposed to be evaluative; it's supposed to be factual." Plus, when parents go into explanatory or pejorative diatribes, they are doing precisely the opposite of withholding attention and likely reinforce the book throwing. (Christophersen advises parents to keep explanations even shorter: "No hitting," say, or "Time-out: hitting." Then shut up.)

That brings us to another mistake parents commonly make with time-outs: They don't really give time-outs. Instead, they keep fretting over their kids, which can turn the time-out from a deterrent into a positive reinforcement. If your daughter cries during a time-out, don't attend to her; she is understandably up-set, but she will learn to self-soothe. If she laughs and pretends to be having a blast, don't yell at her to be quiet. Just leave her be. And don't require her to apologize or fess up at the end of the time-out, either. "The popular press has been quick and persis-tent in making up rules for the use of time-out that are not evidence-based and, in fact, seem to have no factual basis what-soever," Christophersen explained in an article he wrote for the AAP's *Developmental and Behavioral News*.

Another common misconception is that you have to physi-cally isolate a child during a time-out. The important thing is not where your child is but that he doesn't get to interact with any-thing interesting, including you. This means that you can initiate

time-outs in strollers, cars, chairs, even on the changing table—
the key is to withhold attention for a certain period of time or as
long as the bad behavior persists. As for how long the time-out
should be, research suggests that somewhere between four and
ten minutes will suffice; one popular rule of thumb is one minute
per year of the child's life. One study found, however, that for
four-to-eight-year-olds, contingency-based releases, i.e., *You can
be done once you sit still on the chair for five minutes*, were more
effective than time-based releases.

Siegel and Bryson, the authors of *No-Drama Discipline*, argued that time-outs can be helpful but are often misunderstood
and misused. "The 'appropriate' use of time-outs calls for brief,
infrequent, previously explained breaks from an interaction used
as part of a thought-out parenting strategy that is followed by
positive feedback and connection with a parent. This seems not
only reasonable, but it is an overall approach supported by the
research as helpful for many children," they wrote in a piece published in *HuffPost*. "However, in actual practice it seems that
many parents instead use what we can term an 'inappropriate' or
'punitive time-out' as the popular go-to reaction, which unfortunately often appears to be frequent, prolonged and done as a punishment and coupled with parental anger and frustration."

In other words, time-outs shouldn't be the default disciplinary
response, but when time-outs are done sparingly and appropriately, they are safe and effective.

In fact, Christophersen said, time-outs can even create the
conditions for children to learn self-control: In time, kids will
"discover that they have the skills to self-quiet or to cope," which
can be empowering, he said. And let's not forget the importance
of time-outs for parents. They give us the excuse to focus on

ourselves for a few minutes rather than our kids and take some deep breaths. Then we can remind ourselves just how much we love our little devils—even though they really should stop throwing books at our heads.

Behavior-Shaping Strategy #3
Model healthy emotional behavior.

To me, one of the hardest aspects of parenting is staying calm in the face of all the insanity. You might walk in on your kid feeding the cat a marshmallow and go absolutely ballistic—which might feel ridiculous, until you remember that you're on a deadline at work and you're coming down with a cold and your other kid woke you up three times last night and your husband just said he's going to be home late. The marshmallow feeding isn't so bad in and of itself, but it's essentially the last straw—the thing that makes you shriek *You're such a nightmare!* to your poor three-year-old, who just thought he was doing a nice thing for the kitty.

In these moments, losing your temper feels like the only option—well, really, it's less of a choice and more of an involuntary reaction. To other people, you might look cruel and ridiculous, but to you, it's just . . . life. In a powerful 2019 essay in *The New York Times*, mother Minna Dubin wrote, "Only a few years ago, I remember judging a mother on the bus for smacking her child. Now I have only empathy for her. Mother rage can change you, providing access to parts of yourself you didn't even know you had." Of course, this rage isn't limited to mothers—fathers, grandparents, aunts, and uncles can feel it, too, when they spend enough time around children.

At a certain point, I had just kind of accepted that this was what parenthood was—moments of joy and laughter interrupted by rage and screaming. But I also knew that my anger really affected my kids; it worried and scared them. Was there anything I could do to stop?

There was. I learned how to better control my temper from my friend and clinical social worker Carla Naumburg, the author of *How to Stop Losing Your Sh*t with Your Kids*. As Naumburg explained in her book, conflict and big feelings are a normal part of being a parent, and they don't mean you're doing anything wrong. "As a clinical social worker, I worry more about the folks who say they never fight than the ones who acknowledge and own the tension that exists in their families," she wrote. So many things can make parenting hard—your life circumstances, your children, exhaustion, and lack of support, among other things. But, she said, it's possible to learn how to be angry and overwhelmed and still "not lose your shit."

To get to that point, we first need to identify our triggers—the buttons that, when pressed, cause us to lose our temper. There are universal triggers, like exhaustion and pain, and then there are triggers unique to each person, like loud noises or stressful work projects. (Of course, our kids can also push our buttons.) Some triggers aren't modifiable, but others are—so if you know loud noise is a trigger for you, you might ask your teenager to turn down the music in his room today, so that you don't throw his speakers across the room.

In her book, Naumburg provided ideas for ways you can tamp down your triggers and minimize your stress. She also provided ways to handle anger in the moment. First, she wrote, you have to notice when you're about to lose your cool. Maybe certain thoughts pop into your head, or your head starts hurting, or you feel your shoulders tense up, or you hear yourself respond or react to your kids a certain way. The key is to work on noticing those tells—to practice observing what happens when you're about to explode. Over time, with this practice, you'll get better at realizing you're about to explode *before* you actually do.

When this happens, and you're about to lose it, you then make yourself *pause*. Give yourself a minute. Then do *anything* you want—anything!—other than lose your temper. You might breathe, talk, stretch, move, repeat a mantra, turn on some music, or make silly noises. My husband sometimes walks outside and screams at a tree, while I have been known to lock myself in the bathroom. Basically: Do anything that directs your attention away from losing it. The idea sounds ridiculous, too simple to work, I know—but I've tried it, and it does.

Of course, it doesn't work *all* the time. If I'm not tuned in to my triggers, then I don't notice when I'm about to explode, and then I'll lose it. And that's all right; it happens. Naumburg suggested that you check in with your kids after calming down, to make sure they're OK, and apologize for losing your temper. Take responsibility for what you did, say you're sorry, and make a plan for how you're going to do things differently in the future.

But most important, after losing your temper, don't beat yourself up. This is important, Naumburg said, because when we blame ourselves, we only make things worse. "*There is no reason to punish yourself for losing your shit with your kids,*" she wrote (emphasis hers). "It's not going to fix anything or make the situation any better. In fact, it's almost certainly going to trigger you even more, making it even more likely that you'll explode all over again." We want to have compassion for ourselves when we make mistakes, just as we want to show compassion toward our kids when they do. The goal is for all of us to learn and grow from the experience.

· ·

KEY POINTS

· ·

1. Research suggests that when parents are warm and responsive but also set clear limits—espousing a parenting style known as *authoritative* parenting—children thrive. This approach differs from *authoritarian* parenting, in which parents discourage negotiation and are quick to punish.
2. Respond to kids' misbehavior first with positive discipline: Acknowledge feelings, gather information, and explain how their actions affect others.
3. If your kids keep misbehaving, it's OK to occasionally use mild disciplinary tactics like time-outs, but make sure you're doing them correctly.
4. Learn how to identify your own temper triggers. When you're about to explode, do literally anything else.

CHAPTER 9

"I Hate My Brother."

Helping Siblings Get Along

O NE DAY IN a quiet suburban neighborhood in Green Bay, Wisconsin, a father drove home after a long day at work. As he neared his house, he saw two kids sprinting, one a few paces behind the other. The one in back was his seven-year-old son. He was red-faced—and brandishing a butcher knife. The one in front was his ten-year-old daughter. The dad slowed his car down, allowing his daughter to jump in. She was practically crying with relief.

"So," he said to her, "what did you do to him this time?"

The girl in the story is one of my good friends, and she did, in fact, do something to spark murderous thoughts in her little brother. One of their house rules was that the television couldn't be on while either of the kids practiced the piano. Knowing this, my friend devised a devious plan: She waited until right before her brother's favorite TV show was about to start, and then she announced it was time for her to practice. This wasn't the first time she'd done it, and this time, her brother began incoherently screaming and opened up the knife drawer—at which point my friend wisely fled out the front door. "I'm not saying I deserved to get *stabbed*," she told me, "but I was definitely a pretty mean older sister sometimes."

Oh, the things siblings do to torment each other. If only they could apply half that ingenuity and effort toward their homework. I know of kids who've staple-gunned their siblings' hands, made their siblings drink gasoline, set their siblings on fire, and convinced their siblings to bite down on live electrical wires. No, I'm not kidding. Yes, everyone (miraculously) survived.

Sometimes, too, kids fight over the darnedest things—things that don't seem worth thinking about, much less fighting over. My kids, for instance, relentlessly argue over timing: who gets to brush their teeth first in the morning and who gets to wash their hands first before dinner. Pick a verb, any verb, and I'll bet you ten dollars that my kids have, at some point, injured one another in a squabble over who gets to do it first.

I've dug into the research on this issue, and I'll start by reassuring you: Sibling conflict is normal. When kids—who naturally struggle with emotional regulation anyway—are forced to spend tons of time together under the same roof (sometimes for months at a time, without reprieve, like during a pandemic), they're bound to start yelling. Sprinkle in potentially complicated family dynamics and the fact that kids often have different wants and needs, and your house is sometimes going to feel more like *Game of Thrones* than *The Brady Bunch*. When, as part of a study, researchers watched toddler and preschool-aged brothers and sisters as they interacted with one another, they saw that siblings had more than six fights *every hour*. And that's just the average.

Although siblings have been fighting since the dawn of time, recent research on sibling conflict is actually quite illuminating.

Studies have uncovered surprising details about the reasons that siblings fight, challenging centuries-old Freudian ideas. And according to new research, the traditional advice given to parents on how best to handle children's fights is pretty much all wrong. In light of the science, I've changed how I intervene in my kids' arguments, and things at home have been improving. A few months ago, I kid you not, my daughter walked up to me with a stuffed animal in her hand and role-played how she and the stuffed animal would resolve an argument if one ever were to arise. I wondered, at first, if she was some kind of alien clone.

So no: The fact that sibling conflict is normal doesn't mean you're doomed to another decade of pretending you don't hear your kids scream at one another while you cook dinner. There are steps you can take to reduce conflict before it happens, even things you can do to help your kids start resolving disputes *by themselves*. And sibling relationships really matter. They can shape the trajectory of kids' entire lives. When researchers surveyed Harvard students and then followed up with them more than four decades later, they found that one of the strongest predictors of the subjects' well-being at age sixty-five was the quality of their sibling relationships, especially later in life. I'll fill you in on what has worked for us—and why—in just a minute, but first, I want to bust a few myths.

IT'S OK TO HAVE JUST ONE

I know this is a chapter about siblings, but I want to reassure those of you who have only one child: Ignore the relatives and "friends" who tell you you're cruel for not giving your kid the gift of siblings. The myth of "only-child syndrome" arose from several questionable studies conducted in the nineteenth century that claimed that kids without siblings are more spoiled and strange than kids with siblings. Child psychologist Granville Stanley Hall went so far as to conclude that "being an only child is a disease in itself."

Yeah, well, it's not. Research suggests that only children have just as many friends as other kids do, and that they are equally happy, if not more so (perhaps because they don't have siblings lighting them on fire). So if you're inclined to stop after one kid, don't feel guilty. You're in good company: According to the Pew Research Center, from 1976 to 2015, the percentage of mothers who had only one child doubled from 11 percent to 22 percent, and the number is still on the rise.

WHY KIDS FIGHT

Sibling conflict isn't all bad. When kids fight with one another in moderation, they can learn better conflict management skills, which they can use over the course of their lives. They also practice regulating their emotions and taking other people's perspectives. Certainly sibling conflict can be detrimental, especially when it involves significant power discrepancies, bullying, or abuse. But conflict can also be a learning experience for kids, especially when we as parents teach them productive ways to resolve their disagreements (more on that in a minute).

Recently, child psychology has undergone a significant shift in

terms of explaining why siblings fight. At the turn of the twentieth century, psychoanalyst Sigmund Freud argued that the root
of most sibling conflict was jealousy. The older child, he said,
feels displaced by his younger sibling. He goes from having
his parents all to himself to suddenly having to share them, and
this unwelcome change breeds resentment. Freud's idea is now
more than one hundred years old, and it's still quite popular. In
an analysis of forty-seven parenting books and book chapters,
Northeastern University psychologist Laurie Kramer and her
colleague Dawn Ramsburg found that two-thirds follow Freud's
lead, arguing that firstborns typically feel angry and resentful of
their younger siblings, and that they punish their little sisters and
brothers for it.

Yet new research questions this claim. "The science doesn't
support it," said Brenda Volling, a psychologist who studies sibling relationships at the University of Michigan. In a 2012 paper,
Volling analyzed thirty studies that evaluated the various ways
firstborn children adjusted to their new siblings. She found that
while some kids are indeed upset by the arrival of a new sibling,
many are not.

Of course, older siblings do often act up after a sibling is born,
because let's face it, a new baby is a big transition. The first few
months after the birth of a baby are tumultuous and stressful for
the entire family, and family dynamics often suffer for a while.
But usually, by the time four months have gone by, Volling said,
families have found a new routine, and the conflicts diminish.
When social and developmental psychologist Judy Dunn and
her colleague Carol Kendrick observed families in order to understand sibling dynamics, she concluded that most kids feel

relatively ambivalent about new siblings—they shift between positive and negative feelings. They certainly aren't all quietly seething in a cloud of resentment. "It's a mistake to expect that all children will feel jealous," Kramer agreed.

I'm telling you all this because parents' beliefs about how their kids feel toward each other shape how they handle sibling drama. If you've been primed to think that little Jack knocked his sister over because he despises her, you're going to react differently than if you thought he was being just a little too enthusiastic when trying to play with her. Volling said that far too many parents overreact when siblings misbehave toward one another. Parents assume that siblings "have malintent when, really, they just don't understand what they're doing or they don't understand what they're saying," Volling explained.

Granted, a generous interpretation may not always be warranted (and if you're worried about sibling abuse, please talk to your pediatrician or a child psychologist). But even when kids do egregiously stupid and seemingly cruel things—like staple-gun their little sisters' hands—they often aren't fully aware of their actions and their consequences, and it's not necessarily a sign that your child is a psychopath.

Sometimes, Volling said, siblings do terrible things to each other because they're curious about cause and effect, and siblings are convenient objects on which to carry out their experiments. Kids' frontal lobes are smaller and less developed than those of adults, and this means they are not so good at planning and thinking things through—especially when those things involve their siblings and, you know, electrical wires.

Siblings may also get unhelpful messages from TV shows,

movies, and books, which help to fuel the (sometimes literal) fire. Once, Kramer and her team pored over more than 250 children's books to see how they portrayed sibling relationships. She found that although some books portrayed sibling warmth and close- ness, many featured siblings insulting or devaluing each other, and the books rarely showed siblings resolving their conflicts constructively.

So what, exactly, do kids fight *over*? When researchers sur- veyed 108 pairs of siblings about their fights as part of a 2004 study, 78 percent of the older siblings, and 75 percent of the younger siblings, admitted that they generally fought over physi- cal possessions. Toys, clothes, art supplies, iPads, pillows—name something in your house, and chances are your kids will argue over it at some point. My neighbor's kids recently got into a screaming fight over whose turn it was to hold *an empty potato chip bag*. Sounds silly, but it's all about perceived fairness and value. An empty potato chip bag may not seem like anything spe- cial when it's sitting in the trash, but the minute your daughter has it in her hands, your son will notice how shiny and pretty and crinkly it is and *need it right this instant*.

This all said, some sibling conflicts do at least indirectly in- volve parents. For instance, if a child perceives that a parent fa- vors her sibling over her, she'll inevitably become disgruntled and lash out. Likewise, if parents constantly compare or contrast their kids, even in well-meaning ways—*Jenny is the artistic one, but, Josh, you really are the athlete*—that, too, can incite sibling rivalry and resentment. The ways we engage with our kids matter in terms of how well they get along. Put another way, parents have some control over how much their kids argue and how peacefully and equitably they resolve their arguments. Here are some strategies for wielding that control in the best possible way.

Sibling Strategy #1
Teach your kids to consider their siblings' feelings.

A few months ago, after my kids got into their forty-second fight of the day and I was pulling clumps of my hair out, I signed up for my very first clinical trial. It wasn't a trial testing a new drug or diet—it was a trial testing a new online intervention for parents. Called the More Fun with Sisters and Brothers Program, the approach was designed by Kramer and her colleagues to test whether parents can teach their kids skills that will help them get along better.

Kramer and her team devised this method more than a decade ago, and research suggests it really works. In a 2008 trial, Kramer and psychologist Denise Kennedy taught their approach to ninety-five sets of parents and their kids. Afterward, the siblings interacted with each other more warmly and needed less parental direction to control their negative emotions compared with kids who had not been taught the approach. The trial in which I was enrolled involved the same method, but it was taught online rather than in person. Via the computer, I learned four main lessons over the course of several months, and then I tested them out on my kids.

One of Kramer's goals is to help siblings understand each other's feelings and perspectives. One key reason siblings squabble is because they often come to situations with different points of view and desires. My six-year-old, for instance, loves to knock on my nine-year-old's door to get him to play with her when she's bored. But my nine-year-old, who likes to read alone, interprets her frequent requests as bothersome—that she is *intentionally* trying to annoy him. "She won't leave me alone! She's trying to make me mad!" he yells.

To help kids understand each other's point of view, Kramer teaches families to use the phrase *See it your way, see it my way.* In the door-knocking situation, I might ask my son to explain what he thinks is going on in his sister's head. He might say something like *She knows I want to be alone and she's trying to bother me!* Then I could turn to my daughter and ask if that's really what she was thinking and intending. She might explain, *No, I just really want to play with him.* Then I'd ask my daughter to explain what she thinks her brother is thinking. She might say, *He just wants to be mean to me because he doesn't like me!* And then he might clarify that *Actually, I'm really tired and just want to be alone for a while.*

When kids learn to consider—and eventually predict—other people's feelings and perspectives, they develop a skill known as theory of mind, and kids who have it have healthier sibling relationships. In a 2017 study, Volling and developmental psychologist Ju-Hyun Song found that older siblings with more well-developed theory of mind skills played better with their younger siblings, probably because they were better able to see things from their sibling's perspective. In another study, Volling found that preschool-aged kids who had better emotional understanding skills (an aspect of theory of mind) were less likely to get upset and lash out when they were made to feel that their mothers were giving too much attention to their younger siblings.

If you're planning to have a second child but haven't yet, you can still teach your firstborn to engage in perspective-taking in ways that will make things easier down the line. In research conducted in the 1970s and 1980s, Dunn and Kendrick observed forty families before and then after the birth of a second child. They found that older siblings were more likely to be affectionate toward their baby siblings if their mothers had referred to the baby in humanizing ways, even before the baby was born. *Do you think she is sleeping in my belly now? How do you think she feels?* In other words, "Talk about the baby as a person who has wants and needs and desires," suggested Holly Recchia, a psychologist at Concordia University in Montreal, who studies how relationships shape kids' social and moral development. Dunn and Kendrick also found that when mothers emphasize that their older kids can help care for the baby, those kids then behave in more helpful and caring ways toward their little siblings.

If your older child is still a little rough with your baby, remember, again, that the behavior doesn't necessarily reflect dislike or resentment. Gently explain to your child why the behavior isn't OK, referring to both your older child's and the baby's feelings. *You're mad that the baby grabbed your teddy bear! But she doesn't understand that it's yours, and no matter how upset you feel, it's not OK to hit the baby, because that hurts her.* Certainly these are conversations you will want to have with your younger child, too, when she gets old enough. Acknowledge her feelings even as you teach her how to treat her older siblings with respect.

Finally, it's worth outright telling your kids that you hope they will like hanging out with each other. Kramer, who has interviewed hundreds of kids over the course of her research, said that many kids don't even know their parents *want* them to get along. Sometimes, we really do need to spell out the obvious things to our children.

Sibling Strategy #2
Don't compare your kids.

As parents, we can't help noticing the ways in which our kids are unique, and we often try to celebrate their differences. But we need to be careful, because when we highlight one child's strengths, our other kids might interpret our comparisons as critiques or, worse, as self-fulfilling prophecies. "When parents say things like 'You're good at science, and your sister is creative,' they're trying to bolster each child's self-esteem by acknowledging unique areas of competence," wrote Eileen Kennedy-Moore in her book *Kid Confidence*. "Unfortunately, kids tend to hear these remarks as *Your sibling owns that area, and you're not allowed to venture near it!* This interpretation is quickly followed by their internal calculations about which area of competence is more desirable." In her book *Peaceful Parent, Happy Siblings* (not to be confused with her other book, *Peaceful Parent, Happy Kids*), clinical psychologist Laura Markham explained that these kinds of "you're this, she's that" labels limit kids, undermine their self-esteem, and fuel sibling rivalry.

I remember this from when I was a child myself: My parents sometimes described my sister as the "gregarious one," which anyone would agree is true. But sometimes it felt like a criticism of me, as well as a prediction of who I would become, even what kind of career would be appropriate for me. And it made me jealous of my sister! This is obviously *not* what my parents meant to do, but kids don't always interpret parents' well-meaning comments as we intend them to.

It's also best not to compliment your kids by comparing them to one another. Avoid saying, *Oh, you're kicking the soccer ball almost as far as your brother does!* The compliment itself is OK—it just doesn't need to involve the sibling as a point of comparison. *Look how far you kicked the soccer ball!* gets the point across just fine. Likewise, try not to say, *When your brother was five, he got himself dressed every day. Why can't you do that?* I may have said this exact thing to my daughter a few months ago in a moment of frustration, but these kinds of comments can make kids feel bad about themselves and, again, fuel sibling resentment.

Sibling Strategy #3
Try for equality, but don't fret over it.

As a parent, I've often found myself worrying over whether I'm treating my kids exactly the same. This is in part because my kids seem obsessed with fairness ("She got the bigger half of the cookie! No fair!"). But in her work with siblings, Kramer has found that kids are often quite generous in how they interpret "fair treatment." In one study, she and a colleague interviewed sibling pairs and found that three-quarters of kids who perceived that their parents treated them and their siblings differently nevertheless felt that this differential treatment was fair.

Kramer's work suggests that when siblings are not being treated the same, they go through a process in which they try to figure out why: They hunt for a reason, and if they can come up with one that seems reasonable, they'll cut their parents quite a bit of slack. "A lot of times kids will say, 'Well, my mom spends more time with my brother than me . . . but I think it's okay because my brother really is going through a hard time,'" she explained.

Plus, it's important to remember that equal treatment isn't always the same as fair treatment. If both your four-year-old and your eight-year-old have to go to bed at the same time, that's certainly equal, but the older child isn't going to consider it fair. Kramer's research suggests that kids much prefer to be treated fairly than equally—they want parents to act in accordance with what each child needs. "They want their individuality to be respected and understood," Kramer told me.

That said, as every parent knows, kids are also really good at misinterpreting our actions. So if you know you're treating your kids differently in significant ways, it may be wise to sit down and explain your rationale to the child who's getting the short end of the stick. Maybe, because of your work schedule, you always make it to your daughter's dance recitals but never to your son's basketball games. Explain to your son why you're not able to attend so that he doesn't assume the worst: that it's because you don't love him as much as his sister. If you find your kids still insist that your behavior is unfair, you might want to make some changes so that things feel more equitable—because when children feel their parents *aren't* treating them fairly, their self-esteem can take a hit as a result.

What should you do if your kids outright ask you which child is your favorite? Here, again, equality might not be the best strategy. In their book *Siblings Without Rivalry*, Adele Faber and Elaine Mazlish recommend against reassuring kids that you love them exactly the same—kids often don't buy it anyway—and suggest instead that parents accentuate their kids' individuality, such as by saying, *Each of you is special to me. You're my only Freddie, and there's no one else in the whole world like you.*

Sibling Strategy #4
Don't force your kids to share on your timeline.

My kids are always fighting over toys. *She's been playing with that ball for like four hours!* is a complaint I've heard at least ninety-three times. As parents, we often feel forced into the role of deciding when one child's turn is over, which means we also have to strong-arm that kid into handing the toy over to their sibling, which means that we then have to deal with the first kid's disgruntled wails, too. It's a thankless job that leads to more thankless jobs, and in the end, pretty much everyone winds up grumpy.

But there's another way. It's counterintuitive, and you're going to think I'm insane for suggesting it, and sure, it might take some getting used to (both by you and your kids). I first learned about it from Laura Markham, who learned about it from Heather Shumaker in her (aptly named) book *It's Okay Not to Share.*

Consider what happens when you step in to force your first-born to hand something over to your second-born. He's suddenly going to feel angry at you—the person in power who has taken away his toy—and he's also rather mad at his little sibling, who now gets the thing he desperately wants. He's left feeling mad and unfairly treated. The whole experience is not going to teach him to *learn how to share.* And your other kid? Your other kid has just learned that if he yells loudly enough, he will get exactly what he wants.

As Markham explained, the entire scenario reinforces bad behavior: It tells kids that it's OK to grab toys away from one another, since you as the parent *just did that yourself.* It also tells kids that the more they yell and complain, the more they get.

These are not exactly the behaviors we want to be reinforcing. Plus, "When children learn that adults will snatch a toy away once the adult's arbitrary idea of 'long enough' has passed, they become more possessive," Markham wrote in *Peaceful Parent, Happy Siblings*. They know that at any point, you might swoop in to take the toy away to give it to their sibling, so they become singularly obsessed with keeping the toy for themselves. It's the opposite of what we actually want.

What Markham suggested is that parents instead let their kids take what she calls "self-regulated turns." When a child has a toy, that child gets to decide how long his turn is before he shares it. Yeah, I know what you're thinking: *Well then my other kid is never going to get it.* And also, *What am I supposed to do with my other kid, who is going to be wailing the entire time he is forced to wait?*

Yes, it's going to be hard. You can start by acknowledging your waiting child's feelings and frustration. *You're so mad that you have to wait for him to finish playing with the ninja sword!* Maybe you encourage the waiting child to play with something else until his turn comes. Maybe you just deal with the inevitable tantrum—your kid might need to get out those feelings and may feel better afterward. And when his sibling does finally hand over the toy, the great thing is that it will happen *willingly*, and the siblings will both feel positive feelings toward one another during the exchange, which will reinforce the joy they can get from giving, and the benefits that come from being patient.

It's also OK to set certain limits on how long a child's turn can be, although I recommend choosing something that doesn't require you to pull out a stopwatch. Perhaps each child's turn has to end by bedtime at the latest, so the next morning, no matter what, the other child automatically gets their turn. (It's also OK for kids to have a box in their room full of their special possessions—things that others have to ask to play with and that they don't have to readily share.)

The first time you try this approach, it might not go well. The kid with the toy might enjoy watching his sibling suffer for as long as possible. But once both kids get used to the approach, they might end up being a bit kinder to each other. And make your life a little bit easier. Hey, it's worth a shot.

Sibling Strategy #5
Be a mediator, not an arbitrator.

As I learned more about Kramer's approach through the clinical trial, I discovered that much of it centers on how parents should respond to sibling conflicts—and that her recommendations challenge conventional wisdom. Psychologists used to recommend for parents to stay out of sibling conflicts, thinking that this approach helped kids learn how to solve problems by themselves.

But starting in the 1990s, research began to suggest that this approach largely backfires, because when left to their own devices, siblings rarely resolve conflicts respectfully and constructively—often, the older or more dominant child "wins" through strength or coercion, leaving the other one feeling deflated and helpless. Research suggests that siblings who are left to resolve conflicts on their own use compromise or reconciliation only 12 percent of the time. Ultimately, these experiences can teach kids that coercion and bullying are the best ways to resolve problems—not exactly the conclusion you want them to draw.

At the same time, parents shouldn't "arbitrate" sibling fights, either. For instance, I shouldn't storm into the room and demand that my nine-year-old hand his little sister the toy flashlight because I've decided he's been hogging it, which I absolutely did *not do* a few months ago. There are several reasons you shouldn't play judge and arbiter: First, you won't always know who's "right" and who's "wrong." Second, even when you do, the minute you take one child's side over the other, the losing child feels resentment that degrades the sibling relationship and fuels further conflict. "The kid who won feels like 'I won, and Mom loves me better,' and the other kid feels like 'I lost—wait till I get my hands around my sibling's neck,'" Markham said.

Research by Kramer and others suggests that the best way for parents to intervene in sibling fights is to act as a mediator—not to decide who's right or wrong or how the conflict should be resolved, but to instead stay calm, treat siblings equally, and help them answer these questions themselves. "Slow it down and help them hear each other, as opposed to deciding how it's going to end," Recchia explained.

This kind of mediation typically involves four steps:

1. Lay down ground rules that prevent further fighting as the issue is being worked out. *You two sound so upset! We're going to take some deep breaths, and I'm going to take the bear you're fighting over and put it up on the cabinet. Then we'll talk about this, with no interrupting. OK?*

2. Ask each sibling to describe what happened, one after the other, and identify points of contention and common ground. *So you both agree that Connor was playing with the bear. Jayden says he asked for a turn, but, Connor, you said*

you didn't hear him? Which made Jayden feel frustrated, because he thought you were ignoring him, and then he hit you.

3. Foster mutual understanding and empathy between the siblings by encouraging them to discuss their feelings and asking each child to repeat what the other said. *So, Connor, why did Jayden say he got so mad? Jayden, why did Connor start yelling when you hit him?*

4. Help the siblings brainstorm solutions to the problem (and if their ideas are far-fetched, try to rein them in). *What are some ways you two could fix this? What could you do differently next time? Hmm, but if we buy six hundred more of these bears so you never have to share, what might happen?*

If this seems long-winded and difficult to do in the heat of the moment, yeah, I thought so, too. Kramer has also come up with a more condensed approach, which involves three short steps that are essentially the same as what I wrote above: Stop, Think, and Talk. In the "Stop" phase, kids are asked to stop fighting, calm down a bit, and focus their attention on what's happening. In the "Think" phase, they think about what they want and feel and also about what their siblings might want and feel (the *see it your way, see it my way* approach). And in the "Talk" phase, the siblings talk to each other about their feelings and desires. Eventually, the goal is for them to brainstorm ways to come to a resolution. (If they don't have a clue how to resolve their issue, it's OK for you to provide suggestions.)

One key aspect of mediation is to acknowledge your kids' emotions rather than trying to quell them. When we yell at our kids to *stop arguing*, we send them the message that the feelings they are having—the feelings driving their yells and cries—aren't valid. Mediation essentially does the opposite: It validates everyone's feelings. This not only makes each child feel heard and respected, but it also helps each child learn how to respect everyone else's feelings. In *Siblings Without Rivalry*, Faber and Mazlish explained that in their decades of clinical experience, they have learned that insisting upon good feelings between siblings tends to lead to bad feelings, while acknowledging bad feelings between siblings tends to lead to good feelings. "A circuitous route to sibling harmony. And yet, the most direct," they wrote.

Of course, if you walk in on a dangerous situation between your kids, you can and should intervene quickly and directly. As Faber and Mazlish suggested, you might start by inquiring whether the fighting is play fighting or real fighting (if you can't tell), and then stating what you see—*I see two very angry children about to hurt each other!* Then separate the siblings and oversee a cooling-off period before moving on to the thinking and talking phases. If any house rules have been broken during the spat, you can point that out and mete out appropriate consequences, too.

Research suggests that mediation works and has lasting effects. In a 2007 study, twenty-four sets of parents were taught how to mediate and then did so over the course of several weeks at home while recording details about sibling conflicts. Another set of twenty-four parents were told to intervene in conflicts as they normally did. When the researchers compared the sibling conflicts and how they were resolved, they found that the mediation families used more constructive resolution strategies and compromised more often. Conflicts in the control families, on the other hand, more often ended in "wins" or "losses."

Then the researchers invited the families into the lab and watched the sibling pairs as they attempted to resolve a recurring conflict on their own. Compared with the kids of parents who weren't taught mediation, those who were taught the approach could better recognize their siblings' perspectives, and their resolutions were more "equal" in that they were less likely to be decided by the older sibling. A month later, the researchers called the mediation parents and asked them whether they'd kept on using the approach. Eighty percent had, with most saying they continued to see improvements in how their children engaged with each other.

In a separate 2014 study, researchers found that after parents were taught to use mediation techniques, their kids were better able to discuss their and their siblings' feelings, identify potential solutions, and arrive at compromises. As the study concluded, mediation seems to "empower the children to do the future-oriented planning that will enable them to resolve their differences."

As for me, I have also found that the mediation approach works well—when I have the mind and energy to use it. (I'll admit, sometimes I regress back to my earlier "Just stop fighting already!" approach, which, as you can imagine, doesn't work that well.) But thankfully, Kramer's three-step process is easy to teach kids so they can then use it themselves. When my kids used the technique to resolve a fight that transpired after my daughter threw my son's Uno cards across the room, I was amazed: They each (willingly!) apologized to each other and cleaned up the cards together afterward. Of course, not every time works quite that well, and yes, they still sometimes fight over who gets to brush their teeth first. But slowly, I'm seeing changes. Every time I facilitate a mediation, it feels like an investment in my sanity—and in my kids' well-being. By fostering in our kids the ability to understand other perspectives, we build skills that will last a lifetime.

··

KEY POINTS

··

1. Teach kids to consider their siblings' feelings.
2. Try to treat kids equally, but don't worry too much about making things exactly the same for them. Try not to compare kids to each other.
3. Don't force kids to share when you want them to. Let them share when they are ready.
4. Don't ignore or arbitrate sibling fights. Be a mediator: Help kids hear each other, understand each other's perspective, and brainstorm solutions.

CHAPTER 10

"Where's the iPad?"

Managing Screens, Games, and Social Media

WHEN IT COMES to kids and screens, I'm pretty sure I've broken all the rules. No screen use before eighteen months? I used to let my toddler watch *Classical Baby* on repeat while I made dinner. Kids between the ages of two and five should only watch one hour a day of high-quality programs? That didn't happen, unless you count *My Little Pony* as a high-quality program (and I assure you, it's not). My guilt over screen time grew exponentially during the coronavirus pandemic, when our iPads morphed into babysitters so that my husband and I could get (some of) our work done.

If you're a busy parent—and honestly, what parent isn't?—then screens have probably been essential to your mental health and overall survival. Yet the dire warnings about their risks may also be giving you angina. Eliminate screens from our kids' lives and we lose our minds; allow our kids to use them and we poison *their* minds. We just can't win!

If there's one thing that (sort of) gives me reassurance about screens, it's that I know I'm not the only one struggling to limit them. The American Academy of Pediatrics recommends that babies and toddlers under eighteen months should never use screens other than for video chatting; yet according to a 2017 survey conducted by the nonprofit group Common Sense Media, children under two watch screens about forty-two minutes a day. Kids ages two to five should be limiting screen time to an hour a day of high-quality programs, but two-to-four-year-olds actually spend more than two and a half hours a day on screens (mostly watching TV). For kids over six, the AAP moves away from specific time-based recommendations and advises parents to put consistent limits on screen use and make sure it doesn't take the place of sleep, physical activity, and other healthy behaviors. But in reality, kids this age use screens for nearly three hours a day, which means it is almost certainly supplanting some of these healthy behaviors. Whoops!

Then there are tweens and teens, who are on digital devices pretty much all the time. According to a 2018 Pew Research Center report, 95 percent of American teens either own or have access to a smartphone, and 45 percent say they are on the internet "almost constantly." Overall, teens say they spend seven and a half hours a day on screens, and that's not even including time spent on screens at school or doing homework. Kids between the ages of eight and twelve use screens a bit less, but they are still using them an average of more than four and a half hours a day.

WHY THE IMPACT OF SCREENS
IS HARD TO NAIL DOWN

But how much does all this matter? How much does this screen time actually affect our kids? This is the million-dollar question—but alas (sorry!), there isn't a clear answer yet. In fact, right now, there isn't much of an answer at all, and that's largely because this is such a complicated and convoluted issue.

Ideally, if you wanted to determine exactly how screen time affected kids, you would design an interventional trial that randomly assigned some kids to tons of screen time and some to none, and then you would watch them for years to see what happened to the kids in each group. But of course we can't do that—these kinds of trials are hideously expensive, for one. But more important, since there's an assumption that screens are harmful, it would be unethical for researchers to plop kids in front of screens just to see what screens did to them.

So instead, the studies that have been done on screen time have generally compared how much time kids spend on screens with measures of overall well-being or diagnoses like anxiety or depression. Yet these findings only provide correlations—a study might find that four hours of screen use a day is linked to a higher risk of depression in kids—and they don't actually say anything about cause and effect. They don't tell us how screens affect kids over time, nor can they determine whether screens are actually the cause of the outcome they're investigating.

For instance, kids who spend a lot of time on screens can differ in many ways from kids who spend little time on screens. They may have different family backgrounds, go to different kinds of schools, and have different levels of privilege, just to name a few possibilities. Researchers try to statistically "control" for these other factors, but the controls don't always work well.

Even observational studies that follow kids over time can't establish causality with certainty. If a study finds that three-year-olds who watch TV for more than two hours a day are more likely than other kids to have attention problems at the age of eight, we can't be sure TV was the instigator. There may be lots of differences among these kids that shape their risk for attention problems. Maybe kids with burgeoning attention problems tend to like or use screens more, or perhaps some third variable drives the relationship (maybe kids with unstable family situations use screens more, and the unstable family situation is what increases their risk for attention problems).

Another problem is that the outcomes researchers look at can be vague. Many studies assess the relationship between screen use and overall well-being, but findings can differ depending on the definition of well-being researchers use. When Amy Orben, a research fellow at the University of Cambridge, and Andrew Przybylski, a researcher at the University of Oxford, analyzed all the possible ways in which screen use could correlate with well-being in adolescents based on various definitions of the word and other plausible variations, they found that there were literally *thousands* of ways to interpret the data, and that some conclusions directly contradicted others.

And, of course, kids can do many different things on screens. They can watch videos, create videos, chat with one another, build apps, use apps, surf the internet, use social media, and more—yet most studies lump these activities together into a single "screen time" measure, even though they undoubtedly each have distinct effects.

The type of app or video matters, too; watching cute cat videos, Orben said, is almost certainly going to have a different impact than watching videos of people harming themselves or others. (Orben pointed out that researchers generally *have* to lump all kinds of screen use together, because even though technology companies collect data on what individuals specifically do or watch, the companies usually don't share these details with independent researchers. Sure would be nice if they did!)

When kids use their screens might matter, too. In a 2017 study, Przybylski and his colleague Netta Weinstein found that screens are linked with fewer negative effects when used on weekends. And most research looks at how screen time relates to outcomes *on average*, when there can be wide variations in terms of how screen time affects different individuals.

Finally, studies tend to rely on people estimating how much time they spend on screens, yet self-reports are hugely unreliable—both because people aren't very good at gauging how much time they spend online and because sometimes they intentionally fib. A 2016 study found that only one-third of individuals accurately and honestly report how much time they spend online; 42 percent overestimate it, and 26 percent underestimate it. Parents, too, are terrible at gauging how much time their kids spend on screens. A 2020 study found that 36 percent of parents underestimate their kids' screen time, while 35 percent overestimate it.

When I spoke with Orben, she used a helpful analogy. If a scientist walked up to you right now and said, *I know exactly how your child is going to react after eating the equivalent of five sugar cubes*, you would probably laugh in her face. How a child reacts to sugar depends on a lot of things. If a child has uncontrolled diabetes, the sugar could be deadly; if a kid just finished an exhausting basketball game, the sugar might provide a source of much-needed fuel. Also, is the sugar provided during a meal, or on its own? Is it in the form of gummy worms, or applesauce? The context matters—and the same is true for screens. Yet right now, with screen research, we don't have this kind of context, so we really can't make meaningful conclusions.

At this point, you're probably thinking, *Why is this lady harping so much on how bad the research is—I just want to know how long I can let my kid use the iPad without breaking her brain.* I hear you. But I think it's important to understand the limitations of the research on screen time because we are all constantly being bombarded with news reports about studies "proving the dangers of screens" or "showing that screen time is harmless." In reality, no study conducted today can provide us with this kind of clear conclusion—and I think it's empowering to know to be skeptical of such sweeping claims.

Case in point: In a September 2017 article titled "Have Smartphones Destroyed a Generation?" published in *The Atlantic*, Jean Twenge, a psychologist at San Diego State University, argued that screens make kids unhappier, lonelier, more sleep deprived, and more depressed. Twenge, who has conducted much of the research behind these claims herself, is regularly cited in articles about the dangers of screen time for kids. One of her arguments is that, because adolescent well-being and happiness have precipitously dropped since 2012, and that's the same year that half of all Americans began owning smartphones, digital media must be the cause of this plunge in teen mental health.

But the scientists I spoke to, and the research I read, was largely skeptical of Twenge's findings and how she interprets them. Because again, these kinds of broad claims are not warranted based on the research we have. In fact, one study, published directly in response to one of Twenge's papers, used longitudinal data—which tracks people over time—to analyze the relationship between social media use and depression in adolescents, and it found no evidence that social media leads to depression. Instead, it found evidence to suggest that the causal arrow might point the other way: Teens who are *first* depressed (especially girls) are *then* more likely to use social media.

So what can we say based on the research we have? On average, the size of possible screen effects on kids appears quite small—perhaps even too small to be meaningful. In a study published in January 2019, Orben and Przybylski analyzed data involving more than 350,000 adolescents. They found that digital technology use is associated with only 0.4 percent of the overall variation known to exist in adolescent well-being—meaning that kids who use screens a lot are, on average, only *very slightly* different on measures of well-being compared with kids who rarely use screens.

In fact, when Orben and Przybylski compared the association between screen time and well-being with other things, they got amusing results. They found, for instance, that screens are linked with decreases in well-being that are about the same size as the decreases in well-being associated with *eating potatoes*, and that wearing glasses is linked with even bigger well-being drops.

In other words, when people argue that screens ruin kids' brains, they should also know that eating potatoes and wearing glasses are potentially just as dangerous—the size of the possible effect is about the same. Now, importantly, we're talking about *average* effects—so screens could be particularly harmful or helpful for certain kids, and again, the impact almost certainly depends on the content and the context.

In a way, from what we know about how different kids can be from one another and how broad and heterogeneous the term *screen time* is, parents, *not* scientists, are probably the best equipped to assess how screens affect their kids—because the impact largely depends on details that parents know best. Parents are also the best equipped to tell if their kids are becoming anxious or depressed, at which point they can investigate whether screen use or social media might be a cause.

All these same limitations, by the way, apply to research investigating the link between violent video games and aggression. Studies do suggest that kids who play more violent video games are more aggressive—but we don't really know what that means yet.

In a meta-analysis of two dozen studies on the topic published in 2018, researchers found that after statistically controlling for several other factors, the relationship between violent games and aggression was very small, and that games accounted for less than 1 percent of the variation in aggressive behavior among US teens and preteens. But again, the effect on a specific child will almost certainly depend on the game, the kid, and how regularly he or she plays.

Keep in mind, too, that our instincts about the dangers of screens and games are nothing new—society *always* freaks out about new types of media. In ancient Greece, Socrates worried that if enough people learned how to write, it would "create forgetfulness in the learners' souls, because they will not use their memories." In 1854, Henry David Thoreau griped that inventions like the telegraph were an "improved means to an unimproved end." And in the 1740s, a moral panic arose over the potentially dangerous effects of novels, which critics worried would lead people to lose touch with reality and emulate the dangerous characters they read about. They particularly worried about the effects of fiction on women—that it might take women away from their domestic duties and inspire them to run off with new suitors. (I wonder what those eighteenth-century prudes would think of *Fifty Shades of Grey*?)

It's also important to mention a few good things about digital technology for balance. Ninety-four percent of teens say that they use social media to connect with people they already know in real life. Most teens who play games say the same, and they also say they feel more connected with friends for doing so. In a 2018 Common Sense Media survey of American teenagers between the ages of thirteen and seventeen, most said that social media had a positive, rather than negative, effect on how they felt about themselves. Only 3 percent of surveyed teens said that social media made them feel more lonely or depressed.

Kids have created some cool and constructive apps and websites, too—like Sit with Us, an app made by a sixteen-year-old in 2016 that ensures that kids don't have to eat lunch alone. In 2017, a teenage boy created an app to organize the caregivers who looked after his grandmother with dementia. It's now called CareZare and is available for free. Many apps and games can be educational and creative, too. I'm pretty sure my son learned to read in part because he was obsessed with the app Endless Alphabet when he was a preschooler. Today, he spends much of his screen time playing online chess and coding on the site Bitsbox, which I suspect are building, rather than destroying, his brain.

"For many of us, social media is an exercise in (mostly) consumption," wrote digital citizenship expert Devorah Heitner in her book *Screenwise*. "But for others, social media is a creative outlet. It's a chance to make new things, to show off creativity, to get feedback, and to share and learn."

SO ... WHEN SHOULD I LET
MY KID HAVE A PHONE?

I know you desperately want practical information, so I'm going to do my best to provide you with some. But I really can't tell you when you should let your child have a phone, because it depends on the kid, the community, the need, and your values. Some kids get phones in elementary school; others wait (or shall I say *are forced to wait*) until middle school or high school.

Many parents in my community have expressed support for Wait Until 8th, a movement that advocates for waiting until at least eighth grade before giving kids phones. I'm on board for that. But it does depend on the community. If all the other students in your child's grade get phones in sixth grade, it can be difficult to deny your child one for two more years—you might disrupt his social life by doing so, because kids make plans and connect with one another in meaningful ways through their phones. (I will say, though, that the experts I interviewed for this chapter all said things like *Look, you're not going to ruin your kid's life by making them wait*.) If you do want to wait until eighth, you might want to rally support for the movement in your community early, because the more families you can get on board, the easier it will be for you to follow through.

But—back to the question at hand. When are kids ready? "I feel strongly that technology requires that people have the ability to think abstractly and ethically in order to manage it," said Liz Repking, founder of Cyber Safety Consulting. Common Sense Media recommends answering the following questions before you decide—and if you answer any of them with "no," your child may not be ready.

- Does your kid show a sense of responsibility, such as letting you know when they leave the house? Do they show up when they say they will?
- Does your kid tend to lose things, such as backpacks or homework folders? If so, expect them to lose a (expensive!) phone, too.
- Does your kid need to be in touch with you for safety reasons?
- Would having easy access to friends benefit your kid socially?
- Do you think your kid would use a cell phone responsibly— for example, not text during class or disturb others with their phone conversations?
- Can your kid adhere to limits you set?
- Will your kid use text, photo, and video functions responsibly and not to embarrass or harass others?

In her book *Raising Humans in a Digital World*, digital literacy educator Diana Graber poses a few additional questions you might want to consider as well:

- Has your kid developed the social and emotional skills necessary to use their gadgets wisely—to show empathy, kindness, and respect?
- Does your kid know how to manage their online reputation?
- Does your kid know how to unplug?

- Does your kid know how to make and maintain safe and healthy relationships?
- Does your kid know how to protect their privacy and personal information?
- Does your kid know how to think critically about the information they find online?
- Is your kid equipped to be a digital leader (e.g., someone who stands up to bullies or creates inspiring content)?

Of course, you have to use your own best judgment on what your child can handle. One option, if you're not quite sure, is to get a "family" phone first, suggested public health scientist Julianna Miner in her book *Raising a Screen-Smart Kid*. Maybe one kid has the phone every Thursday to bring to soccer practice, and the other has it for play practice on Fridays. Plus, when you share the phone, you can monitor what they've been doing and downloading, which will give you an idea of what skills your kids might need to work on. Another option, if you think your child needs a phone for safety reasons (maybe she walks to school by herself), would be to get her a "dumb" phone—one that doesn't allow apps.

Even if you answered "no" to some of the questions, you can remedy the situation in a short amount of time by teaching the skills your child needs. Have conversations about how important it is to manage online reputation, explaining that colleges and employers often check social media accounts and that nothing can ever truly be deleted on the internet. Talk to your child about sexting—the sharing of any sexually explicit or sexually suggestive message or image on digital devices—and the fact that doing it is illegal for people under the age of eighteen in most states (see chapter 11). Help your kids understand how to protect their privacy, too.

If you really feel your child needs a phone, you don't necessarily have to wait months or years—but you do need to take steps to ensure that they will use the phone safely and responsibly. Here are the key tips I've gleaned about phones—and other forms of technology and social media—based on research and recommendations from digital media experts.

Screen Strategy #1
Don't monitor; mentor.

When I started researching this issue, I hunted for themes. Was there anything that *all* the experts recommended regarding screens and phones? I quickly found one, and it's this: Rather than monitoring or limiting your kids' technology use, be a mentor instead.

Mentorship, for instance, is the overarching strategy recommended in Heitner's book *Screenwise*. "Helping [kids] make good decisions is a better and more effective strategy than trying to protect them from everything that is out there," she wrote.

In her book *The Art of Screen Time*, NPR correspondent Anya Kamenetz summarized her overarching advice as follows: "Enjoy screens. Not too much. Mostly with others." (If this sounds familiar, that's because it's based on Michael Pollan's famous eating advice "Eat food. Not too much. Mostly plants.") Also, the AAP's latest guidelines for parents on media use emphasize that parents should ideally be engaging in media *with* their children, rather than having kids always use screens by themselves.

There's a reason everyone is advocating for mentorship: Because as much as we wish we could, we can't shield our kids from screens and social media. Even if you ban them at home, they'll have access at school or at friends' houses. It's far better to help your kids understand how to navigate screens and social media safely and responsibly than it is to ignore the issue entirely or try to keep screens out of your house.

Research supports this idea, too. Alexandra Samuel, a technology researcher and writer, surveyed North American parents about how they manage media with their kids. She found that parents generally fall into one of three camps:

- "Limiters," who try to restrict their kids' screen time as much as possible;
- "Enablers," who take a permissive approach and let their kids do what they want, often by themselves;
- "Mentors," who engage with their kids about technology and often play games or explore apps with them.

Samuel then asked parents when and how their kids have gotten into trouble online. She found that during the school-age years, the kids of limiters were twice as likely as kids of mentors to access pornography or post rude comments online, and that they were three times as likely to impersonate classmates or adults online. "Shielding kids from the Internet may work for a time, but once they do get online, limiters' kids often lack the skills and habits that make for consistent, safe, and successful online interactions," Samuel wrote in a piece about her research in *The Atlantic*.

Kids of enablers were *also* more likely than kids of mentors to access porn, she found, and they were the most likely to engage in online chats or email exchanges with people they didn't know.

As Samuel concluded, mentors "may be the parents who are most successful in preparing their kids for a world filled with screens, working actively to shape their kids' online skills and experiences."

Young kids learn more from educational content when their parents engage with them about it, too. In a 2016 study, researchers split kids between the ages of two and six into four groups. In the first group, parents watched ten episodes of *Daniel Tiger's Neighborhood* with their kids over the course of two weeks and talked to their kids about the shows as much as possible. In the second group, parents watched the *Daniel Tiger* shows with their kids but didn't talk with their kids about what they'd seen. In the third group, kids watched the *Daniel Tiger* episodes alone and their parents didn't talk about them. And in the fourth group, the parents played ten episodes of a nature documentary for their kids but were given no further instructions.

The researchers found that kids who watched the Daniel Tiger shows developed higher levels of empathy—but *only* when their parents had also engaged with them about what they had seen. They also found that the benefits were most pronounced for younger preschoolers and those who were low-income.

Watching screens with our kids also helps us gauge whether the content they're viewing is truly appropriate. In 2015, YouTube launched YouTube Kids, which was intended to include child-friendly videos and educational content. But in 2017, journalists with *The New York Times* reported that the channel was also exposing kids to questionable and even disturbing content—videos that had somehow slipped past their filters (with so much new content created every day, it's hard for even a big company to keep up). YouTube claims it has fixed the problem, but the fact is, we can never be sure that harmful media won't make it past our filters.

So how do we do this mentoring thing? Well, for one, we can talk to our parent friends and crowd source ideas. In *The Art of Screen Time*, Kamenetz explained that because the prevailing wisdom among middle- and upper-class parents is that screens are bad and shouldn't be used, parents rarely talk to other parents about them—they're considered a somewhat taboo and shameful topic. But we could learn a lot if we talked to one another about what we're doing with our kids and why, what apps our kids are using and what games they're playing, and how we're navigating the ever-changing digital landscape with our kids.

Ultimately, too, mentoring is fairly simple: The idea is to research, explore, and use screens *with* our kids, rather than separate from them. "Any form of media that supports a positive interaction between a caregiver and a child can be enriching and educational," Kamenetz wrote, based on what developmental psychologist Rachel Barr had told her. So if your kid comes to you asking to get Minecraft or try a new app or check out a new cool website she heard about, you might *both* look it up online—check it out together, read the user agreement together, read reviews of it together on Common Sense Media—because you'll inevitably share your values and concerns with your child as you do, and these conversations will educate her and help her understand what safe media use looks like.

Of course, we can't *always* use screens with our kids—sometimes, especially when kids are home all day with us and we're trying to work, we have to take important calls or finish making dinner—but we should try to do it regularly. A 2014 study found that when parents knew what websites their adolescents were visiting and talked to them about it, their kids were far less likely to experience online harassment than were teens whose parents simply tried to restrict their internet use.

Screen Strategy #2
Create a digital road map for your family.

If you feel you have too little control over your kids' screen use, or you want to structure rules and expectations, consider sitting down for a family meeting in which you discuss and create a family screen plan or digital road map.

Before the family meeting, you'll want to come to some kind of agreement with your partner, if you have one, on what you're hoping to accomplish. "There should be a lot of prework done up front by the parents to understand where they're going to allow their kids to have a voice and what their bottom line is on a particular item," Repking said.

For instance, if you really don't want your kid watching TV after 9:00 p.m., make sure your partner knows this and doesn't argue against you during the meeting. Discuss, too, what you're comfortable letting your kids do—and not do—on their devices. My husband and I don't want my kids to engage with strangers online, so we have been selective about the apps we let them use. We signed my son up for a kids' email that requires us to review and approve any emails that come from, or are sent to, people who aren't on his preapproved contact list.

Then sit down as a family and explain what you're hoping to do. You might say that your goal is to help the family figure out ways to use screens constructively—to bring the family joy, connect the family with others, and help the family learn. You might add that you hope to minimize the bad things that can come with screens, like fights and sleep loss. The goal of the meeting, you might say, is to come up with rules and guidelines to create an ideal balance.

Here are some things to keep in mind for the discussion:

- Do you want to create daily (or weekly) time limits, or do you feel it's OK for your kids to use screens whenever they want, provided they have finished their homework, chores, and other essential activities? Check out the AAP's Media Time Calculator at healthychildren.org (perhaps with your kids), which will help you figure out how much time, on average, your kids will have left for screen time each day after doing what they need to do.
- Will you expect your kids to ask your permission, or at least check in with you, before using a screen? Some experts say this can be helpful because it communicates to kids that screens deserve respect and thoughtfulness. "By just pausing at that permission getting, you're already asking a child to be conscious about what they're doing," said Liz Kline, the vice president of education programs at Common Sense Media.
- Consider a media curfew—like that all phones have to be downstairs charging by 9:00 p.m. Screens emit blue light, which reduces the body's production of the sleep hormone melatonin, so the use of screens right before bedtime (or nap time) can make it harder for kids to fall asleep.

- Think about how the layout of your house could be tweaked to make it easier to manage screen use. Maybe all phones and tablets have to be stored in a specific place. A central charging hub (and no chargers in the bedrooms) could help.
- Where will kids be able to use their devices? Perhaps they can do certain activities (like online reading) in their rooms but others (like chats and video chats) must be done in shared spaces, so you can check on what they're doing. If that sounds intrusive, consider that when your kids have real-life playdates, you're likely to pop in every so often to check in and offer snacks; digital playdates should be no different, Heitner said.
- What could you do to encourage shared media use? Should you have a family movie night each week, or Sunday afternoon game watching?
- What should happen if kids want to get a new app or try out a new game or social media site? Should they come to you first? What kind of research has to be done? Who pays?
- If there's only one TV or tablet, what's the process for determining who gets to use it and when?
- What rules should you have about creating and sharing photos and other content?

Screen Strategy #3
Teach your kids about privacy.

Diana Graber, the author of *Raising Humans in a Digital World*, has taught cyber civics to hundreds of American middle schoolers. In one of her seventh-grade lessons, she makes a special announcement. She says, "The school principal just hired a research firm to help him customize the school to better meet your needs. To accomplish this task, researchers will be on campus for a week. During this time, they'll be collecting personal information about you, such as your name, age, address, and so forth. They'll also be following you around and tracking your habits, like where you go (including the restroom, lunch area, playground, etc.), how long you spend there, who you spend time with, and basically everything you do all day."

As you can imagine, her seventh graders do not take this information well. In fact, they tend to go ballistic, complaining that this "research" is an egregious violation of their privacy. Graber then invites her students to write letters complaining to the school administration. In these letters, the students say things like *This to me is an invasion of privacy and stalking* and *These people have no right to know my habits or personal information.*

Graber is, in fact, making the entire story up in order to make a point. She next explains to the students that, in reality, no researchers are coming to the school—but that kids share this exact kind of personal information, including where they go and with whom, with social media apps and companies every time they use their phones. The lesson, Graber said, is always a powerful one—her students have rarely thought about how much information they give away via their devices, and they are often eager to learn how to update their privacy settings and use their phones more responsibly.

Although it might be hard to duplicate this lesson at home, consider asking your kids how they might feel if their principal made a similar kind of announcement, and use it to start a conversation about online privacy and data mining. If you're not sure where to start, Common Sense Media has free lesson plans available on talking to kids about privacy, tailored by grade, in their digital citizenship curriculum.

Another great way to teach your kids the importance of privacy (and consent and boundaries), even from a young age, is to ask them for their permission before posting photos of them to social media. This shows them that it's important to respect others and their privacy when using social media, and that people should have control over how their pictures are shared.

The same thing goes when camps and schools ask if they can use images of your children for their marketing literature. Explain to your kids what they're requesting and then ask for *their* consent. Parents aren't often aware that kids care about this: In a 2016 study, researchers asked parents and their kids, aged ten to seventeen, about their rules and expectations for technology use. Twice as many children as parents said that parents shouldn't share pictures of kids without asking first.

Screen Strategy #4
Put down *your* phone.

At the beginning of her book *It's Complicated: The Social Lives of Networked Teens*, technology and social media researcher danah boyd (her legal name is uncapitalized) shared what she saw while attending a high school homecoming football game in Nashville, Tennessee, in 2010. All the teens at the game had cell phones, but they were not spending their time engrossed in their devices. Usually, boyd said, when they looked at their phones, it was to briefly share something with people around them. "Although many parents I've met lament their children's obsession with their phones, the teens in Nashville were treating their phones as no more than a glorified camera plus coordination device," she wrote.

But some people, she saw, *were* glued to their devices almost the entire time. The parents.

According to a 2016 Common Sense Media survey, parents spend more time on screens than their kids do—an average of nearly 9.5 hours a day, with more than 80 percent of that time devoted to personal screen use (not work-related use). And yet, this survey also found that 78 percent of parents think they are good media and technology role models for their children. Ha!

Part of the problem is that our kids notice when we are using screens—but we don't notice them noticing it. In a study published in 2014, pediatrician Jenny Radesky, then at Boston Medical Center, and her colleagues observed fifty-five caregivers while they dined in fast food restaurants with at least one young child. Even when the caregivers had other adults with them, forty of the fifty-five spent most of the meal engrossed in their phones or tablets. When the children tried to talk to them or otherwise get their attention, the caregivers often scolded them or responded robotically to them without looking up. One woman pushed a young boy's hands away when he tried to repeatedly lift her face from the screen to engage her in conversation.

When we're not responsive to our kids, they can become not just frustrated but despondent. In a highly cited experiment from 1975, developmental psychologist Edward Tronick and his colleagues asked mothers and their two-month-old babies to engage in normal play together. Then they asked the mothers to suddenly make their facial expressions flat and expressionless for three minutes (as undoubtedly happens when we get engrossed in our phones). Tronick watched what the babies did in response: They first tried to get their mothers' attention. Then, when the mothers didn't respond, they pulled away from their mothers, looking withdrawn and hopeless. Is this what our kids go through every time we get sucked into social media and ignore their pleas for attention? It's heartbreaking to think about, but I fear the answer might be yes.

Researchers who engage with kids about media issues say that kids frequently complain that their parents are always glued to their screens. As Heitner explained in *Screenwise*, her students once created an app to solve the problem, which they named Stop Texting, Enjoy Life. It shuts down a parent's phone when triggered by their child's voice. "As parents, we have put timers on our kids' use of technology, and these clever kids are letting us know that they want the same consideration," Heitner wrote. Consider asking your kids which of your tech habits they find the most annoying—and see if you can do something to change them.

It's important to monitor and manage our media use for another crucial reason, too: We can't expect our kids to have a healthy relationship with screens if we don't. As I've written over and over again in this book, kids do as we do, not as we say. We need to model the behaviors and choices we want to see in our children.

If picking up your phone every four seconds to check social media is a reflexive habit, what can you do to crack down on your use? First, disable notifications, at least during periods when you're typically with your family. My husband is really good at this; I could be better, but I've been making progress.

Designate some strict "no screen" times for yourself, too. Perhaps you put your screens away for the half hour after your kids come home from school (if you're home); the hour after you get home from work; during meals; and during family outings (like trips to museums and zoos). Repking said that when she picks up her kids from school, she always arrives ten minutes early so that she can catch up on her emails and social media, and then as soon as she sees her daughter walk out of the building, she puts her phone down for the entire ride home.

Another strategy you can use, especially with young kids, is to explain why you're using your phone whenever you use it, Graber suggested. You might say, *I'm just going to go look up the recipe we wanted to make*, or *Daddy just texted me to say he's on his way home, so I'm going to reply that I got it.* Engaging in a tech play-by-play also helps us recognize when we're using our devices when we don't need to be, Graber said. *I'm just going to check my Instagram for the third time in five minutes* doesn't sound very reasonable, does it? When we have to admit to ourselves what we're doing, it makes us ease up and put our phones down, and it helps us model the values we hope to see in our children.

1. The research so far doesn't tell us anything clear about how screens and digital media affect kids.
2. Help your child develop essential skills before letting them have their own phone.
3. As much as possible, use screens *with* your kids, and talk to them about what they are doing and seeing.
4. Create a family media plan.
5. Model healthy screen use yourself.

CHAPTER 11

"When I Touch It, It Gets Bigger!"

Talking to Kids About Sex and Pornography

JUST BEFORE THE coronavirus hit, my then eight-year-old had a friend over for a playdate. At one point, they asked if they could borrow the iPad to listen to music, and I agreed. For half an hour, I heard songs blaring from his room—including "Weird Al" Yankovic's "Eat It," which cracked me up—and then suddenly, all went quiet.

The kids had been loudly bantering for almost the entire playdate, and I wondered about the sudden silence. I knocked on my son's door, and when he said "come in," I saw both boys huddled over the iPad on the bed.

"What are you doing?" I asked.

"We were . . . looking at . . . pictures," his friend answered. My son looked horrified.

"Well, I'll take the iPad now," I said. They handed it to me immediately, and my curiosity dial went up to 11.

As I walked away, I turned the iPad on, and saw that they'd just finished a Google search.

They had searched for "naked people."

It was actually (kind of) funny that this happened when it did, because earlier that week, I had interviewed a handful of sex educators for this chapter. Everyone encouraged me to talk to my kids about pornography, saying that it's never too early and that many kids encounter porn by the age of eight. *Whatever—my son couldn't possibly need to know about that yet*, I scoffed to myself. Clearly, the joke was on me.

Parents, it turns out, very often underestimate what they need to tell their kids about sex and pornography—and even when we want to have these conversations, we don't know how. Some of us end up waiting years for the "right moment," when of course, there is no such thing. Who can blame us, though? Many of us were raised by parents who considered sex an extremely private subject. Talking about sex with our kids seems about as fun as getting a colonoscopy.

But we need to get over our fears, because research suggests that many kids reach adulthood without having received *any* information on the subject from their parents—and that's not OK. In a 2015 study, researchers analyzed the results of a national CDC-sponsored survey of nearly two thousand young women between the ages of fifteen and twenty-four. Three out of four said that before the age of eighteen, they had never learned anything from their parents about sex or birth control, a finding that is all the more shocking when you consider that parents are much more likely to talk to girls about sex than they are to talk to boys (probably because they desperately do not want their daughters to get pregnant).

In their 2020 book *Sexual Citizens*, Columbia University anthropologist Jennifer Hirsch and sociologist Shamus Khan interviewed more than 150 Columbia students about the conversations they'd had—or shall I say didn't have?—with their parents about sex. "Time and again, we thought of how disappointed we were, not in young people, but in the communities that had raised them," Hirsch and Khan wrote. "Almost no one related an experience where an adult sat them down and conveyed that sex would be an important and potentially joyful part of their life, and so they should think about what they wanted from sex, and how to realize those desires with other people in a respectful way."

It is bizarre when you stop and think about it. We spend decades preparing our kids for so many aspects of their adult lives, yet for some reason, we ignore a part of their life that's typically a cornerstone of love and relationships and drives the propagation of our species. This topic we gloss over also happens to be extremely complicated and difficult to navigate, yet we just shrug our shoulders and assume our kids will figure it all out by themselves.

If your response is *But kids are getting sex education in school, so it's fine*, um, no. According to the nonprofit Guttmacher Institute, nineteen US states do not require that sex education be taught in school at all, and of those that do, only seventeen mandate that the information be medically accurate. When the New York American Civil Liberties Union evaluated the quality of New York's sex education in 2012, the organization found that one school district described the penis as a "sperm gun" and the vagina simply as "penis fits in here." Most school programs promote abstinence—only twenty states, along with Washington, DC, require that their programs even mention contraception—even though, according to a 2008 study, teenage girls who receive abstinence-only sexual education are no less likely to get pregnant than girls who receive no sex education at all.

Research also suggests that abstinence-only programs don't

lower the risk of sexual assault, but that more comprehensive sex education that includes teaching refusal skills does. "If there were a vaccine that could prevent half of all campus rapes, and it was only provided to young people in half the school districts in the country and those whose parents could afford a progressive private education, there'd be a national outcry," Hirsch and Khan wrote in *Sexual Citizens*. "And yet that is essentially the situation in the United States." According to a 2017 study based on a survey of more than 1,600 Columbia and Barnard College students, more than one in four female and one in eight male college students experience sexual assault on college campuses. An even higher proportion of gender-nonconforming students—more than one in three—experiences a sexual assault. In a 2017 CDC national survey, nearly one in ten high school students said they had been forced to do "sexual things" they didn't want to do in the past year.

Even if you live in a state that provides comprehensive sex education, your kids still might not be learning what you think they are. Among other things, most comprehensive sex ed programs focus only on the bad things that can happen when teens have sex, such as pregnancy and STDs. Fewer than half of high schools and fewer than a fifth of middle schools teach *all* the topics recommended by the CDC, which include what healthy relationships look like and navigating the issue of consent (only taught by nine states and Washington, DC).

So no—kids don't learn much about sex in school. We need to educate them ourselves. Still, some of you might be wondering: Won't conversations about sex at home increase the chance that our kids will start doing it? Actually, no—although *how* parents talk to kids about sex does seem to matter. A 2015 study found that when parents introduce their kids to the issue of sex with a stern, scaremongering lecture, kids are more likely to have sexual intercourse during adolescence. On the other hand, when parents have supportive and receptive conversations with their kids about sex, kids are less likely to take sexual risks. In a 2012 nationwide survey, 87 percent of teens said it would be much easier for them to postpone sexual activity and avoid pregnancy if they were able to have more open and honest conversations about sex with their parents.

If it's hard for you to stomach the idea of talking to your kids about sex itself, frame it in your mind as being more about *sexuality*. Sexuality is a broader topic that encompasses gender roles, relationships, desire, and consent, and these are issues our kids have to grapple with every day.

"As soon as they are out in the world, they are seeing people in relationships; people are interacting with them based on what they perceive the kids' gender to be. When they start watching TV or consuming any other kind of media, they're learning a lot about sexuality," said Elizabeth Schroeder, a New Jersey–based sex educator who has worked internationally with schools, parent groups, and other youth-serving organizations for over twenty-five years. "It's really important, therefore, for parents to talk with their kids proactively from the very beginning to help the kids understand the world around them."

MASCULINITY IN CRISIS

Parents of boys have an especially difficult and important job, because boys are growing up in a world that sends them strong, and often dangerous, messages about masculinity and sex. A

2018 national survey of American kids found that 72 percent of boys feel pressure to be physically strong, while one in three boys believes that society expects them to hide or suppress feelings of sadness or fear. In addition, 40 percent of heterosexual boys between the ages of fourteen and nineteen say they feel pressure to "hook up" with girls, while 32 percent of all boys this age feel pressure to "join in when other boys talk about girls in a sexual way." Nearly half of boys aged fourteen to nineteen said they had heard their fathers or other male family members make sexual jokes and comments about women.

The media sends boys dangerous messages, too. In one disturbing study, researchers at the University of Massachusetts edited together scenes from the R-rated movies *Showgirls* and *9½ Weeks* that depicted women as sexual objects (none of the scenes involved overt physical violence). They showed these clips to a group of mostly college-aged young adults, while another group of young adults watched cartoons. Afterward, the researchers asked both groups to read fictitious magazine accounts describing stranger and acquaintance rape and then asked them questions about what they read.

The men in the study who had watched the degrading sexual videos were much more likely than the men who'd watched cartoons to think that the girls being raped by an acquaintance actually enjoyed it and secretly "got what she wanted." (No matter which videos the women in the study watched, they did not think women enjoyed being raped.) The men in the study were also asked whether they might commit acquaintance rape themselves. Compared with the men who hadn't watched the degrading videos, twice as many of those who had—nearly one in every five—admitted that yes, sure, they might commit rape.

Every year, high school and college scandals come to light involving groups of boys (often athletic teams or fraternities— groups that celebrate and reinforce certain types of masculinity) acting in horrifically misogynistic ways. Who knows how many more things happen that never make it into the national media. Many of these incidents involve otherwise so-called good or smart young men—guys, in other words, who really should know better.

In 2016, for instance, the Harvard men's soccer team was caught rating new recruits to the women's team based on their hotness, which they'd been doing since 2012; at Columbia, the men's wrestling team referred to the school's female students as "ugly socially awkward cunts"; and at Amherst, the men's cross-country team sent around an email that contained photos of eight women along with their alleged sexual histories. In many of these examples, the perpetrators said that they were just trying to be funny. But as journalist Peggy Orenstein explained in her 2020 book, *Boys & Sex*, for sexual harassment to seem funny, it has to feel harmless—which means that the boys perpetrating it have to, in her words, "systematically ignore the humanity of the girls involved—and that is not harmless at all."

While interviewing boys for her book, Orenstein also noticed that they tended to describe hookups with girls in violent ways: They would tell their friends they "destroyed her" or "ripped her up" or "slammed her." Orenstein interpreted this framing as evidence that this kind of locker room banter is not really about sex but about power: "[It's] asserting masculinity through the control of women's bodies," she wrote, "using symbolic aggression toward women to bond and validate their heterosexuality."

And then there's pornography, which may skew boys' expectations and beliefs about sex and consent in dangerous ways—but it's hard to know for sure. A 2019 study reported that the more that teens are exposed to sexually explicit material, the more likely they are to believe rape myths and to be skeptical of the #metoo movement. Another 2019 study found that tenth-grade boys who watched violent pornography were more than three times as likely to perpetrate teen dating violence as boys who didn't watch violent pornography. Yet it's difficult to discern which direction the causal arrow points in studies like this. It's possible that boys who already hold sexist beliefs, and who are predisposed to dating violence for other reasons, are more likely than other boys to watch pornography—perhaps the attitudes drive the pornography use rather than the other way around. Still, considering the ways that pornography portrays sex and women, it's unlikely to shape boys' sexual expectations and attitudes in healthy ways.

RECLAIMING FEMALE SEXUALITY

I have a daughter, too, so I worry a lot about the sexual messages our culture sends to girls. My six-year-old recently started posing for photos with her head cocked and her hip jutting out, which tells me that even at this sweet young age, she's already internalizing that girls should look a certain way. (My son, who's nine, hasn't yet moved beyond the "goofy smile" phase.)

If you look around, you can easily see where girls get this idea. Many female characters in kids' books and TV shows are obsessed with their appearance; even in movies where girls are the heroes, they still have eyelashes longer than their waist circumference. Girls are constantly bombarded by well-meaning appearance-related comments, too—the old lady in the grocery store saying "I love your dress!" or "Don't you look pretty today!" On their own, these comments wouldn't necessarily be a problem, but they are part of a near-constant onslaught of messages girls receive that indicate that their value stems largely from their looks. As developmental psychologist Deborah Tolman wrote in a 2012 paper, adolescent girls are "being barraged by a deafening one-note anthem: Their appearance is what matters, and looking sexy is what counts."

It hasn't always been this bad. When Cornell social historian Joan Jacobs Brumberg read and compared the diaries written by adolescent girls over the course of a century, she found that when girls in the nineteenth century talked about wanting to improve themselves, they typically meant doing better in school or giving more to others. These days, however, girls almost exclusively discuss self-improvement in terms of enhancing their appearance. "Girls today are concerned with the shape and appearance of their bodies as a primary expression of their individual identity," she wrote in her book *The Body Project*.

This focus on appearance feeds into a bigger and more pernicious problem: Girls "think of and treat their own bodies as objects of others' desires," according to a 2007 report from the American Psychological Association. This then shapes their sexual health, because girls start to believe that their partners' physical and sexual desires matter more than their own. A 2009 study found that young women are four times as willing as young men to engage in sexual activities they don't like. Some girls totally lose touch with their feelings and desires. In a 2014 study, researchers asked young women to describe key indicators of their own sexual satisfaction, and some highlighted their partner's satisfaction—and specifically their partners' orgasm—as being among the most important. (Some young men in the study said they enjoyed when their partners climaxed, but those men did not cite their partners' orgasms as *key aspects* of their own sexual satisfaction.)

Orenstein encountered this issue over and over again while interviewing girls for her 2016 book *Girls & Sex*. "The concern with pleasing, as opposed to pleasure, was pervasive among the girls I met, especially among high schoolers, who were just starting sexual experimentation," she wrote. "Girls have long been made the gatekeepers of male desire, charged with containing it, diverting it, controlling it. Providing reliable release from it had now become their responsibility as well."

To be honest, I don't want to think about my six-year-old ever being sexually active. But one day she will be, and when she is, I want her to have knowledge and agency. I want her to understand her body and what she wants (and doesn't want) and be able to clearly advocate for it. Girls are not going to get this information from sex education—and the information they get from the media and their peers will likely be skewed—so we as parents really need to help them. We need to make sure our daughters recognize that their worth is not based on their looks and that their own desires and experiences matter just as much as those of their partners.

So yes, we need to talk to our kids about sex, sexual stereotypes, and pornography—and we need to do it early and often. "After nearly a decade of reporting on teenagers and sex, if I know anything for sure, it's that parents just have to get over it," Orenstein wrote. "I know it's awkward. I know it's excruciating. I know it's unclear how to begin. You may have never even been able to have such conversations with your own spouse and partner. I get that. But this is your chance to do better." Here's how.

Sex and Porn Strategy #1

Talk about it all—body parts, boundaries, privacy, harassment, consent, and gender stereotypes.

Kids say and do the darnedest things, and that's especially true when it comes to body parts. Young kids in particular often have no concept of privacy, and they're more than happy to share their thoughts and observations with anyone who will listen. One of my favorite stories involves a conversation that took place between a five-year-old boy—a good friend of my son's from preschool—and his seventy-year-old grandmother:

> FIVE-YEAR-OLD: Grandma, do you have a pagina or a penis?
> GRANDMA: What?
> FIVE-YEAR-OLD, LOUDER: Do you have a PAGINA or a PENIS?
> GRANDMA: Oh. I have a vagina.
> FIVE-YEAR-OLD: Oh, I have a penis.
> GRANDMA: Yes, you do.
> FIVE-YEAR-OLD: Mine gets bigger.
> GRANDMA: Yes, as you grow, it gets bigger.
> FIVE-YEAR-OLD: No, Grandma. When I touch it, it gets bigger!!

Grandma, I think, deserves a gold medal for how she handled that conversation. When I was growing up, it was rare for parents to even use the correct anatomical names when referring to body parts; I'm not sure I knew the word *vulva* until I was in high school.

But it's wise to jump right in with the correct words—to teach your kids about their penises and testicles and vulvas and vaginas from the time they are babies. Among other things, research shows that kids who know the correct names are less likely to be sexually abused and are more successful when they try to report abuse. In her book *The Sex-Wise Parent*, Janet Rosenzweig, the executive director of the American Professional Society on the Abuse of Children, told the heartbreaking story of a girl who told her teacher that her father "hurt her cookie," by which she meant her vagina; her teacher, of course, had no idea what she was trying to convey and simply offered her a snack. We need to "ensure that they have the right words to use when they need to communicate with you about anything, including sex," Rosenzweig wrote.

I agree—although I think the reasons to use accurate terms go far beyond preventing sexual abuse. When we invent euphemisms for body parts, we communicate to our kids that there are parts of their body that aren't OK for them to discuss with us. It sends them the message that sex and bodies are taboo topics, which does not bode well for keeping lines of communication open down the line, when we want our kids to come to us with questions or concerns. Put another way, by keeping silent about sex and bodies, we don't keep the topics out of our children's lives; we just ensure that the information they receive does not come from us. "There's a lot in the world that's going to be teaching your child about sex and sexuality. And so you have to put your voice in there as one of the strongest," said Eva Goldfarb, a sexuality educator at Montclair State University in New Jersey.

We should also regularly reinforce the concept of boundaries. Parents are usually good at talking about boundaries when it comes to overt violence and body violations—we tell our kids not to hit or pinch others and not to grab each other's toys. But we need to go further. Ideally, we should tell our kids that they're in charge of their own bodies (and that other people are in charge of theirs)—and that they shouldn't touch other people's bodies without their explicit consent, nor should anyone touch theirs. We often don't use the word *consent* with our kids, but experts recommend introducing the concept early and referring to it regularly. One book that's great for introducing young kids to this topic is *Consent (for Kids!)* by Rachel Brian.

Sometimes, too, we directly violate our children's body autonomy in our well-meaning attempts to teach them to be polite. We'll tell them that they are in charge of their bodies, then turn around and instruct them to give Aunt Joyce a hug (I've certainly done this). The same goes for making kids give their friends hugs at the ends of playdates or as an apology—it's not a good idea, because it sends mixed messages about consent and body autonomy. "What feels most comfortable to me is when people say, 'I would love a hug from you if you'd like to give me a hug,'" said Poco Kernsmith, a violence prevention researcher at Wayne State University. But reassure them that it's fine if they don't want to.

Whenever you need to invade your child's personal space, you might also want to "make a big underlined point of asking them for their consent," said Emily Rothman, a community health scientist at the Boston University School of Public Health. *Is it OK if I lift up your shirt to look at this scratch? Mind if I give you a snuggle?* This may sound over-the-top, but showing your kids that you respect their body autonomy and personal space affirms that it's

OK for them to take ownership of their bodies—and that other people's bodies are their own, too.

We also need to have clear conversations with our kids about what they should do if someone else touches them in a way they don't want. It's a complicated message to convey, because unwanted touching can sometimes feel good—we can have physiological reactions that do not match our desires, which is why even people who despise being tickled will sometimes still giggle. Advise your kids to tell you or another adult (such as a camp counselor or teacher) if someone touches them in a way that feels confusing, or that they didn't really want, even if the touching itself didn't hurt or they didn't know how to refuse it.

You can also be specific about what kind of touching you're referring to. You might say, *Tell me right away if someone kisses you, asks you to take your clothes off, or touches your penis or other parts of your body in a way you don't like or want, or asks you to touch them in ways you don't want.* Say that it's not fair for people to ask them to keep these kinds of experiences secret, and that it's always OK to tell you, even if that person says not to. You might want to add that *every* grown-up knows that it's not OK to touch a child's private parts, and that if they say otherwise, they're lying. (If you're worried that your child might have been sexually abused, talk to your pediatrician, the police, or the Childhelp National Child Abuse Hotline.)

Also, emphasize and respect the notion of privacy with your kids. If you're a family that's generally comfortable with nudity, that's fine, but still signify that being naked is something that some people do in private. When your kid waltzes into the bathroom while you're getting into the shower, maybe say, *Just so you know, you are in my bathroom and I'm naked, and that's OK with me, but next time could you knock?* This kind of acknowledgment "shows that you have boundaries, and that you know how to assert your boundaries, and that you want them to respect your boundaries," Rothman said. The more your kids encounter and navigate boundaries, the more comfortable and accepting they'll be in the future when they meet other people who assert theirs.

This all said, it's perfectly OK for kids to touch *themselves*. This happens from the time kids are babies, and it's normal. (You can and should explain to kids that this is something that they should do in private, though, not in front of other people, including you.) In fact—and I know, this might seem crazy—you might want to go so far as to encourage it, especially for girls in high school. Many young women have sex for the first time without ever having had an orgasm—and when that happens, how do they know what to ask for, or even what they want? Having some prior knowledge about what feels good (and what doesn't) can give young women confidence and agency. As clinical psychologist Lisa Damour wrote in her book *Under Pressure*, "Girls who aren't well acquainted with their own sexual wishes are the ones who are most likely to make compromises in their physical relationships, to go along with sexual activity they don't actually want, and to put their health at risk." Maybe you say something like, *It's OK and even good to touch yourself to figure out how you like being touched, because one really important thing about our bodies is that they can give us pleasure. And one day, you'll want to be able to tell someone you care about what makes your body feel good.*

It's also important to help kids recognize—and put into context—the sexist and sexualized messages that pervade our culture and the media. After the 2020 Super Bowl halftime show featuring Jennifer Lopez and Shakira, my son confided in me that he didn't know what to make of it; he said he thought the show was "inappropriate." (My husband snapped a particularly amusing picture of him and a friend watching the halftime show, mouths agape.) I used his comment as an opportunity to talk with him about gender stereotypes and culture; we discussed the vast differences in the ways masculinity and femininity are portrayed on TV, and also talked about differences in what the world expects from boys versus girls and what it's like for people who don't fit neatly into "boy" or "girl" categories. (For more on gender stereotypes, see chapter 5.) I also pointed out that both Jennifer Lopez and Shakira are Latin American women, and that some aspects of their performance reflected and celebrated their cultural and ethnic heritage.

Kids' books and movies often present opportunities for discussion, too. When I see female characters acting in stereotypically feminine ways, I often make a point of mentioning it to my kids and asking them what they think of it. Likewise, if all the heroes in a movie I see are boys, I sometimes mention that, too. And when male characters are portrayed as macho and unemotional—reinforcing the idea that men aren't allowed to feel emotions like sadness or fear—that can also be something good to discuss.

By the time your kids are in late elementary or early middle school, you'll want to have talked with them about sexual harassment, too. In *Under Pressure*, Damour suggested that parents ask girls whether the boys they know are treating them respectfully. We should explain that harassment is a sexualized form of bullying and that it's never OK and never their fault. We should also let our kids know that we're there to help and support them if needed.

We need to ask our boys whether they and their friends are treating girls respectfully, too—and explain why harassment is never funny or something to shrug off. Damour has found that when girls call boys on their harassment, the boys often insist that they were "just kidding" or that the girl is making too big a deal of it. That is, in effect, gaslighting—a manipulative response that causes the person being harassed to question her own sanity or reality. "The more we pull sexually aggressive behavior out of the shadows, the more we minimize the needless shame girls feel about being mistreated," Damour wrote.

I choose to discuss these issues with my kids because I don't want them to implicitly accept what they see as the way things have to be or always will be. I don't want them to see girls harassed or portrayed as objects of desire without pushing back on the narrative and making sure they understand that these expectations and ideas aren't fair or right. Nor do I want my kids to believe that they have to act or look a certain way because of their gender. I want my kids to know, too, that they can help rewrite this sexist narrative.

Sex and Porn Strategy #2
Answer questions honestly and briefly,
and don't worry if you mess up.

When my daughter was four and my son was seven, my husband and I bought them Robie Harris's book *It's Not the Stork!* It's a wonderful picture book that describes body parts, sex, how and where fetuses grow, and what happens when babies are born—and we bought it in part because we didn't know how to have these conversations without a script.

For whatever reason, my kids never asked me to read the whole book from start to finish; they typically picked specific pages for me to read aloud and they never requested the page that talked about the mechanics of sexual intercourse.

Then one day, when my daughter was five, we finally read that page together. When I got to the part that explained intercourse, my daughter stopped and looked aghast. "Wait. Mom. Did you and Daddy do this?!" she asked.

"Yes," I replied, trying to sound as casual and normal as possible. (I did not feel casual and normal at all.)

"Why didn't you tell me?" she demanded, sounding hurt.

"I'm telling you now," I said.

A half second passed. Then: "OK, keep going," she said matter-of-factly, and that was that.

It can be really hard to know how to answer your kids when they ask you questions about sex—especially when they're young. And sometimes we read more into their questions than we should. Goldfarb shared with me the story of a school principal whose four-year-old turned to him one day and said, "Daddy, how did I get here?" The father immediately started stumbling over his words, eventually launching into a barely coherent lecture about seeds and eggs. His son looked at him, perplexed, and said, "But, Daddy, I know you said I came from Puerto Rico. Did I get here by boat or by plane?"

So when your child asks you a question that you assume is about sex, take a second to probe what they're *really* asking. You might say, *What made you think of that?* or *What do you think?* Or *What do you already know about that?* It's also OK to give kids a short (but honest) answer and then wait for them to ask follow-ups.

If you completely mess up your response, that's fine, too—you can say to your child, *You know how you asked me yesterday about how babies are made? I don't think I gave you a very good answer, so I'd like to try again now.* It's also OK to have boundaries in terms of what you talk about with your kids. If your child asks you a question that feels private or that you don't really want to answer, you are perfectly within your rights to tell them that. Or, Schroeder said, you can answer it, but in a way that feels comfortable. Say, "'Honey, I am going to choose to not share with you how old I was when I first started having sex, but I do want to talk about what people need to think about before making that decision,'" Schroeder suggested.

What if you want to talk to your kids about sex but have no idea how? It's hard—really, really hard. One acceptable crutch is to rely on books to at least introduce the topic, as my husband and I did. Author Robie Harris has written a series of excellent books for kids of various ages, including the one I mentioned earlier—*It's Not the Stork!*—for kids four and up. Her other books include *It's So Amazing!* (which I recently bought for my son), for kids seven and up; and *It's Perfectly Normal*, for kids ten and up, which is all about puberty, sex, and sexual health.

You also don't have to (and probably shouldn't) try to tell your kids "everything" in one talk. "We hold on to the idea that there's a fixed quantity of sexual information adults need to keep close to the chest until we think the kids are ready, and then we can safely turn it over—whole," wrote sex educator Deborah Roffman in her book *Talk to Me First*. But that's kind of like never telling kids about math and then trying to teach them arithmetic, algebra, and geometry all in one sitting—it doesn't make sense.

Another thing Roffman suggested is for parents to convey to their kids that sex is a topic that deserves respect. Kids (and adults) often giggle and make jokes when talking about sex or body parts, because the topic makes us uncomfortable, and humor is a way to defuse the tension. But kids can misinterpret these reactions as conveying that sex itself is a funny topic, and we should push against that and convey instead that sex is important and powerful, and that it deserves respect and a degree of seriousness.

What if your kid walks in on you having sex? Try your best not to get mad (although it's OK if you do; you can always apologize later and say you were surprised). If you can, stay calm and be direct—maybe say, *We're having some private time, can you please close the door and go play somewhere else?* Then, later, talk about what happened, because your kid might have questions (eek). Reassure younger kids that what you were doing was OK; explain to them that what you were doing is called sex and that it's something that grown-ups do with each other that feels good and can express love. And it's perfectly fine to lock your door, or at least ask your kids to knock next time—we all deserve privacy when we want it, and especially when we're having sex!

Sex and Porn Strategy #3
With older kids, regularly discuss the rules of consent—and accept that they can have loving relationships.

Once your kids are old enough to be romantically interested in others—around middle school, if not before—you should be regularly talking with them about sexual consent and entitlement.

Boys, in particular, don't always understand what consent means or how it looks. This can be dangerous, considering that they also often feel entitled to sexual pleasure.

For her book *Boys & Sex*, Orenstein interviewed more than one hundred high school and college boys about their sex lives. Whereas girls often feel pressured to submit to boys' advances or to ensure that their partners climax, boys don't always feel the same, she found—and they also may not recognize the subtle (or not so subtle) pressure they put on girls to appease their sexual desire. "The narcissism of male desire is instilled early, reinforced by media, peers and parental silence, and by girls who have themselves been trained from an early age to take men's needs and desires more seriously than their own," Orenstein wrote.

Among other things, boys tend to overestimate how interested girls are in having sex with them. When social psychologist Antonia Abbey interviewed college students, 72 percent of women told her that men had sometimes misperceived their friendliness as a come-on. Her work has also found that young men are much more likely to overestimate a woman's interest when they have been drinking alcohol, and that they are more likely to assume that a woman is sexually available and interested if *she* has been drinking, too, regardless of her behavior.

We need to talk to our sons about these inclinations so that when they find themselves in these situations, they second-guess their assumptions and make sure their partners are truly on the same page. We need to talk to them about the fact that they are not "entitled" to sex or oral sex or anything else if they dance with someone or walk someone home from a party, or if they get invited back to someone's house to hang out. We also need to spell out what consent does and doesn't look and sound like. We need to tell our kids that silence isn't consent; that saying yes to one activity at one time doesn't imply consent for other activities or the same activity at other times; that consent shouldn't be coerced or manipulated; and that a person can't consent while intoxicated, asleep, or restrained. You might even want to suggest some questions for your kid to ask periodically to help them check in with a partner. These might include *Are you enjoying yourself? Are we moving too fast? Are you still okay with this?*

We should convey, too, that rape and sexual assault are not just things that "bad guys" or "monsters" do—they are things that otherwise good guys can do when they make assumptions or think more about themselves than their partners. "Among the young men I've talked to, some that I liked enormously—friendly, thoughtful, bright, engaging guys—have 'sort of' raped girls; pushed girls' heads down to get oral sex; taken a Snapchat video of a prom date giving them a blow job without her knowledge and sent it to the basketball team; shot an iPhone video of a girlfriend performing a blow job (again, without her immediate knowledge) for 'personal use,'" Orenstein wrote. "They all described themselves as 'good guys.' And they were, most of the time. But the truth is, a really good guy can do a really bad thing."

We should talk to our girls about consent, too—and about ensuring that they set a high bar for their sexual experiences. Girls have been conditioned to avoid and resolve conflict and to be generous and nurturing. In sexual situations, this can translate into girls doing things they don't want to do because they don't want to disappoint or anger their sexual partners. Because of this, we need to teach our daughters that their desires are no less important than their partners', and that whatever they've heard about boys "needing" sexual release is untrue. We should explain that if their partners pressure them to do more than they want, they absolutely do not owe them anything, no matter what they've already done or what else has happened between them. We should encourage them to do things only when they really want to, and that it's OK for them to say no if they sort of want to do it but aren't sure. "To require mere consent sets an incredibly low bar for entering into what should be the shared pleasure of physical romance," Damour wrote. "A healthy love life centers on finding areas of joyful agreement. As we're welcoming young people into the world of romance, we should hold them to the highest possible standards—not the lowest."

Damour suggested that parents help their daughters brainstorm gentle ways to say no to sexual activities they don't want. Although it should be perfectly OK for a girl to say "I'm not into this" in the middle of a hookup and get up and leave, the reality is that many girls are too afraid to do this—they worry about hurting their partner's feelings and whether their refusal will trigger an angry, or even violent, response. (This is, again, why we need to tell our boys to regularly check in with their partners and give them an easy out if they don't want to keep going.) Damour suggested trying out phrases like *Hey, this is really fun. I'm not sure what you had in mind, but I don't want to have sex tonight*, or even *I just remembered that I told my friend I'd take her home. I have to leave now.* "I'd rather have teenagers tell a white lie than do something dangerous, or something they don't want to do, for lack of a handy way of saying 'no,'" Damour wrote. I want to emphasize that this is not how things should be; girls should not have to worry that refusing sex could lead to violence. But the reality is it may be wise to help girls come up with ways of saying no that make them feel comfortable and safe.

On the flip side, we should also let our daughters know that they are entitled to sexual desire and should not be ashamed of it. Our culture frames boys' sexual desire as normal and girls' desire as shameful, which is why sexually permissive boys are called "players" yet sexually permissive girls are called "sluts" and "hos." We should talk to our girls about this double standard so they recognize that it's unfair. We should also communicate to them that sex is a normal and healthy part of life, for both men and women, and that it should be a source of pleasure, not shame or stress. Damour suggested saying to tween and teen girls, *As you're thinking about the physical side of your own romantic life, you should start by reflecting on what you want. You should tune into what you would like to have happen, what would be fun for you, what would feel good.* And then you might also emphasize the importance of being in a trusting relationship, Damour wrote, by saying something like *The next thing to consider is what your partner would like to have happen. This will require some communication—you'll need to know each other well enough to learn this.*

This underscores another important point: We shouldn't assume that our kids are too young or immature for real, loving relationships. American parents tend to pooh-pooh the idea that teenagers can experience love, and as a result we often assume that they are not ready or mature enough for sex. But whether or not we think it's time, kids do what they want—on average, American teens lose their virginity at age seventeen. And teens fare better when we show them respect in the conversations we have with them about sex and relationships.

In her book *Not Under My Roof,* University of Massachusetts at Amherst sociologist Amy Schalet compared the ways in which

American and Dutch parents engage with their kids on the topic of sex. Although teens from both countries lose their virginity at around the same age, American teenage girls are nearly six times as likely to give birth compared with Dutch girls.

Schalet's work suggests that this difference stems in large part from how American parents—and the American culture at large—frame and discuss the issue of sex and love with kids and what kinds of expectations we have of them. She found, for instance, that Dutch parents talk to their boys regularly about love and relationships and think of their sons as being able to make strong emotional connections. American parents, on the other hand, she found, often write off their boys as sex crazed and hormone driven and consider them unable to truly fall in love. One self-described American liberal parent said to her, "Most teenage boys would fuck anything that would sit still."

American teens do tend to have more sexual partners than Dutch teens do, but it's unlikely that there is a biological reason to explain this discrepancy. It's more likely that American boys play to the stereotype of them as sex crazed and unable to make deep connections—they have more sex in part because our culture expects them to, and because the media tells them that this is what they are supposed to do. And because we (and our schools) don't provide information about how to have sex safely, American teens get into a lot more trouble when they do start doing it.

Schalet argued that kids would be far better off if parents helped them understand their sexual feelings and desires in positive ways, rather than always framing them as negative and dangerous. Hirsch and Khan agreed. "It's a parent's right to tell young people, 'Not under my roof.' But they shouldn't fool themselves into thinking that the rule will keep young people from having sex. What it does do is effectively convey a refusal to see them as sexually maturing young adults," they wrote in *Sexual Citizens*. Put another way, what we say and do as parents may not affect whether or not our kids have sex—but it will absolutely shape whether our kids will make wise and safe choices about how, why, and where they have sex.

Sex and Porn Strategy #4
Talk to your kids about sexting and pornography.

You knew this one was coming: Yes, you've got to talk to your kids about porn. After discovering my son's "naked people" search on the iPad, I pondered what to do. (Also, I felt extremely grateful for adult content controls, which, thanks to my husband, were in place on the iPad, so their curious search did not actually produce photos of naked people.)

I wondered: Should I have a conversation with both boys about it during the playdate? Or should I wait and just talk to my son about it afterward? I didn't want to embarrass my son in front of his friend, and I also wasn't sure how the other boy's parents would want me to handle the situation, so I decided not to mention anything during the playdate. But I did tell the other boy's father what happened when he picked him up.

Then I sat down to chat with my son, trying to remember everything I'd learned from my interviews about how to talk—and not talk—to kids about porn.

First, it's totally normal for kids to be curious about sex and nakedness. So I started the conversation by telling my son, calmly and kindly, that I'd seen what he and his friend had searched for on the iPad, and that he was not in trouble, because it was natural to be curious.

Then I brought up the fact that, as he knew, there are some things that adults do that aren't so good for kids—like drinking beer and coffee. I said that looking at naked pictures can be a little bit like that. Sometimes, I explained, when kids search for things like naked people, they'll end up seeing things that are weird, or confusing, or unrealistic, and that are not meant for their eyes. So, I said, it's best not to search for things like that on computers or iPads.

That's when my son piped up and said, oh yes—he'd already seen a weird and confusing video at a friend's house that involved naked women dancing. His friend had been excited to show it to him. Not exactly what I wanted to hear, but I was glad that he felt comfortable enough to share that tidbit with me.

So then I said: "Well, you should always talk to me or Dad if you see things that confuse or upset you like that." I promised him he wouldn't get into trouble for telling us about them. I also reminded him that I'd just bought him a new book all about sex and body parts—I'd just gotten him Robie Harris's *It's So Amazing!*—and I said that it has some safe-for-kids illustrations of naked people that he could look at any time he wanted. I added that if he had any questions about any of it, he should always ask me or his father.

So the talk went fine—and wow, did I feel good getting all that off my chest. I encourage you to do the same with your kids. In fact, Rothman recommends that parents talk to kids about pornography as early as kindergarten, framing it as being about nakedness (as I did) rather than sex. Surveys suggest that more than half of eleven-to-thirteen-year-olds have seen pornography; often, they first see it by accident because they type the wrong words into a search engine or because older siblings or friends show it to them to freak them out. But by the time boys are in sixth to eighth grade, many start searching for porn intentionally.

To reduce the risk that your kids will accidentally stumble across porn, you might also want to activate content filters on your devices and browsers, as my husband had thankfully done on our tablet. On Apple devices, these options can be found at Settings > Screen Time > Content & Privacy Restrictions > Content Restrictions. These restrictions won't block everything, but they will make it much less likely that your kids will accidentally see something they shouldn't. Once kids are older and more web savvy and (in some cases) actively hunting for porn, these blocks won't do much good, though, since they are pretty easy to circumvent.

If your kids have already seen pornography, you'll also want to help them understand and interpret what they've seen. One key point to make is that a lot of pornography is unrealistic and doesn't depict what most people look like naked, how most people treat others during sex, or how most people like to be treated. "That's the number one message that I think kids of any age need to hear," Rothman said. Explain that, just as impossible, unrealistic things happen in cartoons or movies, "pornography is made to entertain people and to be fantasy. And it's not meant to be an instruction manual or a documentary," she said. Explain, too, that the bodies (and body parts) they see in pornography usually aren't natural or typical.

Of course, there are exceptions; not all pornography is as terrible as parents assume. Sometimes it's really just people having garden-variety sex. So before you launch into a tirade about what your kids saw and how horrible it was, you might first want to inquire about what they've seen so you can put it into appropriate context.

If your kid seems to enjoy watching disturbing pornography, don't totally freak out, Rothman added. Just as your pupils dilate when it gets dark, our bodies can have automatic physiological reactions to disturbing sexual images—even to things you don't want for yourself, or things that go against your ethical principles. (Rothman said that parents sometimes ask her for the names of "ethical" porn sites to recommend to their kids but that she doesn't condone this approach; curating porn for your kids is going a little too far.)

If your kids still keep watching porn, even after you've advised them not to, then you may need to let things go. Certainly you can try upping the ante on your parental controls and explain, again, why pornography is not good for them or why it goes against your values. But if they're teenagers, you might not want to get into a full-on war over the issue, either. "There comes a point where, even if you're not entirely comfortable with it, kids are going to make their own choices about who they are and what they want to do," Rothman said. And as anyone who's ever been a teenager knows, when parents go overboard in terms of being controlling, teens will do everything they can to rebel and break the rules.

What if you're worried that your child might be addicted to porn? Rothman said that, thankfully, porn addiction is relatively rare. Some counseling professionals make scary but inaccurate claims about porn addiction in order to get more clients. But if you are concerned about the compulsiveness of your kid's pornography use, consider finding a therapist who specializes in CBT (cognitive behavioral therapy) for teens. This kind of therapy can effectively treat compulsive behavior.

The other really important thing to discuss with kids is sexting—the sharing of sexually explicit images or sexually suggestive material via digital devices. According to a 2018 systematic review of the research literature, more than one in four teens admits to having received a sext, and nearly one in seven admit to having sent one. Kids often don't realize that sexting is illegal under the age of eighteen—naked pictures can, for instance, be considered child pornography. Although it's rare, some kids who have shared sexts have been forced to register as sex offenders.

In a 2019 commentary, cyberbullying researchers Justin Patchin and Sameer Hinduja argued that when kids receive a sext, they should delete it immediately, without sending or showing it to anyone. The usual advice we give to kids about dealing with online behavior—taking screenshots of the evidence and showing them to trusted adults—might backfire and get them, not to mention the other people involved in the sexting, in lots of trouble. (That said, if kids are being pressured or threatened to send nude photos, Patchin and Hinduja advised that they should take screenshots of those requests or threats.) For more advice, check out cyberbullying.org.

If this is all terribly scary and difficult to think about, I hear you. I didn't want to think about my kids ever encountering porn or sexts—but when my son did, I was really glad I was able to intercept it (at least this time!) and engage with him about it. And I feel much more at ease now that I have planted the seeds for more conversations with him and his sister about sex and sexuality. All of our kids will have to navigate the messy world of sex, porn, and sexting soon enough—so it's smart for us, and for them, to be prepared, and to do all we can to ensure that this part of their lives, like every other, is as healthy and fulfilling as can be.

....

KEY POINTS

....

1. Talk to kids about boundaries, consent, sexuality, harassment, and gender stereotypes from a young age. If you need help, use books.
2. Answer questions about sex honestly and succinctly, and don't fret if you mess up—you can revisit it later.
3. Talk to kids regularly about consent—what it is, what it isn't, and that consent for something at one time does not imply consent again later.
4. Don't pooh-pooh the idea that teens can fall in love. Some teens can have mature and loving relationships.
5. Talk to kids about sexting and pornography and what to do if they encounter it.

Epilogue

OVER THE COURSE of the year in which I wrote this book, I read hundreds of studies and spoke with dozens of child psychologists. I learned *a whole lot* about the most constructive ways to parent my own two kids. So I was a little sad when I found that I didn't magically transform into Super Mom, nor did my kids magically become Perfect Kids. Having everyone home 24–7 during the coronavirus pandemic certainly didn't help: How are we supposed to maintain perspective and patience when our kids are literally climbing all over us all the time?

Much to my own dismay, I often found myself reacting to situations in ways that directly contradicted what I'd spent hours reading the day before. My kids would start screaming at each other, and even though I had just read eight studies on the most effective ways to mediate sibling conflict, I would hear myself barking down at them to stop fighting. My daughter would have her twenty-first meltdown of the day just as I was serving dinner, and even though I would know that she was tired and hungry and it was entirely reasonable for her to have trouble regulating her feelings, I couldn't see the situation through any other lens than *Ugh not again*, and the last thing I wanted to do was empathize.

This might happen to you, too. You might find that even after you've learned new strategies and are excited to use them, you still watch yourself do the exact opposite and wonder what in the ever-living hell is going on. It feels like your brain and your body are disconnected. Your brain is telling you, *Hey, I think I know what to do here!* But your body jumps in first, taunting, *Hahaha nope*.

I struggled at first with what this disconnect meant. Was I incapable of change? Did I just waste a year of my life educating myself only to discover that I will never actually become a better parent?

I don't think so. In fact, the other day I was reading a textbook on authoritative parenting (yes, those exist) and came across a section on *parent training*. As the book explained, "Some of the most difficult challenges in parent training are to encourage parents to (a) take the time and make the effort to acquire new parenting skills, (b) consistently implement those skills learned rather than reverting to relatively automatic maladaptive and coercive responses, and (c) apply parenting skills when they are depressed, tired, worried, and stressed."

If you've read this book, you've already succeeded with (a)—you've taken the time and effort to acquire new parenting skills. Gold star! But (b) and (c) . . . Well, those challenges sure resonated with me. It really is hard to use new parenting skills, especially when you're tired and stressed (which I think all parents are right now, all the time).

Why is it so hard to change our ways? Parenting is deeply rooted in emotion, and it's reactive. Our choices and responses in difficult parenting moments are often driven by the parts of the brain that deal with feelings—the limbic system. When we learn and try to internalize new strategies, on the other hand, we're engaging the prefrontal cortex, the part of our brain that orchestrates thought and action. Sometimes (often?) these two parts of the brain will be at odds with each other. It takes time for our brains to figure out how to be mindful and accepting of our emotional reactions, while also responding to experiences in ways that are consistent with the approaches we've learned. It's like we have to retrain our brain—and if your brain is as stuck in its ways as mine was, well, that could require a wee bit of time.

Thankfully, about six months in, I did start seeing small changes in myself. First, I began having more empathy for my kids when they got upset about seemingly silly things. I started seeing their experiences from their perspective and was able to think, *OK, it makes sense that she got mad when I gave her the cereal in the green bowl rather than the red one.* (Well, OK, maybe not *total* sense.) It was like a door had opened in front of me, but it took me a really long time to amble my way through it. I also think I needed a lot of practice trying out these new approaches before I could start doing them well.

One of the biggest changes I began to see in myself was in how I talked to my kids. I remember, as a new parent, reading articles that said things like *The problem with parents today is that they don't talk enough with their kids.* And I remember thinking, *Surely that doesn't apply to me because I talk to my kids all the time!*

But now, after spending a year deep in the research, I think I finally get what those experts were trying to convey. Of course we all talk to our kids, and we work hard to instill in them the lessons we think they need to learn. But we don't always communicate these lessons in ways our kids can easily understand and absorb. Now I talk much more about feelings, and I try to connect dots much more clearly, and I try my best to stay calm when having important conversations (and if I can't, I revisit the topic later, when I am feeling better). When I talk to my kids about their choices, I now try to connect those choices directly with other people's feelings and lives. When I make requests, I explain my reasoning for those requests and how the requests relate to me or others. I also just have *more* conversations with my kids about values and issues I consider important—like race and sexism and consent. I try to be explicit and specific.

I've described many kinds of suggestions on many different topics. Your head may be spinning a little right now (sorry). But if I had to whittle my advice down into one sentence, it would be this: Try to *show compassion and make connections.* When your kids are pushing your buttons, think about what *they* are experiencing; think about what they might not understand about others and the world and how that lack of understanding may be shaping their choices. Then think of ways to fill in those blanks— to connect them and their actions to other people and the world at large. How you fill in those blanks will depend largely on your kids, the situation you're facing, and your own values.

If this sounds too simple to be effective, I hear you. But these are the things that have changed in my parenting as a result of all this research, and I am starting to see changes in my kids, too. (*Starting* to. But hey, it's progress.)

So do I handle all situations with my kids now with empathy and grace? Nope. The other day, in fact, after a particularly difficult afternoon, I snuck down into the basement to exercise. I needed an hour to sweat and clear my head, but as soon as I got down there, my son came down to play. My daughter soon followed, and they immediately started fighting—right next to me—over a chair. I completely lost it and yelled at them. And then I felt terrible. But I connected with them about it later and apologized, and my son surprised me when he said, "It's OK, Mom. I understand." It was almost as if he was starting to understand *my* perspective better, too.

The fact is, no matter how much we know or how intentional we try to be, we can't always be there for our kids when they need us, especially during difficult times. And that's all right. I think of parenting as a bank—when we're able, we make deposits. We build up a balance. If something bad happens and we can't make more deposits for a little while, our kids still have a balance they can draw from. Our investments give our kids security and guidance and resilience, leaving them with tools that they can use to get through their own difficult moments.

A while back, for an article I was writing for *The New York Times*, I spoke to a philosopher of education, who told me that, in her mind, there are essentially two types of people: those who think that humans are basically good but need guidance and nurturing in order to fare well; and those who think that humans are essentially bad, who need to be controlled and beaten down in order to stay in line.

I am firmly in Camp Good. I think that when kids are provided with ample love, compassion, and guidance (which includes setting limits), they usually grow into loving, compassionate, capable people. We don't have to give our kids everything all the time, but we have to be there for them enough. And the science supports this conclusion, too. Research from a diverse set of disciplines suggests that children—and people in general—are intuitively kind and good when they are given what they need. It's the kids who are denied these needs for much of their lives who struggle—who often make bad choices and have trouble finding their inner moral compass. This helps to explain why kids with neglectful parents fare the worst: They haven't gotten much guidance at all, and their moral compass, over time, loses its way.

One winter day while I was revising some chapters of this book, I looked outside and saw the school bus dropping my kids off at the end of our long driveway. At the beginning of the school year, their walk home from the bus typically ended with my son running into the house, oblivious to the fact that his little sister was far behind him, yelling for me through tears. Usually she was upset because her brother had done something to annoy her while walking off the bus—he didn't let her go first, maybe, or he hurried her down the bus stairs. My son would walk into the house and I would say, "Do you hear your sister crying outside?" and he would shrug and walk upstairs, slamming the door to his room.

But on this particular day, I watched something different unfold. My son had walked halfway down the driveway when I saw him stop and turn around to check on his sister. That morning, she had left her balance bike at the end of the driveway in order to ride it to the house after school, but she was clearly struggling to mount the bike wearing her oversize backpack. I watched as my son slowly turned around from the middle of the driveway and walked back toward her. Then he took the backpack off her, helped her onto her bike, and lumbered down the driveway carrying both backpacks as she rode on her bike next to him.

This may not sound like a big deal to you, but it was to me. My son has always had a big heart, and he's as honest and rule-following as they come, but he has often struggled to put others first. But over the course of his life (and especially this year), I've tried over and over again to help him see himself as part of something bigger—to help him understand how much good he can do in the world, why being generous matters, and why love sometimes means carrying your little sister's backpack home, even if you're tired and need a snack and want to be alone.

So when my son walked down the driveway that day under the weight of two backpacks, I broke out into a smile, ran downstairs, and waited for him to come in so I could tell him how proud I was. I was close to tears, and I gave him a great big hug. Even though this was not a world-changing moment in the broader sense, it was a world-changing moment for me as a mother—and for us as a family.

Parenting is hard—I'll say it yet again. No matter what we do, our kids will constantly challenge us, because that is how they learn and grow. We may wonder at times if they are absorbing any of what we try to instill in them. But every once in a while, if we're watching closely, we will catch glimpses of the fundamental goodness underneath all their layers and be able to envision the kind of people they are becoming. When this happens we should feel proud of them, and we should feel proud of *ourselves*, too, because their grace in these moments is evidence that we are doing OK, that our hard work as parents is paying off—and that our kids aren't growing up to be assholes. They are growing up to be people who will make the world a more beautiful and loving place, and we have helped them get there.

Acknowledgments

IT TAKES A village to raise a child. It takes a much bigger village to write a book about raising children while raising two children. I am indebted to so many people who helped to bring this book to life.

My agents, Larry Weissman and Sascha Alper, have been nothing short of marvelous. When I contacted them in 2018 with only a book title, they wrote back immediately, giving me just the right encouragement. Their instincts, wisdom, and deep knowledge of the publishing industry astound me. They provide exactly what I need without my even having to ask.

I hit the jackpot with Michelle Howry as an editor. I'm convinced she is the kindest, most upbeat, and most talented book editor on the planet. She, Ashley Di Dio, Ashley Hewlett, Emily Mlynek, and the rest of the Putnam team have been extraordinary. I must also thank Eric Nelson, who saw a book writer in me many moons ago and taught me what a book is (and more important, what it isn't). He also helped shape and hone this book's concept from the beginning.

I am exceptionally grateful to my *Slate* editors Chad Lorenz and Allison Benedikt. If it weren't for Allison, who offered me my parenting column and was my first editor, I might never have dipped my toes into parenting journalism. Her faith in my perspective gave me essential confidence, and she helped me recognize the value of humor in this kind of writing. Chad Lorenz, who edited my column for four years, is the kind of editor I wish I had for every story—astute and sharp, yet empathetic and encouraging. He provided incisive comments on many of my chapters. Thanks also to Jessica Grose, Julia Calderone, Melonyce McAfee, and Erik Vance, who have given me myriad opportunities to hone my parenting voice at *The New York Times*.

It's impossible for a mother to write a book without excellent childcare. I am so thankful for beloved babysitter Katrina Campbell—who nurtured my kids while I hid in the bedroom writing—and to the teachers and staff at the Haldane Elementary School, the Randolph School, Hudson Hills Academy, and the Philipstown Recreation Department. I'm also immensely grateful to bibliographer Dani Leviss and to fact-checkers Emily Krieger, Jenni Gritters, Leslie Nemo, and Jen Monnier, whose careful work on the book was absolutely crucial. And to talented photographer Gabrielle Gerard, the first person to make me feel comfortable in front of a camera.

My dear friend and neighbor Virginia Sole-Smith helped me in innumerable ways throughout this process, providing support, encouragement, and answers to my endless questions. She also gave me invaluable feedback on my gnarliest chapters. Close friends Karen Schrock Simring and Meredith Knight showered me with insight and support, as did the women in my neighborhood writing group—Virginia (again), Lauren Daisley, Maria

Ricapito, Pamela Doan, Liesa Goins, Nicki Sizemore, and Lynn Strong. Many thanks to other friends who provided advice, ideas, and encouragement: Molly Webster, Rachele Lenehan, Andrea Anderson, Lisa Jarvis, Tracy Bunye, Emily Poe Boyer, Whitney Woodward, Jenny Muller, Susanna Hegner, Juliet Harvey, Laura Kaufman, Angela Attia, Rachel Moody, Tara Haelle, Jenny Morber, Christie Nicholson, Brooke Borel, Robin Marantz Henig, Maria Konnikova, Dan Fagin, and Josh Fischman.

I could not have written a research-based book about parenting and children without all the fantastic researchers who study parenting and children, many of whom spent hours helping and teaching me. The same goes for the parents, therapists, educators, and other parenting writers who shared their wisdom (and stories). I cannot name everyone, but I am especially thankful to Rebecca Bigler, Bobby McCullough, David Levine, Tovah Klein, Campbell Leaper, Carla Naumburg, Jessica Lahey, Emily Oster, Devorah Heitner, Tina Payne Bryson, Michelle Borba, Jamil Zaki, Laura Markham, Eileen Kennedy-Moore, Angela Duckworth, Christia Spears Brown, Susie Simring, Carol Dweck, Robert Larzelere, Joan Grusec, and the Child Mind Institute. The Julia Butterfield Library, which loaned me many of the books I used for my research, never raised their eyebrows when I checked out fifteen titles at once.

The handful of people over the course of my life who inspired me to write deserve my immense gratitude, too: Dan Fagin, Emily Laber-Warren, Ivan Oransky, Trudy Lieberman, Mariette DiChristina, Rebecca Skloot, Mike Burns, and Suzanne Wilsey.

While working on this book, I have thought a lot about my own childhood. My parents, Marilyn and Dave, taught me so much about kindness, resilience, hard work, and unconditional love.

They have supported me in every way, with everything; my dad was my very first editor (and publisher) when I decided at age eight to publish *Magic* magazine. My older sister, Bethany, the yin to my yang, taught me from a young age that I am stronger than I think, and that I should speak up when I have things to say. Observing her as a mother over the past thirteen years has been a tremendous source of inspiration. My other family members have always been right there, cheering me on, too: Wendy Wenner, Ann and Dean Moyer, Van Crocker Jr., Maggie and Dominic Lacie, Kate Moyer, Travis Bessey, Robert Busk, and my wonderful, bighearted nieces and nephews.

I certainly couldn't have written this book if it weren't for my own kids, in whom I see the whole world—a better world. They challenge me to check my assumptions, consider new perspectives, and find joy in unexpected places. They have helped me understand that parenting is a process worthy of serious consideration and respect.

Throughout everything, my husband, Michael, has been my lifeline. From the moment I blurted out at our anniversary dinner, "I should write a book called *How to Raise Kids Who Aren't Assholes!*" and he replied "That's it!," he has been there to buoy me up whenever I dip below the surface, radiating support and positivity, staying up late to read my chapters. There is nothing I cannot do when he is by my side.

Notes

INTRODUCTION

1 **In 2020, *Parents* magazine surveyed more than 1,200 parents:** Meredith Bryan, "For Parents in 2020, Raising Kind Kids Is Most Important," Parents.com, October 7, 2020. Accessed October 12, 2020. https://www.parents.com/kids /development/social/for-parents-in-2020-raising-kind-kids-is-most-important/.

2 **Similarly, in 2016, Sesame Workshop, the nonprofit organization behind the show *Sesame Street*:** Sesame Workshop, *K Is for Kind: A National Survey on Kindness and Kids*, 2016. Accessed October 12, 2020. http://kindness.sesamestreet .org/view-the-results/.

3 **But the research clearly shows that children (even babies!) do see race:** David J. Kelly, Paul C. Quinn, Alan M. Slater, Kang Lee, Alan Gibson, Michael Smith, Liezhong Ge, and Olivier Pascalis, "Three-Month-Olds, but Not Newborns, Prefer Own-Race Faces," *Developmental Science* 8, no. 6 (November 2005): F31–F36.

4 **In the fall of 2018, K–12 teachers and staff reported to the Southern Poverty Law Center:** Southern Poverty Law Center, *Hate at School*, 2019. https://www.splcenter.org/20190502/hate-school.

5 **Between 2015 and 2018, according to the FBI:** United States Department of Justice, Federal Bureau of Investigation (November 2016), *Hate Crime Statistics, 2015*. Accessed October 9, 2020. https://ucr.fbi.gov/hate-crime/2015/. United States Department of Justice, Federal Bureau of Investigation (November 2019), *Hate Crime Statistics, 2018*. Accessed October 9, 2020. https://ucr.fbi.gov/hate-crime /2018/.

5 **In 2016 and 2017, the Human Rights Campaign surveyed more than fifty thousand American thirteen-to-eighteen-year-olds:** Human Rights

Campaign Foundation, *Human Rights Campaign Post-Election Survey of Youth*, January 2017. Accessed October 19, 2020. https://assets2.hrc.org/files/assets /resources/HRC_PostElectionSurveyofYouth.pdf?_ga=2.38080299.942564036.1603 112422-1567842572.1601165887.

5 **When researchers at the University of California, Los Angeles, surveyed 1,535 public high school teachers:** John Rogers with the Teaching and Learning in the Age of Trump research team: Megan Franke, Jung-Eun Ellie Yun, Michael Ishimoto, Claudia Diera, Rebecca Cooper Geller, Anthony Berryman, and Tizoc Brenes, *Teaching and Learning in the Age of Trump: Increasing Stress and Hostility in America's High Schools*, October 2017. Accessed October 9, 2020. https://idea.gseis.ucla.edu/publications/teaching-and-learning-in-age-of-trump.

5 **In a study published in January 2019, educational psychologists Dewey Cornell and Francis Huang:** Francis L. Huang and Dewey G. Cornell, "School Teasing and Bullying After the Presidential Election," *Educational Researcher* 48, no. 2 (January 8, 2019): 69–83.

6 **A 2017 study published in the journal *Pediatrics* noted that between 2005 and 2014:** Tracy Evian Waasdorp, Elise T. Pas, Benjamin Zablotsky, and Catherine P. Bradshaw, "Ten-Year Trends in Bullying and Related Attitudes Among 4th- to 12th-Graders," *Pediatrics* 139, no. 6 (June 2017): e20162615.

6 **In November 2016, the Southern Poverty Law Center compiled a list of 867 hate incidents:** Southern Poverty Law Center, *Ten Days After: Harassment and Intimidation in the Aftermath of the Election*, November 26, 2016. Accessed October 9, 2020. https://www.splcenter.org/20161129/ten-days-after-harassment -and-intimidation-aftermath-election.

6 **In a 2019 paper published in the *Journal of Child Psychotherapy*, five US child psychologists lamented:** Tracy A. Prout, Leore J. Faber, Emma Racine, Rebecca Sperling, and Rebecca F. Hillman, "Clinical Encounters with Children in the Trump Era," *Journal of Child Psychotherapy* 45, no. 2 (September 19, 2019): 191–208.

7 **In one well-known experiment, Bandura and his colleagues invited three-to-six-year-olds into a room:** Albert Bandura, Dorothea Ross, and Sheila A. Ross, "Transmission of Aggression Through Imitation of Aggressive Models," *Journal of Abnormal and Social Psychology* 63, no. 3 (1961): 575–582.

8 **Research has found that college students are less empathetic than they were a decade ago:** Sara H. Konrath, Edward H. O'Brien, and Courtney Hsing, "Changes in Dispositional Empathy in American College Students over Time: A Meta-Analysis," *Personality and Social Psychology* 15, no. 2 (2011): 180–198.

9 **In a 2019 study, researchers followed nearly 450 kids for three years:** Elisabeth Malonda, Anna Llorca, Belen Mesurado, Paula Samper, and M. Vicenta Mestre, "Parents or Peers? Predictors of Prosocial Behavior and Aggression: A Longitudinal Study," *Frontiers in Psychology* 10 (October 22, 2019).

9 **Research consistently shows that when people (including kids) are kind and generous to others:** Lee Rowland and Oliver Scott Curry, "A Range of

Kindness Activities Boost Happiness," *Journal of Social Psychology* 159, no. 3 (2018): 340–343.

9 **And in a 2019 analysis of thirty years' worth of data that controlled for the effects of family economic status and child IQ:** Francis Vergunst, Richard E. Tremblay, Daniel Nagin, Yann Algan, Elixabeth Beasley, Jungwee Park, Cedric Galera, Frank Vitaro, and Sylvana M. Cote, "Association Between Childhood Behaviors and Adult Employment Earnings in Canada," *JAMA Psychiatry* 76, no. 10 (June 19, 2019): 1044–1051.

9 **In his research-based book *Give and Take*:** Adam Grant, *Give and Take: A Revolutionary Approach to Success* (New York: Viking, 2013).

11 **Pediatrician Leonard Sax penned an entire book in 2015:** Leonard Sax, *The Collapse of Parenting: How We Hurt Our Kids When We Treat Them Like Grown-Ups* (New York: Basic Books, 2015). Melinda Wenner Moyer, "There Has Been No Collapse of Parenting," Slate.com, January 22, 2016. Accessed October 9, 2020. https://slate.com/human-interest/2016/01/leonard-sax-is-wrong-authoritarian-parenting-can-be-bad-for-kids.html.

CHAPTER 1: "IT'S ALL ABOUT *ME*!"

19 **In March 2019, the parenting website Fatherly published an article:** Joshua A. Krisch, "Should Parents Want to Raise Nice Kids? Probably Not," Fatherly.com, March 1, 2019. Accessed October 10, 2020. https://www.fatherly.com/love-money/altruism-kids-nice/.

20 **Research suggests that generous individuals live longer and have better health:** Stephanie L. Brown and R. Michael Brown, "Connecting Prosocial Behavior to Improved Physical Health: Contributions from the Neurobiology of Parenting," *Neuroscience and Biobehavioral Reviews* 55 (2015): 1–17.

20 **Being kind and helpful also reduces symptoms of depression, anxiety, and stress:** Jennifer L. Trew and Lynn E. Alden, "Kindness Reduces Avoidance Goals in Socially Anxious Individuals," *Motivation and Emotion* 39 (June 5, 2015): 892–907. Myrian Mongrain, Caroline Barnes, Ryan Barnart, and Leah B. Zalan, "Acts of Kindness Reduce Depression in Individuals Low on Agreeableness," *Translational Issues in Psychological Science* 4, no. 3 (2018): 323–34. Elizabeth B. Raposa, Holly B. Laws, and Emily B. Ansell, "Prosocial Behavior Mitigates the Negative Effects of Stress in Everyday Life," *Clinical Psychological Science* 4, no. 4 (2015): 691–698. Allan Luks, "Doing Good: Helper's High," *Psychology Today* 22, no. 10 (October 1988): 39.

20–21 **In a 2012 study, psychologists at the University of British Columbia gave toddlers crackers:** Lara B. Aknin, J. Kiley Hamlin, Elizabeth W. Dunn, "Giving Leads to Happiness in Young Children," *PLoS One* 7, no. 6 (2012).

21 **After researchers asked nine-to-eleven-year-olds to perform three acts of kindness each week:** Kristin Layous, S. Katherine Nelson, Eva Oberle,

Kimberly A. Schonert-Reichl, and Sonja Lyubomirsky, "Kindness Counts: Prompting Prosocial Behavior in Preadolescents Boosts Peer Acceptance and Well-Being," *PloS One* 7, no. 12 (2012).

21 **A 2018 study reported that kids who were rated by peers as more helpful:** Maria Gerbino, Antonio Zuffiano, Nancy Eisenberg, Valeria Castellani, Bernadette Paula Luengo Kanacri, Concetta Pastorelli, and Gian Vittorio Caprara, "Adolescents' Prosocial Behavior Predicts Good Grades Beyond Intelligence and Personality Traits," *Journal of Personality* 86, no. 2 (April 2018).

21 **And in a 2015 study, researchers followed a group of children from kindergarten:** Damon E. Jones, Mark Greenberg, and Max Crowley, "Early Social-Emotional Functioning and Public Health: The Relationship Between Kindergarten Social Competence and Future Wellness," *American Journal of Public Health* 105, no. 11 (November 2015).

23 **In a 2013 study, Celia Brownell, a psychologist at the University of Pittsburgh:** Celia A. Brownell, Margarita Svetlova, Ranita Anderson, Sara R. Nichols, and Jesse Drummond, "Socialization of Early Prosocial Behavior: Parents' Talk About Emotions Is Associated with Sharing and Helping in Toddlers," *Infancy* 18 (March 1, 2013): 91–119.

25 **In one experiment, third and fourth graders were given money and then encouraged:** Nancy Eisenberg-Berg and Elizabeth Geisheker, "Content of Preachings and Power of the Model/Preacher: The Effect on Children's Generosity," *Developmental Psychology* 15, no. 2 (1979): 168–175.

25 **Other research has shown that the more that mothers consider other people's feelings:** Brad M. Farrant, Tara A. J. Devine, Murray T. Maybery, and Janet Fletcher, "Empathy, Perspective Taking and Prosocial Behavior: The Importance of Parenting Practices," *Infant and Child Development* 21 (2011): 175–188.

25 **Their research found that when parents discipline kids with explanations:** Martin L. Hoffman and Herbert D. Saltzstein, "Parent Discipline and the Child's Moral Development," *Journal of Personality and Social Psychology* 5, no. 1 (1967): 47–57.

26 **In a 1996 study designed to test Hoffman's theory:** Julia Krevans and John C. Gibbs, "Parents' Use of Inductive Discipline: Relations to Children's Empathy and Prosocial Behavior," *Child Development* 67, no. 6 (December 1996): 3263–3277.

26 **In another study, researchers found that the children of mothers who clearly explained:** Carolyn Zahn-Waxler, Marian Radke-Yarrow, and Robert A. King, "Child Rearing and Children's Prosocial Initiations Toward Victims of Distress," *Child Development* 50 (1979): 319–330.

27 **Research suggests that when parents are responsive to their children's feelings of distress:** Maayan Davidov and Joan E. Grusec, "Untangling the Links of Parental Responsiveness to Distress and Warmth to Child Outcomes," *Child Development* 77, no. 1 (January/February 2006): 44–58.

27   **The theory, which is backed by research, suggests that when parents respond sensitively and consistently:** Inge Bretherton, "The Origins of Attachment Theory: John Bowlby and Mary Ainsworth," *Developmental Psychology* 28, no. 5 (1992): 759–775.

28   **In a multiyear study published in 2016, researchers at Penn State and the University of California, Riverside:** Meghan B. Scrimgeour, Elizabeth L. Davenport, and Kristin A. Buss, "You Get What You Get and You Don't Throw a Fit!: Emotional Socialization and Child Physiology Jointly Predict Early Prosocial Development," *Developmental Psychology* 52, no. 1 (January 2016): 102–116.

28   **And in a 2019 study, researchers found that when mothers made an effort to help their toddlers:** Nancy Eisenberg, Tracy L. Spinrad, Zoe E. Taylor, and Jeffrey Liew, "Relations of Inhibition and Emotion-Related Parenting to Young Children's Prosocial and Vicariously Induced Distress Behavior," *Child Development* 90, no. 3 (May/June 2019): 846–858.

30   **In a 2018 paper, Brownell and Hammond interviewed more than five hundred parents:** Stuart I. Hammond and Celia A. Brownell, "Happily Unhelpful: Infants' Everyday Helping and Its Connections to Early Prosocial Development," *Frontiers in Psychology* 9 (September 21, 2018): 1770.

30   **In a 2015 study, Hammond and his colleague Jeremy Carpendale watched mothers interact:** Stuart I. Hammond and Jeremy I. M. Carpendale, "Helping Children Help: The Relation Between Maternal Scaffolding and Children's Early Help," *Social Development* 24, no. 2 (May 2015): 367–383.

31   **In a 1997 study, she and her colleagues interviewed mothers about the kinds of jobs:** Joan E. Grusec, Jacqueline J. Goodnow, and Lorenzo Cohen, "Household Work and the Development of Concern for Others," *Developmental Psychology* 32, no. 6 (1996): 999–1007.

31   **In a 2017 study, researchers found that five-year-olds (particularly girls) who were given the choice:** Diotima J. Rapp, Jan M. Engelmann, Esther Herrmann, and Michael Tomas, "The Impact of Choice on Young Children's Prosocial Motivation," *Journal of Experimental Child Psychology* 158 (2017): 112–121.

32   **Research by psychologist Edward Deci has shown that when people do things out of choice:** Edward L. Deci, "Effects of Externally Mediated Rewards on Intrinsic Motivation," *Journal of Personality and Social Psychology* 18, no. 1 (1971): 105–115.

32   **Indeed, a 2014 meta-analysis of forty-nine studies found that teens who participate in community service:** Anne van Goethem, Anne van Hoof, Bram Orobio de Castro, Marcel Van Aken, and Daniel Hart, "The Role of Reflection in the Effects of Community Service on Adolescent Development: A Meta-Analysis," *Child Development* 85, no. 6 (November/December 2014): 2114–2130.

37   **In a large 2014 study, researchers at Indiana University and the University of Indianapolis:** Mark Ottoni-Wilhelm, David B. Estell, and Neil H.

Perdue, "Role-Modeling and Conversations About Giving in the Socialization of Adolescent Charitable Giving and Volunteering," *Journal of Adolescence* 37 (2014): 53–66.

37 **In a 2016 study, psychologists found that people donated more money to charities:** Erik C. Nook, Desmond C. Ong, Sylvia A. Morelli, Jason P. Mitchell, and Jamil Zaki, "Prosocial Conformity: Prosocial Norms Generalize Across Behavior and Empathy," *Personality and Social Psychology Bulletin* 42, no. 8 (2016): 1045–1062.

CHAPTER 2: "THIS IS TOO HARD."

41 **In a 2010 study conducted by psychologists Chia-Jung Tsay and Mahzarin R. Banaji:** Chia-Jung Tsay and Mahzarin R. Banaji, "Naturals and Strivers: Preferences and Beliefs About Sources of Achievement," *Journal of Experimental Social Psychology* 47 (December 2010): 460–465.

41 **In a follow-up study, Tsay performed the same experiment:** Chia-Jung Tsay, "Privileging Naturals over Strivers: The Costs of the Naturalness Bias," *Personality and Social Psychology Bulletin* 42, no. 1 (2015): 40–53.

42 **As Stanford University psychologist Carol Dweck explained in her book** *Mindset:* Carol Dweck, *Mindset: The New Psychology of Success* (New York: Ballantine, 2007).

42 **In 1926, for instance, a Stanford psychologist named Catharine Morris Cox published:** Catharine M. Cox, *Genetic Studies of Genius, Vol. II: The Early Mental Traits of Three Hundred Geniuses*, ed. Louis M. Terman (California: Stanford University Press, 1926).

43 **In a study published in 1972, California education researcher Calvin Edlund gave IQ tests:** Calvin V. Edlund, "The Effect on the Test Behavior of Children, as Reflected in the I.Q. Scores, When Reinforced After Each Correct Response," *Journal of Applied Behavior Analysis* 5, no. 3 (Fall 1972): 317–319.

43 **In a similar study conducted by University of South Florida researchers, kids from various socioeconomic backgrounds:** Joy Clingman and Robert L. Fowler, "The Effects of Primary Reward on the I.Q. Performance of Grade-School Children as a Function of Initial I.Q. Level," *Journal of Applied Behavior Analysis* 9 (Spring 1976): 19–23.

44 **Passion combined with perseverance is what University of Pennsylvania psychologist Angela Duckworth calls "grit":** Angela Duckworth and Lauren Eskreis-Winkler, "Grit," *International Encyclopedia of the Social & Behavioral Sciences* 10 (2015): 397–401.

45 **In one study, Duckworth and her colleagues assessed new cadets at West Point military:** Angela L. Duckworth, Abigail Quirk, Robert Gallop, Rick H. Hoyle, Dennis R. Kelly, and Michael D. Matthews, "Cognitive and Noncognitive

Predictors of Success," *Proceedings of the National Academy of Sciences* 116, no. 47 (2019): 23499–23504.

45 **In other research, Duckworth has found that grit scores predict which students will do well:** Angela Lee Duckworth, Teri A. Kirby, Eli Tsukayama, Heather Berstein, and K. Anders Ericsson, "Deliberate Practice Spells Success: Why Grittier Competitors Triumph at the National Spelling Bee," *Social Psychology and Personality Science* 2, no. 2 (2010): 174–181.

45 **which soldiers will finish the US Army's rigorous Special Operations Forces selection course, and which students:** Lauren Eskreis-Winkler, Elizabeth P. Shulman, Scott A. Beal, and Angela L. Duckworth, "The Grit Effect: Predicting Retention in the Military, the Workplace, School and Marriage," *Frontiers in Psychology* 5, no. 36 (February 2014).

46 **Grit, as Duckworth wrote in her aptly titled book *Grit*, comes into play:** Angela Duckworth, *Grit: The Power of Passion and Perseverance* (New York: Scribner, 2016).

46 **In a classic study, education researcher Deborah Stipek, now at Stanford University:** Deborah Stipek, Rachelle Feiler, Denise Daniels, and Sharon Milburn, "Effects of Different Instructional Approaches on Young Children's Achievement and Motivation," *Child Development* 66 (1995): 209–223.

48 **For his book *Developing Talent in Young People*, University of Chicago psychologist Benjamin Bloom:** Benjamin S. Bloom, ed., *Developing Talent in Young People* (New York: Ballantine, 1985).

48 **In his book *The Procrastination Equation*, University of Calgary motivation scientist Piers Steel:** Piers Steel, *The Procrastination Equation: How to Stop Putting Things Off and Start Getting Stuff Done* (New York: HarperPerennial, 2012).

49 **In one of the most famous studies in the mindset field, psychologist Carol Dweck:** Claudia M. Mueller and Carol S. Dweck, "Praise for Intelligence Can Undermine Children's Motivation and Performance," *Journal of Personality and Social Psychology* 75, no. 1 (1998): 33–52.

53 **In one of the first studies to suggest that negative emotions fuel procrastination:** Dianne M. Tice, Ellen Bratslavsky, and Roy F. Baumeister, "Emotional Distress Regulation Takes Precedence over Impulse Control: If You Feel Bad, Do It!" *Journal of Personality and Social Psychology* 80, no. 1 (2001): 53–67.

56 **A 2016 article in *The Atlantic*, "Against the Sticker Chart," warned me that:** Erica Reischer, "Against the Sticker Chart," *Atlantic*, February 22, 2016. Accessed October 10, 2020. https://www.theatlantic.com/health/archive/2016/02/perils-of-sticker-charts/470160/.

56 ***Money* magazine ran a story in 2015 titled:** Kerri Anne Renzulli, "The Hidden Downside to Rewarding Your Kids for Good Behavior," *Money*, March 6, 2015. Accessed October 10, 2020. https://money.com/downside-treating-kids-for-good-behavior.

56 **Education guru Alfie Kohn has written an entire book on the subject:**
Alfie Kohn, *Punished by Rewards: The Trouble with Gold Stars, Incentive Plans, A's,
Praise, and Other Bribes* (New York: Houghton Mifflin, 1993).

56 **Faced with this conundrum, I dug into the research myself, and
eventually wrote an article for *Slate*:** Melinda Wenner Moyer, "Go Ahead,
Heap Rewards on Your Kid," *Slate*, August 22, 2017. Accessed October 15, 2020.
https://slate.com/human-interest/2017/08/rewards-systems-for-kids-are
-effective-if-you-use-them-correctly.html.

57 **In my piece, I unpacked one of the earliest and most famous studies on
rewards, published in 1971 by Edward Deci:** Edward L. Deci, "Effects of
Externally Mediated Rewards on Intrinsic Motivation," *Journal of Personality and
Social Psychology* 18, no. 1 (1971): 105–115.

59 **In a well-known 1973 study, for instance, Stanford University
researchers placed drawing paper:** Mark R. Lepper, David Greene, and
Richard E. Nisbett, "Undermining Children's Intrinsic Interest with Extrinsic
Reward: A Test of the 'Overjustification' Hypothesis," *Personality and Social
Psychology* 28, no. 1 (1973): 129–137.

61 **But, Deci wrote, there is no magic wand for getting kids to do what you
want:** Edward Deci and Richard Flaste, *Why We Do What We Do: Understanding
Self-Motivation* (New York: Penguin, 1996).

61 **In a classic study published in 1984, Deci's colleague and frequent
collaborator Richard Ryan:** Richard Koestener, Richard M. Ryan, Frank J.
Bernieri, and Kathleen D. Holt, "Setting Limits on Children's Behavior: The
Differential Effects of Controlling vs. Informational Styles on Intrinsic Motivation
and Creativity," *Journal of Personality* 52, no. 3 (1984): 233–248.

CHAPTER 3: "YOU'RE DUMB AND UGLY!"

64 **Parents often worry that their kids will be bullied—a 2017 national
survey found:** "Bullying and Internet Safety Are Top Health Concerns
for Parents," *Mott Poll Report* 30, no. 1 (August 21, 2017): https://mottpoll
.org/reports-surveys/bullying-and-internet-safety-are-top-health-concerns
-parents.

64 **When researchers at the University of New Hampshire surveyed kids
and parents:** Melissa K. Holt, Glenda Kaufman Kantor, and David Finkelhor,
"Parent/Child Concordance About Bullying Involvement and Family
Characteristics Related to Bullying and Peer Victimization," *Journal of School
Violence* 8, no. 1 (January 2, 2009): 42–63.

65 **A 2014 meta-analysis of eighty studies estimated:** Rashmi Shetgiri,
"Bullying and Victimization Among Children," *Advances in Pediatrics* 60, no. 1
(July 12, 2013): 33–51.

65   **while nearly one in six engages in cyberbullying via digital devices:** Kathryn L. Modecki, Jeannie Minchin, Allen G. Harbaugh, Nancy Guerra, and Kevin Runions, "Bullying Prevalence Across Contexts: A Meta-analysis Measuring Cyber and Traditional Bullying," *Journal of Adolescent Health* 55, no. 5 (November 2014): 602–611.

65   **"The way we usually talk about bullying":** Rosalind Wiseman, *Queen Bees and Wannabes: Helping Your Daughter Survive Cliques, Gossip, Boys, and the New Realities of Girl World*, 3rd ed. (New York: Harmony Books, 2016).

65   **Although the boys' actions didn't appear to be a response to bullying:** Deborah Temkin, Victoria Stuart-Cassel, Kristy Lao, Brissa Nuñez, Sarah Kelley, and Claire Kelley, "The Evolution of State School Safety Laws Since the Columbine School Shooting," *Child Trends*, February 12, 2020. Accessed October 14, 2020. https://www.childtrends.org/publications/evolution-state-school-safety-laws-columbine.

67   **In her book *Sticks and Stones*:** Emily Bazelon, *Sticks and Stones: Defeating the Culture of Bullying and Rediscovering the Power of Character and Empathy* (New York: Random House, 2014).

67   **In a 2007 study, former Duke University psychologist and neuroscientist Kristina McDonald:** Kristina L. McDonald, Martha Putallaz, Christina L. Grimes, Janis B. Kupersmidt, and John D. Coie, "Girl Talk: Gossip, Friendship, and Sociometric Status," *Merrill-Palmer Quarterly* 53, no. 3 (July 2007): 381–411.

68   **"When a group decides to exclude one girl":** Katie Hurley, *No More Mean Girls: The Secret to Raising Strong, Confident, and Compassionate Girls* (New York: TarcherPerigee, 2018).

69   **In 2018, more than two-thirds of US teens said that bullying:** Amanda Lenhart, "Cyberbullying," Pew Research Center, June 27, 2007. Accessed October 14, 2020. https://www.pewresearch.org/internet/2007/06/27/cyberbullying/.

69   **Bullying researchers have found that when schools effectively tackle regular bullying:** Konstanze Schoeps, Lidón Villanueva, Vicente Javier Prado-Gascó, and Inmaculada Montoya-Castilla, "Development of Emotional Skills in Adolescents to Prevent Cyberbullying and Improve Subjective Well-Being," *Frontiers in Psychology* 9 (October 26, 2018): 2050.

69   **Being bullied can be incredibly scarring:** Suzet Tanya Lereya, William E. Copeland, E. Jane Costello, and Dieter Wolke, "Adult Mental Health Consequences of Peer Bullying and Maltreatment in Childhood: Two Cohorts in Two Countries," *The Lancet Psychiatry* 2, no. 6 (June 1, 2015): 524–531.

69–70   **When researchers surveyed young LGBT adults:** Stephen T. Russell, Caitlin Ryan, Russell B. Toomey, Rafael M. Diaz, and Jorge Sanchez, "Lesbian, Gay, Bisexual, and Transgender Adolescent School Victimization: Implications for Young Adult Health and Adjustment," *Journal of School Health* 81, no. 5 (May 2011): 223–230.

71   **In the powerful 2013 book *Bullying Under Attack*:** Stephanie Meyer, John Meyer, Emily Sperber, and Heather Alexander, eds., *Bullying Under Attack: True*

Stories Written by Teen Victims, Bullies & Bystanders (Deerfield Beach, FL: Health Communications, Inc., 2013).

71 **Research suggests, for instance, that when kids don't get the supervision:** "Why Do Kids Bully?" STOMP Out Bullying. Accessed October 14, 2020. https://www.stompoutbullying.org/why-kids-bully.

71 **Bullies are also more likely than non-bullies:** Suzet Tanya Lereyaa, Muthanna Samara, and Dieter Wolkec, "Parenting Behavior and the Risk of Becoming a Victim and a Bully/Victim: A Meta-analysis Study," *Child Abuse & Neglect* 37, no. 12 (December 2013): 1091–1108.

71 **Ultimately, the parents who are least likely to end up with kids who bully others:** Stelios N. Georgiou, Myria Ioannou, and Panayiotis Stavrinides, "Parenting Styles and Bullying at School: The Mediating Role of Locus of Control," *International Journal of School & Educational Psychology* 5, no. 4 (2017): 226–242.

71–72 **Research has shown that *authoritarian* parents:** Hamid Masud, Muhammad Shakil Ahmad, Ki Woong Cho, and Zainab Fakhr, "Parenting Styles and Aggression Among Young Adolescents: A Systematic Review of Literature." *Community Mental Health Journal* 55, no. 6 (August 1, 2019): 1015–1030.

72 **In a 2003 study, researchers in Spain and Italy gave 179 kids:** Ersilia Menesini, Virginia Sanchez, Ada Fonzi, Rosario Ortega, Angela Costabile, and Giorgio Lo Feudo, "Moral Emotions and Bullying: A Cross-National Comparison of Differences Between Bullies, Victims and Outsiders," *Aggressive Behavior: Official Journal of the International Society for Research on Aggression* 29, no. 6 (December 2003): 515–530.

72 **Other research suggests that 15 to 20 percent of kids:** Gianluca Gini, Tiziana Pozzoli, Francesco Borghi, and Lara Franzoni, "The Role of Bystanders in Students' Perception of Bullying and Sense of Safety," *Journal of School Psychology* 46, no. 6 (December 2008): 617–638.

73 **Research has also found that some kids who bully:** Sania Shakoor, Sara R. Jaffee, Lucy Bowes, Isabelle Ouellet-Morin, Penelope Andreou, Francesca Happé, Terrie E. Moffitt, and Louise Arseneault, "A Prospective Longitudinal Study of Children's Theory of Mind and Adolescent Involvement in Bullying," *Journal of Child Psychology and Psychiatry* 53, no. 3 (March 2012): 254–261.

73 **As part of the Youth Voice Research Project:** Stan Davis and Charisse Nixon, "Preliminary Results from the Youth Voice Research Project: Victimization & Strategies," Youth Voice Research Project, March 2020. Accessed October 15, 2020. https://njbullying.org/documents/YVPMarch2010.pdf.

74 **In a 2018 study, researchers watched as parents advised their fourth- and fifth-grade:** Stevie N. Grassetti, Julie A. Hubbard, Marissa A. Smith, Megan K. Bookhout, Lauren E. Swift, and Michael J. Gawrysiak, "Caregivers' Advice and Children's Bystander Behaviors During Bullying Incidents," *Journal of Clinical Child & Adolescent Psychology* 47, no. sup1 (2018): S329–S340.

79   **Studies suggest that as many as 40 percent of kids who are bullied:**
James D. Unnever and Dewey G. Cornell, "Middle School Victims of Bullying:
Who Reports Being Bullied?" *Aggressive Behavior: Official Journal of
the International Society for Research on Aggression* 30, no. 5 (October 2004):
373–388.

79   **But you can look for warning signs:** Kathy Robison, "Bullies and Victims: A
Primer for Parents," *Helping Children at Home and School III—Handouts for
Families and Educators* (2010): S4H6-1–S4H6-3.

79   **Victims who fight back tend to lose:** Michael Tholander, "The Making and
Unmaking of a Bullying Victim," *Interchange* 50, no. 1 (February 2019): 1–23.

81   **Mediation can work when people of equal stature:** "Misdirections in
Bullying Prevention and Intervention," Anti-Defamation League. Accessed October
15, 2020. https://www.adl.org/education/resources/tools-and-strategies
/misdirections-in-bullying-prevention-and-intervention.

81   **Researchers also suggest that schools move away from zero-tolerance
punishments:** American Psychological Association Zero Tolerance Task Force,
"Are Zero Tolerance Policies Effective in the Schools? An Evidentiary Review
and Recommendations," *American Psychologist* 63, no. 9 (December 2008):
852–862.

81   **respond to bullying with more restorative approaches:** Jessica Swain-
Bradway and Sarah Sisaye, "Restorative Justice Practices and Bullying Prevention,"
StopBullying.gov, March 2, 2016. Accessed October 15, 2020. https://www
.stopbullying.gov/blog/2016/03/02/restorative-justice-practices-and-bullying
-prevention.

81   **While a handful of school anti-bullying programs:** David Scott Yeager,
Carlton J. Fong, Hae Yeon Lee, and Dorothy L. Espelage. "Declines in Efficacy of
Anti-bullying Programs Among Older Adolescents: Theory and a Three-Level Meta-
analysis." *Journal of Applied Developmental Psychology* 37 (March/April 2015):
36–51.

81   **That's because schools all too often implement these programs:** Dorothy
L. Espelage, "Why Are Bully Prevention Programs Failing in U.S. Schools?" *Journal
of Curriculum and Pedagogy* 10, no. 2 (2013): 121–124.

82   **In a two-year clinical trial involving thirty-six schools:** Dorothy L.
Espelage, Sabina Low, Joshua R. Polanin, and Eric C. Brown. "Clinical Trial of
Second Step© Middle-School Program: Impact on Aggression & Victimization,"
Journal of Applied Developmental Psychology 37 (March/April 2015): 52–63.

82   **A 2011 meta-analysis also found that kids who underwent SEL
programs:** Joseph Durlak, Roger P. Weissberg, Allison Dymnicki, Rebecca Taylor,
and Kriston Schellinger, "The Impact of Enhancing Students' Social and Emotional
Learning: A Meta-analysis of School-Based Universal Interventions," *Child
Development* 82, no. 1 (January/February 2011): 405–432.

CHAPTER 4: "I'M TELLING THE TRUTH, DAMMIT!"

85   **"Don't think you can prevent swearing":** Timothy Jay, *What to Do When Your Kids Talk Dirty* (San Jose: Resource Publications, 1998).

85   **By the time kids enter school:** Timothy Jay and Kristin Janschewitz, "The Science of Swearing," *Observer* 25, no. 5 (May/June 2012): https://www .psychologicalscience.org/observer/the-science-of-swearing.

86   **Studies also find that half of all kids start lying around age two or three:** Victoria Talwar, Jennifer Lavoie, and Angela M. Crossman, "Carving Pinocchio: Longitudinal Examination of Children's Lying for Different Goals," *Journal of Experimental Child Psychology* 181 (May 2019): 34–55.

86   **As one paper concluded, "The emergence of lying":** Victoria Talwar and Angela Crossman, "From Little White Lies to Filthy Liars: The Evolution of Honesty and Deception in Young Children," in *Advances in Child Development and Behavior* 40, ed. Janette B. Benson (2011): 139–179.

87   **(One study even found that after initially honest three-year-olds . . .):** Xiao Pan Ding, Henry M. Wellman, Yu Wang, Genyue Fu, and Kang Lee, "Theory-of-Mind Training Causes Honest Young Children to Lie," *Psychological Science* 26, no. 11 (November 1, 2015): 1812–1821.

87   **Researchers say that lie-telling in kids:** Angela D. Evans and Kang Lee, "Emergence of Lying in Very Young Children," *Developmental Psychology* 49, no. 10 (October 2013): 1958–1963.

88   **In a classic 1989 study:** Michael Lewis, Catherine Stanger, and Margaret W. Sullivan, "Deception in 3-Year-Olds," *Developmental Psychology* 25, no. 3 (May 1989): 439–443.

88   **In a similarly designed 2002 study:** Victoria Talwar and Kang Lee, "Development of Lying to Conceal a Transgression: Children's Control of Expressive Behaviour During Verbal Deception," *International Journal of Behavioral Development* 26, no. 5 (September 1, 2002): 436–444.

88   **Kids also lie for personal gain:** Victoria Talwar, Jennifer Lavoie, and Angela M. Crossman, "Carving Pinocchio: Longitudinal Examination of Children's Lying for Different Goals," *Journal of Experimental Child Psychology* 181 (May 2019): 34–55.

88   **Research suggests that self-serving lies:** Victoria Talwar and Angela Crossman, "From Little White Lies to Filthy Liars: The Evolution of Honesty and Deception in Young Children," in *Advances in Child Development and Behavior* 40, ed. Janette B. Benson (2011): 139–179.

89   **In a 2019 study, Victoria Talwar and her colleagues at McGill University:** Victoria Talwar, Jennifer Lavoie, and Angela M. Crossman, "Carving Pinocchio: Longitudinal Examination of Children's Lying for Different Goals," *Journal of Experimental Child Psychology* 181 (May 2019): 34–55.

91 **Interestingly, too, kids are more likely to lie:** Pooja Megha Nagar, Shanna Williams, and Victoria Talwar, "The Influence of an Older Sibling on Preschoolers' Lie-Telling Behavior," *Social Development* 28, no. 4 (January 30, 2019): 1095–1110.

91 **In a 2014 study, University of California psychologists:** Chelsea Hays and Leslie J. Carver, "Follow the Liar: The Effects of Adult Lies on Children's Honesty," *Developmental Science* 17, no. 6 (March 17, 2014): 977–983.

92 **Kids are also more likely to lie if they observe:** Paraskevi Engarhos, Azadeh Shohoud, Angela Crossman, and Victoria Talwar, "Learning Through Observing: Effects of Modeling Truth- and Lie-Telling on Children's Honesty," *Developmental Science* 23, no. 1 (January 2020): e12883.

96 **It sounds arbitrary, but hear me out:** Kang Lee, Victoria Talwar, Anjanie McCarthy, Ilana Ross, Angela Evans, and Cindy Arruda, "Can Classic Moral Stories Promote Honesty in Children?" *Psychological Science* 25, no. 8 (June 13, 2014): 1630–1636.

97 **A 2011 study illustrated this phenomenon:** Victoria Talwar and Kang Lee, "A Punitive Environment Fosters Children's Dishonesty: A Natural Experiment," *Child Development* 82, no. 6 (November/December 2011): 1751–1758.

98 **And if you're facing a situation:** Angela D. Evans and Kang Lee, "Promising to Tell the Truth Makes 8- to 16-Year-Olds More Honest," *Behavioral Sciences & the Law* 28, no. 6 (November/December 2010): 801–811.

98 **In a similar study, three-to-seven-year-olds:** Victoria Talwar, Kang Lee, Nicholas Bala, and R. C. L. Lindsay, "Children's Conceptual Knowledge of Lying and Its Relation to Their Actual Behaviors: Implications for Court Competence Examinations," *Law and Human Behavior* 26, no. 4 (August 2002): 395–415.

98–99 **Excessive lying *can* be a symptom of conduct disorder:** Victoria Talwar and Angela Crossman, "From Little White Lies to Filthy Liars: The Evolution of Honesty and Deception in Young Children," in *Advances in Child Development and Behavior* 40, ed. Janette B. Benson (2011): 139–179.

99 **Research suggests yes:** Hali Kil, Joan E. Grusec, and Maria Paula Chaparro, "Maternal Disclosure and Adolescent Prosocial Behavior: The Mediating Roles of Adolescent Disclosure and Coping," *Social Development* 27, no. 3 (August 2018): 652–664.

CHAPTER 5: "GIRLS CAN'T DO THAT."

102 **As one peer-reviewed paper I read concluded:** Susan A. Gelman, Marianne G. Taylor, Simone P. Nguyen, Campbell Leaper, and Rebecca S. Bigler, "Mother-Child Conversations About Gender: Understanding the Acquisition of Essentialist Beliefs," *Monographs of the Society for Research in Child Development* 69, no. 1 (2004): i, v, vii, 1–142.

103 **As many as 2 percent of babies are born intersex:** Melanie Blackless, Anthony Charuvastra, Amanda Derryck, Anne Fausto-Sterling, Karl Lauzanne, and Ellen Lee, "How Sexually Dimorphic Are We? Review and Synthesis," *American Journal of Human Biology* 12, no. 2 (March 2000): 151–166.

107 **In a 2003 experiment, researchers asked kindergarten teachers:** Lindsay M. Lamb, Rebecca S. Bigler, Lynn S. Liben, and Vanessa A. Green, "Teaching Children to Confront Peers' Sexist Remarks: Implications for Theories of Gender Development and Educational Practice," *Sex Roles* 61 (May 8, 2009): 361.

107 **In one study, University of Oregon developmental psychologist Beverly Fagot observed preschoolers:** Beverly I. Fagot, "Consequences of Moderate Cross-Gender Behavior in Preschool Children," *Child Development* 48 (1977): 902–907.

108 **In her book *Parenting Beyond Pink and Blue*, developmental psychologist Christia Spears Brown:** Christia Spears Brown, *Parenting Beyond Pink and Blue: How to Raise Your Kids Free of Gender Stereotypes* (New York: Ten Speed Press, 2014).

108 **Just before the 2008 presidential election, she and three colleagues:** Rebecca S. Bigler, Andrea E. Arthur, Julie Milligan Hughes, and Meagan M. Patterson, "The Politics of Race and Gender: Children's Perceptions of Discrimination and the U.S. Presidency," *Analyses of Social Issues and Public Policy* 8, no. 1 (2008): 83–112.

109 **In a 2017 study published in the journal *Science*, developmental psychologists:** Lin Bian, Sarah-Jane Leslie, and Andrei Cimpian, "Gender Stereotypes About Intellectual Ability Emerge Early and Influence Children's Interests," *Science* 355 (January 27, 2017): 389–391.

111 **In a classic study, researchers at Cornell University showed college students:** John Condry and Sandra Condry, "Sex Differences: A Study of the Eye of the Beholder," *Child Development* 47 (1976): 812–819.

111 **In another study, three- and five-year-olds watched videos:** Susan Sterkel Haugh, Charles D. Hoffman, and Gloria Cowan, "The Eye of the Very Young Beholder: Sex Typing of Infants by Young Children," *Child Development* 51 (1980): 598–600.

111 **Research has also found that parents use broader emotional language and explanations:** Amy Kennedy Root and Kenneth H. Rubin, "Gender and Parents' Emotion Socialization Beliefs During the Preschool Years," *New Directions for Child and Adolescent Development* 128 (2010): 51–64.

111–12 **Research has shown that boys who adopt masculine "toughness" behaviors:** Adam A. Rogers, Kimberly A. Updegraff, Carlos E. Santos, and Carol Lynn Martin, "Masculinity and School Adjustment in Middle School," *Psychology of Men & Masculinity* 18, no. 1 (2016): 50–61. Carlos E. Santos, Kathrine Galligan, Erin Pahlke, and Richard A. Fabes, "Gender-Typed Behaviors, Achievement, and Adjustment Among Racially and Ethnically Diverse Boys During Early

Adolescence," *American Journal of Orthopsychiatry* 83, no. 2, 3 (203): 252–264. Adan A. Rogers, Dawn DeLay, and Carol Lynn Martin, "Traditional Masculinity During the Middle School Transition: Associations with Depressive Symptoms and Academic Engagement," *Journal of Youth and Adolescence* 46 (2017): 709–724.

112 **Girls who internalize the idea that their value stems from how they look:** American Psychological Association, Task Force on the Sexualization of Girls, *Report of the APA Task Force on the Sexualization of Girls*, 2007. Accessed October 11, 2020. Sarah J. McKenney and Rebecca S. Bigler, "High Heels, Low Grades: Internalized Sexualization and Academic Orientation Among Adolescent Girls," *Journal of Research on Adolescence* 26, no. 1 (2014): 30–36. Marika Tiggemann and Amy Slater, "The Role of Self-Objectification in the Mental Health of Early Adolescent Girls: Predictors and Consequences," *Journal of Pediatric Psychology* 40, no. 7 (August 2015): 704–711.

112 **Starting as early as age ten, male gender stereotypes start to incorporate ideals of male dominance, aggression, and sexual callousness:** Robert W. Blum, Kristin Mmari, and Caroline Moreau, "It Begins at 10: How Gender Expectations Shape Early Adolescence Around the World," *Journal of Adolescent Health* 61, no. 4 (October 1, 2017): S3–S4.

112 **In a 2018 survey of more than one thousand US adolescents:** Plan International, "The State of Gender Equality for U.S. Adolescents: Full Research Findings from a National Survey of Adolescents," September 12, 2018. Accessed October 11, 2020. https://www.planusa.org/docs/state-of-gender-equality-2018.pdf.

113 **Men who adhere strongly to norms of masculinity are more likely than other men to sexually harass:** Rachel M. Smith, Dominic J. Parrott, Kevin M. Swartout, and Andra Teten Tharp, "Deconstructing Hegemonic Masculinity: The Roles of Antifemininity, Subordination to Women, and Sexual Dominance in Men's Perpetration of Sexual Aggression," *Psychology of Men & Masculinity* 16, no. 2 (2015): 160–169.

114 **To answer these questions, in 1992, Bigler began running a series of experiments:** Rebecca S. Bigler, "The Role of Classification Skill in Moderating Environmental Influences on Children's Gender Stereotyping: A Study of the Functional Use of Gender in the Classroom," *Child Development* 66, no. 4 (August 1995): 1072–1087. Rebecca S. Bigler, Lecianna C. Jones, and Debra B. Lobliner, "Social Categorization and the Formation of Intergroup Attitudes in Children," *Child Development* 68, no. 3 (June 1997): 530–543. Rebecca S. Bigler, Christia Spears Brown, and Marc Markell, "When Groups Are Not Created Equal: Effects of Group Status on the Formation of Intergroup Attitudes in Children," *Child Development* 72, no. 4 (July/August 2001): 1151–1162.

116 **In order for children to develop prejudices about a social group, Bigler has found:** Rebecca S. Bigler and Lynn S. Liben, "Developmental Intergroup Theory: Explaining and Reducing Children's Social Stereotyping and Prejudice," *Current Directions in Psychological Science* 16, no. 3 (2007): 162–166.

118   **One study found that by the time kids are six and a half:** Eleanor E.
Maccoby and Carol Nagy Jacklin, "Gender Segregation in Childhood," *Advances in
Child Development and Behavior* 20 (1987): 239–287.

118   **Research has also shown that the more girls and boys play with same-
gender partners:** Carol Lynn Martin and Richard E. Fabes, "The Stability and
Consequences of Young Children's Same-Sex Peer Interactions," *Developmental
Psychology* 37, no. 3 (2001): 431–446.

119   **As for gender-segregated schools, researchers are largely in agreement
that:** Campbell Leaper and Christia Spears Brown, "Sexism in Schools," *Advances
in Child Development and Behavior* 47 (2014): 189–223.

123   **(Lest you think things have recently improved on the toy front . . .):**
Elizabeth V. Sweet, "Boy Builders and Pink Princesses: Gender, Toys, and Inequality
over the Twentieth Century," ProQuest Dissertations Publishing (2013): 3614279.
Accessed October 11, 2020. https://search.proquest.com/openview
/eaa5f665af82e76329798e40e2b4fbcf/1?pq-origsite=gscholar&cbl=18750&diss=y.

123   **Research suggests that some parents (especially dads) become *very*
uncomfortable when their boys play with dolls:** Judith H. Langlois and A.
Chris Downs, "Mothers, Fathers, and Peers as Socialization Agents of Sex-Typed
Play Behaviors in Young Children," *Child Development* 51 (108): 1217–1247.

123   **Teachers too: One study found that boys were criticized:** Beverly I. Fagot,
"Consequences of Moderate Cross-Gender Behavior in Preschool Children," *Child
Development* 48 (1977): 902–907.

123   **In another study, researchers observed preschool and kindergarten kids
during recess:** Michael E. Lamb, M. Ann Easterbrooks, and George W. Holden,
"Reinforcement and Punishment Among Preschoolers: Characteristics, Effects, and
Correlates." *Child Development* 51, no. 4 (December 1980): 1230–1236.

123   **In one well-known study, University of Oregon researchers Beverly
Fagot and Mary Leinbach:** Beverly I. Fagot and Mary D. Leinbach, "The Young
Children's Gender Schema: Environmental Input, Internal Organization," *Child
Development* 60 (1989): 663–672.

124   **One study observed families at a museum science exhibit:** Kevin Crowley,
Maureen A. Callanan, Harriet R. Tenenbaum, and Elizabeth Allen, "Parents
Explain More Often to Boys Than to Girls During Shared Scientific Thinking,"
Psychological Science 12, no. 3 (2001): 258–261.

124   **And in a 2014 *New York Times* op-ed, former Google data scientist Seth
Stephens-Davidowitz pointed out:** Seth Stephens-Davidowitz, "Google, Tell
Me. Is My Son a Genius?" *The New York Times*, January 18, 2014. Accessed October
11, 2020. https://www.nytimes.com/2014/01/19/opinion/sunday/google-tell-me-is
-my-son-a-genius.html.

124   **Research suggests that boys who are made to feel emasculated:** Dennis E.
Reidy, Joanne P. Smith-Darden, Kai S. Cortina, Roger M. Kernsmith, and Poco D.
Kernsmith, "Masculine Discrepancy Stress, Teen Dating Violence, and Sexual

Violence Perpetration Among Adolescent Boys," *Journal of Adolescent Health* 56, no. 6 (June 2015): 619–624.

125 **Compared with girls the same age, research shows that adolescent boys often maintain superficial friendships:** Matthew Oransky and Jeanne Marecek, "'I'm Not Going to Be a Girl,' Masculinity and Emotions in Boys' Friendships and Peer Groups," *Journal of Adolescent Research* 24, no. 2 (March 2009): 218–241.

125 **But, as child psychologists Dan Kindlon and Michael Thompson explained:** Dan Kindlon and Michael Thompson, *Raising Cain: Protecting the Emotional Life of Boys* (New York: Ballantine, 1999).

126 **Research has shown that transgender and gender-expansive kids have higher self-esteem:** Bruna L. Seibel, Bruno de Brito Silva, Anna M. V. Fontanari, Ramiro F. Catelan, Ana M. Bercht, Juliana L. Stucky, Diogo A. DeSousa, Elder Cerqueira-Santos, Henrique C. Nardi, Silvia H. Koller, and Angelo B. Costa, "The Impact of the Parental Support on Risk Factors in the Process of Gender Affirmation of Transgender and Gender Diverse People," *Frontiers in Psychology* 9 (March 27, 2018): 399. Lisa Simons, Sheree M. Schrager, Leslie F. Clark, Barvin Belzer, and Johanna Olson, "Parental Support and Mental Health Among Transgender Adolescents," *Journal of Adolescent Health* 53, no. 6 (December 2013): 791–793.

126 **Books that might be helpful include:** Stephanie A. Brill and Rachel Pepper, *The Transgender Child: A Handbook for Families and Professionals* (Minneapolis: Cleis Press, 2008). Diane Ehrensaft and Norman Spack, *The Gender Creative Child: Pathways for Nurturing and Supporting Children Who Live Outside Gender Boxes* (New York: The Experiment, 2016).

126 **A few years ago, a family friend bought my daughter the book *Good Night Stories for Rebel Girls*:** Elena Favilli and Francesca Cavallio, *Good Night Stories for Rebel Girls: 100 Tales of Extraordinary Women* (Santa Monica: Rebel Girls, 2016).

127 **One of Bigler's studies, which she coauthored with psychologist Erica Weisgram, found:** Erica S. Weisgram and Rebecca S. Bigler, "Effects of Learning About Gender Discrimination on Adolescent Girls' Attitudes Toward and Interest in Science," *Psychology of Women Quarterly* 31, no. 3 (2017): 262–269.

127 **Devine's research suggests that they'll only stop having them once they learn to recognize these thoughts:** Patricia G. Devine, Patrick S. Forscher, Anthony J. Austin, and William T. L. Cox, "Long-Term Reduction in Implicit Race Bias: A Prejudice Habit-Breaking Intervention," *Journal of Experimental Social Psychology* 48, no. 6 (November 2012): 1267–1278.

128 **In a series of studies published in 2004, psychologists Susan Gelman, Marianne Taylor, and Simone Nguyen:** Susan A. Gelman, Marianne G. Taylor, Simone P. Nguyen, Campbell Leaper, and Rebecca S. Bigler, "Mother-Child Conversations About Gender: Understanding the Acquisition of Essentialist Beliefs," *Monographs of the Society for Research in Child Development* 69, no. 1 (2004): i, v, vii, 1–142.

CHAPTER 6: "I'M PERFECT."

132   **The final report published by the task force:** California Task Force to
Promote Self-Esteem, Personal, and Social Responsibility, *Toward a State of Esteem:
The Final Report of the California Task Force to Promote Self-Esteem and Personal
and Social Responsibility* (California Department of Education, 1990).

132   **In an exhaustive review of the research literature:** Roy F. Baumeister,
Jennifer D. Campbell, Joachim I. Krueger, and Kathleen D. Vohs, "Does High
Self-Esteem Cause Better Performance, Interpersonal Success, Happiness, or
Healthier Lifestyles?" *Psychological Science in the Public Interest* 4, no. 1 (May 1,
2003): 1–44.

133   **Among other things, healthy self-esteem reduces the risk:** Ingvild Oxås
Henriksen, Ingunn Ranøyen, Marit Sæbø Indredavik, and Frode Stenseng, "The
Role of Self-Esteem in the Development of Psychiatric Problems: a Three-Year
Prospective Study in a Clinical Sample of Adolescents," *Child and Adolescent
Psychiatry and Mental Health* 11 (2017): 68.

134   **(Also, you may have heard of well-publicized research . . .):** Kali H.
Trzesniewski, M. Brent Donnellan, and Richard W. Robins, "Do Today's Young People
Really Think They Are So Extraordinary? An Examination of Secular Trends in
Narcissism and Self-Enhancement," *Psychological Science* 19, no. 2 (February 1, 2008):
181–188. Eunike Wetzel, Anna Brown, Patrick L. Hill, Joanne M. Chung, Richard W.
Robins, and Brent W. Roberts, "The Narcissism Epidemic Is Dead; Long Live the
Narcissism Epidemic," *Psychological Science* 28, no. 12 (December 1, 2017): 1833–1847.

134   **Brummelman has been studying this question for years:** Eddie
Brummelman, Sander Thomaes, Stefanie A. Nelemans, Bram Orobio De Castro,
Geertjan Overbeek, and Brad J. Bushman, "Origins of Narcissism in Children,"
Proceedings of the National Academy of Sciences 112, no. 12 (March 24, 2015):
3659–3662. Eddie Brummelman, Sander Thomaes, and Constantine Sedikides,
"Separating Narcissism from Self-Esteem." *Current Directions in Psychological
Science* 25, no. 1 (February 1, 2016): 8–13.

135   **They can bully (because bullying makes them feel . . .):** Albert Reijntjes,
Marjolijn Vermande, Sander Thomaes, Frits Goossens, Tjeert Olthof, Liesbeth
Aleva, and Matty Van der Meulen, "Narcissism, Bullying, and Social Dominance in
Youth: A Longitudinal Analysis," *Journal of Abnormal Child Psychology* 44, no. 1
(January 2016): 63–74.

135   **they can respond to criticism or rejection with anger and aggression:**
Brad J. Bushman and Roy F. Baumeister, "Threatened Egotism, Narcissism,
Self-Esteem, and Direct and Displaced Aggression: Does Self-Love or Self-Hate
Lead to Violence?" *Journal of Personality and Social Psychology* 75, no. 1 (July 1998):
219–229.

136   **At the ten most competitive US universities, the admissions rate
dropped:** Henry Steele, "Analyzing College Admissions & Acceptance Rates Over

Time: A Study Comparing 2006 to 2018 Acceptance Rates," BusinessStudent.com, September 21, 2018. Accessed October 16, 2020. https://www.businessstudent.com/topics/college-acceptance-rates-over-time/.

136 **When the Organisation for Economic Co-operation and Development:** Organisation for Economic Co-operation and Development, *Under Pressure: The Squeezed Middle Class* (Paris: OECD Publishing, 2019).

136 **(Important note: Research suggests that kids who attend play-based schools . . .):** Adele Diamond, Chris Lee, Peter Senften, Andrea Lam, and David Abbott, "Randomized Control Trial of *Tools of the Mind*: Marked Benefits to Kindergarten Children and Their Teachers," *PLoS One* 14, no. 9 (September 17, 2019): e0222447.

137 **In his 2015 book *Our Kids: The American Dream in Crisis*:** Robert D. Putnam, *Our Kids: The American Dream in Crisis* (New York: Simon & Schuster Paperbacks, 2016).

137 **Research suggests that when parents overemphasize achievement:** Suniya S. Luthar, Nina L. Kumar, and Nicole Zillmer, "High-Achieving Schools Connote Risks for Adolescents: Problems Documented, Processes Implicated, and Directions for Interventions," *American Psychologist* 75, no. 7 (October 2020): 983–995.

138 **In a survey published in 2014, Harvard University:** Rick Weissbourd, Stephanie Jones, Trisha Ross Anderson, Jennifer Kahn, and Mark Russell, "The Children We Mean to Raise: The Real Messages Adults Are Sending About Values," Making Caring Common Project, Harvard Graduate School of Education, July 2014. Accessed October 16, 2020. https://mcc.gse.harvard.edu/reports/children-mean-raise.

138 **In her book *Kid Confidence*:** Eileen Kennedy-Moore, *Kid Confidence: Help Your Child Make Friends, Build Resilience, and Develop Real Self-Esteem* (Oakland: New Harbinger Publications, 2019).

138 **Starting in the late 1990s, she and her colleagues studied:** Suniya S. Luthar and Karen D'Avanzo, "Contextual Factors in Substance Use: A Study of Suburban and Inner-City Adolescents," *Development and Psychopathology* 11, no. 4 (Fall 1999): 845–867.

139 **Luthar's research suggests that the problems afflicting these students:** Suniya S. Luthar and Nina L. Kumar, "Youth in High-Achieving Schools: Challenges to Mental Health and Directions for Evidence-Based Interventions," in *Handbook of School-Based Mental Health Promotion*, ed. Alan W. Leschied, Donald H. Saklofske, and Gordon L. Flett (Cham: Springer, 2019): 441–458.

139 **In research conducted in 2019 that involved nine cohorts of kids:** Suniya S. Luthar, Nina L. Kumar, and Nicole Zillmer, "High-Achieving Schools Connote Risks for Adolescents: Problems Documented, Processes Implicated, and Directions for Interventions," *American Psychologist* 75, no. 7 (October 2020): 983–995.

139 **These trends continue after high school, too:** Suniya S. Luthar, Phillip J. Small, and Lucia Ciciolla, "Adolescents from Upper Middle Class Communities:

Substance Misuse and Addiction Across Early Adulthood," *Development and Psychopathology* 30, no. 1 (February 2018): 315–335.

139 **In a 2019 paper, Luthar and her colleagues framed the cause this way:** Suniya S. Luthar, Nina L. Kumar, and Nicole Zillmer, "High-Achieving Schools Connote Risks for Adolescents: Problems Documented, Processes Implicated, and Directions for Interventions," *American Psychologist* 75, no. 7 (October 2020): 983–995.

140 **In a 2017 study, Luthar and her colleagues interviewed:** Lucia Ciciolla, Alexandria S. Curlee, Jason Karageorge, and Suniya S. Luthar, "When Mothers and Fathers Are Seen as Disproportionately Valuing Achievements: Implications for Adjustment Among Upper Middle Class Youth," *Journal of Youth and Adolescence* 46, no. 5 (May 2017): 1057–1075.

140 **Other research has found that when parents accentuate:** Karen E. Ablard and Wayne D. Parker, "Parents' Achievement Goals and Perfectionism in Their Academically Talented Children," *Journal of Youth and Adolescence* 26, no. 6 (December 1997): 651–667.

141 **In 2019, the National Academies of Sciences, Engineering, and Medicine:** National Academies of Sciences, Engineering, and Medicine, *Vibrant and Healthy Kids: Aligning Science, Practice, and Policy to Advance Health Equity* (Washington, DC: National Academies Press, 2019).

141 **And in 2018, the Robert Wood Johnson Foundation published a report:** Mary B. Geisz and Mary Nakashian, "Adolescent Wellness: Current Perspectives and Future Opportunities in Research, Policy, and Practice," Robert Wood Johnson Foundation, July 1, 2018. Accessed October 16, 2020. https://www.rwjf.org/en /library/research/2018/06/inspiring-and-powering-the-future—a-new-view-of -adolescence.html.

144 **In a 2009 study, researchers interviewed ninth graders and their teachers:** Guy Roth, Avi Assor, Christopher P. Niemiec, Richard M. Ryan, and Edward L. Deci, "The Emotional and Academic Consequences of Parental Conditional Regard: Comparing Conditional Positive Regard, Conditional Negative Regard, and Autonomy Support as Parenting Practices," *Developmental Psychology* 45, no. 4 (July 2009): 1119–1142.

144 **When college students were asked in an informal survey:** Steve Henson, "What Makes a Nightmare Sports Parent—and What Makes a Great One," ThePostGame.com, February 15, 2012. Accessed October 16, 2020. http://www .thepostgame.com/blog/more-family-fun/201202/what-makes-nightmare-sports -parent.

145 **Kids with low self-esteem often also struggle with depression:** A. W. Geiger and Leslie Davis, "A Growing Number of American Teenagers—Particularly Girls—Are Facing Depression," Pew Research Center, July 12, 2019. Accessed October 16, 2020. https://www.pewresearch.org/fact-tank/2019/07/12/a-growing -number-of-american-teenagers-particularly-girls-are-facing-depression/.

147   **In a 2014 study, Brummelman and his colleagues found:** Eddie
Brummelman, Sander Thomaes, Bram Orobio de Castro, Geertjan Overbeek, and
Brad J. Bushman. "'That's Not Just Beautiful—That's Incredibly Beautiful!' The
Adverse Impact of Inflated Praise on Children with Low Self-Esteem," *Psychological
Science* 25, no. 3 (March 1, 2014): 728–735.

147   **one survey found that 87 percent of parents believe:** Eddie Brummelman
and Sander Thomaes, "Parents' Beliefs About Praise," unpublished raw data (2011).

147–48   **In a follow-up to the 2014 experiment:** Eddie Brummelman, Sander Thomaes,
Bram Orobio de Castro, Geertjan Overbeek, and Brad J. Bushman. "'That's Not
Just Beautiful—That's Incredibly Beautiful!' The Adverse Impact of Inflated Praise
on Children with Low Self-Esteem," *Psychological Science* 25, no. 3 (March 1,
2014): 728–735.

148   **In a 2005 study, Joanne V. Wood:** Joanne V. Wood, Sara A. Heimpel, Ian R.
Newby-Clark, and Michael Ross, "Snatching Defeat from the Jaws of Victory:
Self-Esteem Differences in the Experience and Anticipation of Success," *Journal of
Personality and Social Psychology* 89, no. 5 (November 2005): 764–780.

149   **Dweck's research has shown that when kids are praised for smarts or
skills:** Melissa L. Kamins and Carol S. Dweck, "Person Versus Process Praise and
Criticism: Implications for Contingent Self-Worth and Coping," *Developmental
Psychology* 35, no. 3 (May 1999): 835–847.

149   **In one study, Dweck and her colleagues found that if kids:** Andrei
Cimpian, Holly-Marie C. Arce, Ellen M. Markman, and Carol S. Dweck, "Subtle
Linguistic Cues Affect Children's Motivation," *Psychological Science* 18, no. 4 (April
1, 2007): 314–316.

149   **Other studies have found that praising kids for being "smart" increases:**
Li Zhao, Gail D. Heyman, Lulu Chen, and Kang Lee, "Praising Young Children for
Being Smart Promotes Cheating," *Psychological Science* 28, no. 12 (December 1,
2017): 1868–1870.

149   **As Dweck and her colleagues have written:** Carol S. Dweck, Gregory M.
Walton, and Geoffrey L. Cohen, *Academic Tenacity: Mindsets and Skills that
Promote Long-Term Learning,* Bill & Melinda Gates Foundation, 2014. Accessed
October 16, 2020. https://files.eric.ed.gov/fulltext/ED576649.pdf.

149   **In another 2014 study, Brummelman and his team measured self-
esteem:** Eddie Brummelman, Sander Thomaes, Geertjan Overbeek, Bram
Orobio de Castro, Marcel A. Van Den Hout, and Brad J. Bushman, "On
Feeding Those Hungry for Praise: Person Praise Backfires in Children with Low
Self-Esteem," *Journal of Experimental Psychology: General* 143, no. 1 (February
2014): 9–14.

150   **Dweck and her colleagues argue that praising for ability:** Melissa L.
Kamins and Carol S. Dweck, "Person Versus Process Praise and Criticism:
Implications for Contingent Self-Worth and Coping," *Developmental Psychology* 35,
no. 3 (May 1999): 835–847.

151 **As part of her research, Indiana University Bloomington sociologist:** Jessica McCrory Calarco, *Negotiating Opportunities: How the Middle Class Secures Advantages in School* (New York: Oxford University Press, 2018).

152 **When I spoke over the phone with psychologist Madeline Levine:** Madeline Levine, *The Price of Privilege: How Parental Pressure and Material Advantage Are Creating a Generation of Disconnected and Unhappy Kids* (New York: HarperCollins, 2006).

152 **In 2015, two parents were charged with felony child neglect:** Lenore Skenazy, "11-Year-Old Boy Played in His Yard. CPS Took Him, Felony Charge for Parents," Reason.com, June 11, 2015. Accessed October 16, 2020. https://reason.com/2015/06/11/11-year-old-boy-played-in-his-yard-cps-t/.

153 **As educator Jessica Lahey explained in her book:** Jessica Lahey, *The Gift of Failure: How the Best Parents Learn to Let Go So Their Children Can Succeed* (New York: HarperCollins, 2015).

CHAPTER 7: "HER SKIN LOOKS DIRTY."

158 **In a study published in 2005, University of Kent psychologist:** David J. Kelly, Paul C. Quinn, Alan M. Slater, Kang Lee, Alan Gibson, Michael Smith, Liezhong Ge, and Olivier Pascalis, "Three-Month-Olds, but Not Newborns, Prefer Own-Race Faces," *Developmental Science* 8, no. 6 (November 2005): F31–F36.

159 **In a seminal 2003 study, developmental psychologist Phyllis Katz:** Phyllis A. Katz, "Racists or Tolerant Multiculturalists? How Do They Begin?" *American Psychologist* 58, no. 11 (November 2003): 897–909.

159 **In another well-known experiment, sociologists Debra Van Ausdale:** Joe R. Feagin and Debra Van Ausdale, *The First R: How Children Learn Race and Racism* (Lanham: Rowman & Littlefield, 2001).

160 **More recently, in 2012, researchers asked white mothers:** Erin Pahlke, Rebecca S. Bigler, and Marie-Anne Suizzo, "Relations Between Colorblind Socialization and Children's Racial Bias: Evidence from European American Mothers and Their Preschool Children," *Child Development* 83, no. 4 (July/August 2012): 1164–1179.

161 **In a 2011 study, Brigitte Vittrup:** Brigitte Vittrup and George W. Holden, "Exploring the Impact of Educational Television and Parent–Child Discussions on Children's Racial Attitudes," *Analyses of Social Issues and Public Policy* 11, no. 1 (December 2011): 82–104.

162 **In 2018, Vittrup interviewed white mothers:** Brigitte Vittrup, "Color Blind or Color Conscious? White American Mothers' Approaches to Racial Socialization," *Journal of Family Issues* 39, no. 3 (February 1, 2018): 668–692.

163 **As Ibram X. Kendi, the founding director:** Ibram X. Kendi, *How to Be an Antiracist* (New York: One World, 2019).

164 In her landmark book *Why Are All the Black Kids Sitting Together in the Cafeteria?*: Beverly Daniel Tatum, *Why Are All the Black Kids Sitting Together in the Cafeteria?: And Other Conversations About Race* (New York: Basic Books, 2017).

165 In a study published in 2003, Bigler and her colleagues interviewed: Rebecca S. Bigler, Cara J. Averhart, and Lynn S. Liben, "Race and the Workforce: Occupational Status, Aspirations, and Stereotyping Among African American Children," *Developmental Psychology* 39, no. 3 (May 2003): 572–580.

166 Researchers have found that both Black and white kids prefer: Anna-Kaisa Newheiser and Kristina R. Olson, "White and Black American Children's Implicit Intergroup Bias," *Journal of Experimental Social Psychology* 48, no. 1 (January 2012): 264–270.

168 Some of my favorites include: Ibram X. Kendi, *How to Be an Antiracist* (New York: One World, 2019). Ijeoma Oluo, *So You Want to Talk About Race* (New York: Hachette Book Group, 2019). Layla F. Saad, *Me and White Supremacy: Combat Racism, Change the World, and Become a Good Ancestor* (Naperville: Sourcebooks, 2020).

171 the author of *Promoting Racial Literacy in Schools*: Howard Stevenson, *Promoting Racial Literacy in Schools: Differences That Make a Difference* (New York: Teachers College Press, 2014).

173 research has shown that kids of color who have these kinds of discussions: Anna-Kaisa Newheiser and Kristina R. Olson, "White and Black American Children's Implicit Intergroup Bias," *Journal of Experimental Social Psychology* 48, no. 1 (January 2012): 264–270.

175 In a 2005 study, Adam Rutland, a social psychologist: Adam Rutland, Lindsey Cameron, Laura Bennett, and Jennifer Ferrell, "Interracial Contact and Racial Constancy: A Multi-Site Study of Racial Intergroup Bias in 3–5 Year Old Anglo-British Children," *Journal of Applied Developmental Psychology* 26, no. 6 (November/December 2005): 699–713.

175 In a 2017 study, Jennifer Steele, a psychologist: Antonya M. Gonzalez, Jennifer R. Steele, and Andrew S. Baron, "Reducing Children's Implicit Racial Bias Through Exposure to Positive Out-Group Exemplars," *Child Development* 88, no. 1 (January/February 2017): 123–130.

175 In another study, five-to-seven-year-old white kids who watched: Brigitte Vittrup and George W. Holden, "Exploring the Impact of Educational Television and Parent–Child Discussions on Children's Racial Attitudes," *Analyses of Social Issues and Public Policy* 11, no. 1 (December 2011): 82–104.

176 In a 2010 study, researchers at Northwestern University: Evan P. Apfelbaum, Kristin Pauker, Samuel R. Sommers, and Nalini Ambady, "In Blind Pursuit of Racial Equality?" *Psychological Science* 21, no. 11 (November 1, 2010): 1587–1592.

178 In a 2007 study, Bigler and her colleagues presented: Julie M. Hughes, Rebecca S. Bigler, and Sheri R. Levy, "Consequences of Learning About Historical

Racism Among European American and African American Children," *Child Development* 78, no. 6 (November/December 2007): 1689–1705.

CHAPTER 8: "YOU CAN'T MAKE ME!"

187 **In his most famous experiment, Lewin and his colleagues:** Kurt Lewin, Ronald Lippitt, and Ralph K. White, "Patterns of Aggressive Behavior in Experimentally Created 'Social Climates,'" *Journal of Social Psychology* 10, no. 2 (1939): 269–299.

188 **Years later, Harvard researcher Alfred Baldwin translated Lewin's findings into the idea of parenting styles:** Alfred L. Baldwin, "Socialization and the Parent-Child Relationship," *Child Development* 19, no. 3 (September 1948): 127–136.

188 **and then Diana Baumrind, a clinical and developmental psychologist at the University of California, Berkeley:** Diana Baumrind, "Child Care Practices Anteceding Three Patterns of Preschool Behavior," *Genetic Psychology Monographs* 75 (1967): 43–88.

189 **Years later, researchers Eleanor Maccoby and John Martin added a fourth parenting style to the mix:** *Neglecting* **parents:** Eleanor Maccoby and John Martin, "Socialization in the Context of the Family: Parent-Child Interaction," in *Handbook of Child Psychology*, ed. Paul Henry Mussen (New York: Wiley, 1983), 1–101.

189 **As research has shown over the years, children of neglectful parents:** Susie D. Lamborn, Nina S. Mounts, Laurence Steinberg, and Sanford M. Dornbusch, "Patterns of Competence and Adjustment Among Adolescents from Authoritative, Authoritarian, Indulgent, and Neglectful Families," *Child Development* 62, no. 5 (October 1991): 1049–1065.

189 **They can have low self-esteem:** Susie D. Lamborn, Nina S. Mounts, Laurence Steinberg, and Sanford M. Dornbusch, "Patterns of Competence and Adjustment Among Adolescents from Authoritative, Authoritarian, Indulgent, and Neglectful Families," *Child Development* 62, no. 5 (October 1991): 1049–1065. Alexandria Meyer, Greg Hajcak Proudfit, Sara J. Bufferd, Autumn J. Kujawa, Rebecca S. Laptook, Dana C. Torpey, and Daniel N. Klein, "Self-Reported and Observed Punitive Parenting Prospectively Predicts Increased Error-Related Brain Activity in Six-Year-Old Children," *Journal of Abnormal Child Psychology* 43, no. 5 (July 2015): 821–829. Keith A. King, Rebecca A. Vidourek, and Ashley L. Merianos, "Authoritarian Parenting and Youth Depression: Results from a National Study," *Journal of Prevention & Intervention in the Community* 44, no. 2 (2016): 130–139.

190 **They do OK, but they tend to be self-centered:** Rikuya Hosokawa and Toshiki Katsura, "Role of Parenting Style in Children's Behavioral Problems Through the

Transition from Preschool to Elementary School According to Gender in Japan,"
International Journal of Environmental Research and Public Health 16, no. 1
(January 2019): 21. Susie D. Lamborn, Nina S. Mounts, Laurence Steinberg, and
Sanford M. Dornbusch, "Patterns of Competence and Adjustment Among
Adolescents from Authoritative, Authoritarian, Indulgent, and Neglectful
Families," *Child Development* 62, no. 5 (October 1991): 1049–1065. Julie A.
Patock-Peckham and Antonio A. Morgan-Lopez, "College Drinking Behaviors:
Mediational Links Between Parenting Styles, Impulse Control, and Alcohol-Related
Outcomes," *Psychology of Addictive Behaviors* 20, no. 2 (June 2006): 117–125.

190 **The kids who thrive the most, by far, are those with authoritative parents:**
Susie D. Lamborn, Nina S. Mounts, Laurence Steinberg, and Sanford M. Dornbusch,
"Patterns of Competence and Adjustment Among Adolescents from Authoritative,
Authoritarian, Indulgent, and Neglectful Families," *Child Development* 62, no. 5
(October 1991): 1049–1065.

190 **They are more likely than their peers to perform well in school:** Laurence
Steinberg, Julie D. Elmen, and Nina S. Mounts, "Authoritative Parenting,
Psychosocial Maturity, and Academic Success Among Adolescents," *Child
Development* (December 1989): 1424–1436. Nancy Darling, Patricio Cumsille, Linda
L. Caldwell, and Bonnie Dowdy, "Predictors of Adolescents' Disclosure to Parents
and Perceived Parental Knowledge: Between-and Within-Person Differences,"
Journal of Youth and Adolescence 35, no. 4 (August 2006): 659–670. Laura M.
Padilla-Walker, Gustavo Carlo, Katherine J. Christensen, and Jeremy B. Yorgason,
"Bidirectional Relations Between Authoritative Parenting and Adolescents'
Prosocial Behaviors," *Journal of Research on Adolescence* 22, no. 3 (September 2012):
400–408.

192 **As sociologists Brian K. Barber and Elizabeth Lovelady Harmon
summarized:** Brian K. Barber and Elizabeth Lovelady Harmon, "Violating the
Self: Parental Psychological Control of Children and Adolescents," in *Intrusive
Parenting: How Psychological Control Affects Children and Adolescents*, ed.
Brian K. Barber (Washington, DC: American Psychological Association, 2002),
15–52.

192 **Studies have linked parental psychological control:** Brian K. Barber and
Elizabeth Lovelady Harmon, "Violating the Self: Parental Psychological Control of
Children and Adolescents," in *Intrusive Parenting: How Psychological Control
Affects Children and Adolescents*, ed. Brian K. Barber (Washington, DC: American
Psychological Association, 2002), 15–52. Nejra Van Zalk and Margaret Kerr, "Shy
Adolescents' Perceptions of Parents' Psychological Control and Emotional Warmth:
Examining Bidirectional Links," *Merrill-Palmer Quarterly* 57, no. 4 (October 2011):
375–401. Xinpei Xu, David Dai, Ming Liu, and Ciping Deng, "Relations Between
Parenting and Adolescents' Academic Functioning: The Mediating Role of
Achievement Goal Orientations," *Frontiers in Education* 3 (January 2018): 1. Brian
K. Barber, "Parental Psychological Control: Revisiting A Neglected Construct,"

Child Development 67, no. 6 (December 1996): 3296–3319. Monica M. Nanda, Beth A. Kotchick, and Rachel L. Grover, "Parental Psychological Control and childhood Anxiety: The Mediating Role of Perceived Lack of Control," *Journal of Child and Family Studies* 21, no. 4 (August 2012): 637–645. Yi-Chan Tu, Hung-Chang Lee, Ho-Yuan Chen, and Tsai-Feng Kao, "A Study on the Relationships Among Psychological Control, Adolescent Depression and Antisocial Behavior in Taiwan," *Procedia-Social and Behavioral Sciences* 122 (March 19, 2014): 335–343. Susanne Frost Olsen, Chongming Yang, Craig H. Hart, Clyde C. Robinson, Peixia Wu, David A. Nelson, Larry J. Nelson, Shenghua Jin, and Jianzhong Wo, "Maternal Psychological Control and Preschool Children's Behavioral Outcomes in China, Russia, and the United States," in *Intrusive Parenting: How Psychological Control Affects Children and Adolescents*, ed. Brian K. Barber (Washington, DC: American Psychological Association, 2002), 235–262.

194 **In their book *No-Drama Discipline*:** Daniel J. Siegel and Tina Payne Bryson, *No-Drama Discipline: The Whole-Brain Way to Calm the Chaos and Nurture Your Child's Developing Mind* (New York: Bantam Books, 2016).

196 **Robert Larzelere, a psychologist at Oklahoma State University:** Robert E. Larzelere, Amanda Sheffield Morris, and Amanda W. Harrist, *Authoritative Parenting: Synthesizing Nurturance and Discipline for Optimal Child Development* (Washington, DC: American Psychological Association, 2013).

196–97 **In a systematic review of forty-one studies published in 2012:** Daniela J. Owen, Amy M. S. Slep, and Richard E. Heyman, "The Effect of Praise, Positive Nonverbal Response, Reprimand, and Negative Nonverbal Response on Child Compliance: A Systematic Review," *Clinical Child and Family Psychology Review* 15, no. 4 (December 2012): 364–385.

197 **In addition, evidence-based parenting programs:** Guy Bodenmann, Annette Cina, Thomas Ledermann, and Matthew R. Sanders, "The Efficacy of the Triple P-Positive Parenting Program in Improving Parenting and Child Behavior: A Comparison with Two Other Treatment Conditions," *Behaviour Research and Therapy* 46, no. 4 (April 2008): 411–427.

197 **Both the American Academy of Pediatrics (AAP) and the Society for Clinical Child and Adolescent Psychology:** Committee on Psychosocial Aspects of Child and Family Health, "Guidance for Effective Discipline," *Pediatrics* 101, no. 4 (April 1, 1998): 723–728. Marc Atkins, Anne Marie Albano, Mary Fristad, Bill Pelham, John Piacentini, Dick Abidin, Kristin Hawley, et al., "Outrageous Claims Regarding the Appropriateness of Time Out Have No Basis in Science," Society for Clinical Child and Adolescent Psychology, September 29, 2014. Accessed October 17, 2020. https://effectivechildtherapy.org/outrageous-claims-regarding-appropriateness-time-no-basis-science/.

197 **Another reason—one cited by the Natural Child Project:** Peter Haiman, "The Case Against Time-Out," The Natural Child Project. Accessed October 17, 2020. https://www.naturalchild.org/articles/guest/peter_haiman.html.

198   **Time-outs are based on the premise:** Edward R. Christophersen, *Beyond Discipline: Parenting That Lasts a Lifetime* (Shawnee Mission, KS: Overland Press, 1990).

200   **"The popular press has been quick and persistent in making up rules . . . ":** Edward Christophersen and Susan Van Scoyoc, "What Makes Time-Out Work (and Fail)?" *Developmental and Behavioral News* 16, no. 1 (Spring 2007).

201   **As for how long the time-out should be, research suggests:** Amy K. Drayton, Melissa N. Andersen, Rachel M. Knight, Barbara T. Felt, Emily M. Fredericks, and Dawn J. Dore-Stites, "Internet Guidance on Time Out: Inaccuracies, Omissions, and What to Tell Parents Instead," *Journal of Developmental and Behavioral Pediatrics* 35, no. 4 (May 2014): 239–246.

201   **One study found, however, that for four-to-eight-year-olds:** Bradley T. Erford, "A Modified Time-Out Procedure for Children with Noncompliant or Defiant Behaviors," *Professional School Counseling* 2, no. 3 (February 1999): 205–210.

201   **Siegel and Bryson, the authors of *No-Drama Discipline,* argued that time-outs:** Daniel J. Siegel and Tina Payne Bryson, "You Said WHAT About Time-Outs?!" *HuffPost*, October 21, 2014. Accessed October 17, 2020. https://www.huffpost.com/entry/time-outs-overused_b_6006332.

202   **In a powerful 2019 essay in *The New York Times*:** Minna Dubin, "The Rage Mothers Don't Talk About," *New York Times*, April 15, 2020. Accessed October 17, 2020. https://www.nytimes.com/2020/04/15/parenting/mother-rage.html.

203   **I learned how to better control my temper from my friend and clinical social worker Carla Naumburg:** Carla Naumburg, *How to Stop Losing Your Sh*t with Your Kids: A Practical Guide to Becoming a Calmer, Happier Parent* (New York: Workman, 2019).

CHAPTER 9: "I HATE MY BROTHER."

207   **When, as part of a study, researchers watched toddler and preschool-age:** Michal Perlman and Hildy S. Ross, "The Benefits of Parent Intervention in Children's Disputes: An Examination of Concurrent Changes in Children's Fighting Styles," *Child Development* 64, no. 4 (August 1997): 690–700.

208   **When researchers surveyed Harvard students and then followed up:** George E. Vaillant and Caroline O. Vaillant, "Natural History of Male Psychological Health: XII. A 45-Year Study of Predictors of Successful Aging at Age 65," *American Journal of Psychiatry* 147, no. 1 (January 1990).

209   **The myth of "only-child syndrome" arose:** E. W. Bohannon, "A Study of Peculiar and Exceptional Children," *Pedagogical Seminary* 4, no. 1 (1896): 3–60.

209   **According to the Pew Research Center, from 1976 to 2015, the percentage of mothers:** Kim Parker, Juliana Menasce Horowitz, and Molly Rohal, "The American Family Today," in "Parenting in America: Outlook, Worries, Aspirations Are Strongly Linked to Financial Situation," Pew Research Center, December 17, 2015. Accessed October 18, 2020. https://www.pewsocialtrends.org/2015/12/17/1-the-american-family-today/.

210   **At the turn of the twentieth century, psychoanalyst Sigmund Freud:** Freud, Sigmund, *Introduction to Psychoanalysis*, trans. G. Stanley Hall (New York: Horace Liveright, 1920).

210   **In an analysis of forty-seven parenting books and book chapters:** Laurie Kramer and Dawn Ramsburg, "Advice Given to Parents on Welcoming a Second Child: A Critical Review," *Family Relations* 51, no. 1 (January 2002): 2–14.

210   **In a 2012 paper, Volling analyzed thirty studies:** Brenda L. Volling, "Family Transitions Following the Birth of a Sibling: An Empirical Review of Changes in the Firstborn's Adjustment," *Psychological Bulletin* 138, no. 3 (May 2012): 497–528.

210   **When social and developmental psychologist Judy Dunn:** Judy Dunn and Carol Kendrick, *Siblings: Love, Envy and Understanding* (London: Grant McIntyre, 1982).

212   **Once, Kramer and her team pored over more than 250 children's books:** Laurie Kramer, Sonia Noorman, and Renee Brockman, "Representations of Sibling Relationships in Young Children's Literature," *Early Childhood Research Quarterly* 14, no. 4 (1999): 555–574.

212   **When researchers surveyed 108 pairs of siblings about their fights:** Shirley McGuire, Beth Manke, Afsoon Eftekhari, and Judy Dunn, "Children's Perceptions of Sibling Conflict During Middle Childhood: Issues and Sibling (DIS) Similarity," *Social Development* 9, no. 2 (May 2000): 173–190.

213   **In a 2008 trial, Kramer and psychologist Denise Kennedy:** Denise E. Kennedy and Laurie Kramer, "Improving Emotion Regulation and Sibling Relationship Quality: The More Fun with Sisters and Brothers Program," *Family Relations* 57, no. 5 (December 2008): 567–578.

214   **In a 2017 study, Volling and developmental psychologist Ju-Hyun Song:** Ju-Hyun Song and Brenda L. Volling, "Theory-of-Mind Development and Early Sibling Relationships After the Birth of a Sibling: Parental Discipline Matters," *Infant and Child Development* 27, no. 1 (January/February 2018): e2053.

214   **In another study, Volling found that preschool-aged kids:** Brenda L. Volling, Nancy L. McElwain, and Alison L. Miller, "Emotion Regulation in Context: The Jealousy Complex Between Young Siblings and Its Relations with Child and Family Characteristics," *Child Development* 73, no. 2 (March/April 2002): 581–600.

215   **In research conducted in the 1970s and 1980s:** Judy Dunn and Carol Kendrick, *Siblings: Love, Envy and Understanding* (London: Grant McIntyre, 1982).

216 **"When parents say things like . . .":** Eileen Kennedy-Moore, *Kid Confidence: Help Your Child Make Friends, Build Resilience, and Develop Real Self-Esteem* (Oakland: New Harbinger, 2019).

216 **In her book *Peaceful Parent, Happy Siblings*:** Laura Markham, *Peaceful Parent, Happy Siblings: How to Stop the Fighting and Raise Friends for Life* (New York: Perigee Books, 2015).

217 **In one study, she and a colleague interviewed sibling pairs:** Amanda Kowal and Laurie Kramer, "Children's Understanding of Parental Differential Treatment," *Child Development* 68, no. 1 (February 1997): 113–126.

218 **In their book *Siblings Without Rivalry*:** Adele Faber and Elaine Mazlish, *Siblings Without Rivalry: How to Help Your Children Live Together So You Can Live Too* (New York: Norton, 2012).

219 **I first learned about it from Laura Markham:** Heather Shumaker, *It's OK Not to Share: And Other Renegade Rules for Raising Competent and Compassionate Kids* (New York: Tarcher, 2012).

221 **Research suggests that siblings who are left to resolve conflicts:** Julie Smith and Hildy Ross, "Training Parents to Mediate Sibling Disputes Affects Children's Negotiation and Conflict Understanding," *Child Development* 78, no. 3 (May/June 2007): 790–805.

224 **In a 2007 study, twenty-four sets of parents were taught how:** Julie Smith and Hildy Ross, "Training Parents to Mediate Sibling Disputes Affects Children's Negotiation and Conflict Understanding," *Child Development* 78, no. 3 (May/June 2007): 790–805.

225 **In a separate 2014 study, researchers found that after parents were taught:** Hildy S. Ross and Marysia J. Lazinski, "Parent Mediation Empowers Sibling Conflict Resolution," *Early Education and Development* 25, no. 2 (2014): 259–275.

CHAPTER 10: "WHERE'S THE IPAD?"

228 **The American Academy of Pediatrics recommends that babies and toddlers:** AAP Council on Communications and Media, "Media and Young Minds," *Pediatrics* 138, no. 5 (November 1, 2016): e20162591.

228 **yet according to a 2017 survey conducted by the nonprofit group Common Sense Media:** Victoria Rideout, "The Common Sense Census: Media Use by Kids Age Zero to Eight," Common Sense Media, 2017. Accessed October 18, 2020. https://www.commonsensemedia.org/sites/default/files/uploads/research /csm_zerotoeight_fullreport_release_2.pdf.

228 **According to a 2018 Pew Research Center report, 95 percent of American teens:** Monica Anderson and Jingjing Jiang, "Teens, Social Media & Technology 2018," Pew Research Center, May 31, 2018. Accessed October 18, 2020.

https://www.pewresearch.org/internet/2018/05/31/teens-social-media-technology
-2018/.

230 **When Amy Orben, a research fellow at the University of Cambridge, and Andrew Przybylski:** Amy Orben and Andrew K. Przybylski, "The Association Between Adolescent Well-Being and Digital Technology Use," *Nature Human Behaviour* 3, no. 2 (February 2019): 173–182.

231 **In a 2017 study, Przybylski and his colleague Netta Weinstein:** Andrew K. Przybylski and Netta Weinstein, "A Large-Scale Test of the Goldilocks Hypothesis: Quantifying the Relations Between Digital-Screen Use and the Mental Well-Being of Adolescents," *Psychological Science* 28, no. 2 (February 1, 2017): 204–215.

231 **A 2016 study found that only one-third of individuals accurately:** Michael Scharkow, "The Accuracy of Self-Reported Internet Use—A Validation Study Using Client Log Data," *Communication Methods and Measures* 10, no. 1 (2016): 13–27.

231 **A 2020 study found that 36 percent of parents underestimate:** Jenny S. Radesky, Heidi M. Weeks, Rosa Ball, Alexandria Schaller, Samantha Yeo, Joke Durnez, Matthew Tamayo-Rios, et al., "Young Children's Use of Smartphones and Tablets," *Pediatrics* 146, no. 1 (July 2020): e20193518.

232 **In a September 2017 article titled "Have Smartphones Destroyed a Generation?":** Jean M. Twenge, "Have Smartphones Destroyed a Generation?" *The Atlantic*, September 2017. Accessed October 18, 2020. https://www.theatlantic .com/magazine/archive/2017/09/has-the-smartphone-destroyed-a-generation/534198/.

232 **In fact, one study, published directly in response to one of Twenge's papers:** Taylor Heffer, Marie Good, Owen Daly, Elliott MacDonell, and Teena Willoughby, "The Longitudinal Association Between Social-Media Use and Depressive Symptoms Among Adolescents and Young Adults: An Empirical Reply to Twenge et al. (2018)," *Clinical Psychological Science* 7, no. 3 (May 1, 2019): 462–470.

233 **In a study published in January 2019, Orben and Przybylski:** Amy Orben and Andrew K. Przybylski, "The Association Between Adolescent Well-Being and Digital Technology Use," *Nature Human Behaviour* 3, no. 2 (February 2019): 173–182.

234 **In a meta-analysis of two dozen studies on the topic published in 2018:** Anna T. Prescott, James D. Sargent, and Jay G. Hull, "Metaanalysis of the Relationship Between Violent Video Game Play and Physical Aggression over Time," *Proceedings of the National Academy of Sciences* 115, no. 40 (October 2, 2018): 9882–9888.

234 **In ancient Greece, Socrates worried that if enough people learned how to write:** Plato, *Phaedrus*, trans. Benjamin Jowett (London: Oxford University Press, 1892). Accessed October 18, 2020. http://classics.mit.edu/Plato/phaedrus.html.

234 **In 1854, Henry David Thoreau griped that inventions like the telegraph:** Henry David Thoreau, *Walden; or, Life in the Woods* (Boston: Ticknor and Fields, 1854).

234 **And in the 1740s, a moral panic arose:** Ana Vogorinčić, "The Novel-Reading Panic in 18th-Century in England: An Outline of an Early Moral Media Panic," *Media Research: Croatian Journal for Journalism and the Media* 14, no. 2 (2008): 103–124.

235 **Ninety-four percent of teens say that they use social media to connect:** Amanda Lenhart, "Chapter 4: Social Media and Friendships," in "Teens, Technology and Friendships," Pew Research Center, August 6, 2015. Accessed October 18, 2020. https://www.pewresearch.org/internet/2015/08/06/chapter-4 -social-media-and-friendships/.

235 **In a 2018 Common Sense Media survey of American teenagers:** Victoria Rideout and Michael B. Robb, "Social Media, Social Life: Teens Reveal Their Experiences," Common Sense Media, 2018. Accessed October 18, 2020. https://www.commonsensemedia.org/sites/default/files/uploads/research /2018_cs_socialmediasociallife_executivesummary-final-release_3_low res.pdf.

235 **"For many of us, social media is an exercise in . . .":** Devorah Heitner, *Screenwise: Helping Kids Thrive (and Survive) in Their Digital World* (New York: Bibliomotion, 2016).

237 **In her book *Raising Humans in a Digital World*:** Diana Graber, *Raising Humans in a Digital World: Helping Kids Build a Healthy Relationship with Technology* (Nashville: HarperCollins Leadership, 2019).

238 **One option, if you're not quite sure, is to get a "family" phone first:** Julianna Miner, *Raising a Screen-Smart Kid: Embrace the Good and Avoid the Bad in the Digital Age* (New York: TarcherPerigee, 2019).

239 **In her book *The Art of Screen Time*:** Anya Kamenetz, *The Art of Screen Time: How Your Family Can Balance Digital Media and Real Life* (New York: PublicAffairs, 2018).

240 **Alexandra Samuel, a technology researcher and writer, surveyed:** Alexandra Samuel, "Parents: Reject Technology Shame," *Atlantic*, November 4, 2015. Accessed October 18, 2020. https://www.theatlantic.com/technology/archive /2015/11/why-parents-shouldnt-feel-technology-shame/414163/.

241 **In a 2016 study, researchers split kids:** Eric E. Rasmussen, Autumn Shafer, Malinda J. Colwell, Shawna White, Narissra Punyanunt-Carter, Rebecca L. Densley, and Holly Wright, "Relation Between Active Mediation, Exposure to Daniel Tiger's Neighborhood, and US Preschoolers' Social and Emotional Development," *Journal of Children and Media* 10, no. 4 (2016): 443–461.

241 **But in 2017, journalists with *The New York Times* reported:** Sapna Maheshwari, "On YouTube Kids, Startling Videos Slip Past Filters," *New York Times*, November 4, 2017. Accessed October 18, 2020. https://www.nytimes.com /2017/11/04/business/media/youtube-kids-paw-patrol.html.

242–43 **A 2014 study found that when parents knew what websites:** Atika Khurana, Amy Bleakley, Amy B. Jordan, and Daniel Romer, "The Protective Effects of

Parental Monitoring and Internet Restriction on Adolescents' Risk of Online Harassment," *Journal of Youth and Adolescence* 44, no. 5 (May 2015): 1039–1047.

244 **Check out the AAP's Media Time Calculator:** "Media Time Calculator," American Academy of Pediatrics. Accessed October 18, 2020. https://www .healthychildren.org/English/media/Pages/default.aspx#wizard.

247 **If you're not sure where to start, Common Sense Media has free lesson plans available:** Erin Wilkey Oh, "23 Great Lesson Plans for Internet Safety," Common Sense Media, February 7, 2020. Accessed October 18, 2020. https://www .commonsense.org/education/articles/23-great-lesson-plans-for-internet-safety.

247 **Parents aren't often aware that kids care about this:** Alexis Hiniker, Sarita Y. Schoenebeck, and Julie A. Kientz, "Not at the Dinner Table: Parents' and Children's Perspectives on Family Technology Rules," *Proceedings of the 19th ACM Conference on Computer-Supported Cooperative Work & Social Computing* (February 2016): 1376–1389.

247 **At the beginning of her book *It's Complicated*:** danah boyd, *It's Complicated: The Social Lives of Networked Teens* (New Haven, CT: Yale University Press, 2014).

248 **According to a 2016 Common Sense Media survey, parents:** Corbie Kiernan and Lisa Cohen, "New Report: Parents Spend More Than Nine Hours a Day with Screen Media," Common Sense Media, December 6, 2016. Accessed October 19, 2020. https://www.commonsensemedia.org/about-us/news/press-releases/new -report-parents-spend-more-than-nine-hours-a-day-with-screen-media.

248 **In a study published in 2014, pediatrician Jenny Radesky:** Jenny S. Radesky, Caroline J. Kistin, Barry Zuckerman, Katie Nitzberg, Jamie Gross, Margot Kaplan-Sanoff, Marilyn Augustyn, and Michael Silverstein, "Patterns of Mobile Device Use by Caregivers and Children During Meals in Fast Food Restaurants," *Pediatrics* 133, no. 4 (April 2014): e843–e849.

249 **In a highly cited experiment from 1975:** Edward Tronick, L. B. Adamson, H. Als, and T. B. Brazelton, "Infant Emotions in Normal and Pertubated Interactions," paper presented at *Biennial Meeting of the Society for Research in Child Development, Denver, CO* 28 (April 1975): 66–104.

CHAPTER 11: "WHEN I TOUCH IT, IT GETS BIGGER!"

253 **In a 2015 study, researchers analyzed the results of a national CDC-sponsored survey:** Rachel H. Vanderberg, Amy H. Harkas, Elizabeth Miller, Gina S. Sucato, Aletha Y. Akers, Sonya B. Borerro, "Racial and/or Ethnic Differences in Formal Sex Education and Sex Education by Parents Among Young Women in the United States," *Journal of Pediatric & Adolescent Gynecology* 29, no. 1 (2016): 69–73.

253 **In their 2020 book *Sexual Citizens*, Columbia University anthropologist Jennifer Hirsch and sociologist Shamus Khan:** Jennifer S. Hirsch and

Shamus Khan, *Sexual Citizens: A Landmark Study of Sex, Power and Assault on Campus* (New York: Norton, 2020).

254 **According to the nonprofit Guttmacher Institute, nineteen US states do not require that sex education be taught in school:** "Sex and HIV Education," Guttmacher Institute. Accessed October 18, 2020. https://www .guttmacher.org/state-policy/explore/sex-and-hiv-education.

254 **When the New York American Civil Liberties Union evaluated the quality of New York's sex education:** New York Civil Liberties Union, *Birds, Bees and Bias: How Absent Sex Ed Standards Fail New York's Students.* September 2012.

254 **even though, according to a 2008 study, teenage girls who receive abstinence-only sexual education are no less likely to get pregnant:** Pamela K. Kohler, Lisa E. Manhart, and William E. Lafferty, "Abstinence-Only and Comprehensive Sex Education and the Initiation of Sexual Activity and Teen Pregnancy," *Journal of Adolescent Health* 42 (2008): 344–351.

254–55 **Research also suggests that abstinence-only programs don't lower the risk of sexual assault:** John Santelli, Stephanie A. Grillo, Tse-Hwei Choo, Gloria Diaz, Kate Walsh, Melanie Wall, Jennifer S. Hirsch, et al., "Does Sex Education Before College Protect Students from Sexual Assault in College?" *PLos One* 13, no. 11 (2018): e0205951.

255 **According to a 2017 study based on a survey of more than 1,600 Columbia and Barnard College students:** Claude A. Mellins, Kate Walsh, Aaron L. Sarvet, Melanie Wall, Louisa Gilbert, John S. Santelli, Martie Thompson, et al., "Sexual Assault Incidents Among College Undergraduates: Prevalence and Factors Associated with Risk," *PLoS One* 12, no. 11 (November 2017): e0186471.

255 **In a 2017 CDC national survey, nearly one in ten high school students said:** Laura Kahn, Tim McManus, William A. Harris, Shari L. Shanklin, Katherine H. Flint, Barbara Queen, Richard Lowry, et al., "Youth Risk Behavior Surveillance— United States, 2017," *MMWR Surveillance Summary* 67, no. SS-8 (2018): 1–114.

255 **Fewer than half of high schools and fewer than a fifth of middle schools teach all the topics recommended by the CDC:** Centers for Disease Control and Prevention, *School Health Profiles 2018: Characteristics of Health Programs Among Secondary Schools.* Atlanta: Centers for Disease Control and Prevention, 2019.

255–56 **A 2015 study found that when parents introduce their kids to the issue of sex with a stern, scare-mongering lecture:** Adam A. Rogers, Thao Ha, Elizabeth A. Stormshak, and Thomas J. Dishion, "Quality of Parent-Adolescent Conversations About Sex and Adolescent Sexual Behavior: An Observational Study," *Journal of Adolescent Health* 57, no. 2 (August 2015): 174–178.

256 **In a 2012 nationwide survey, 87 percent of teens said it would be much easier for them to postpone sexual activity:** Bill Albert, *With One Voice 2012: America's Adults and Teens Sound Off About Teen Pregnancy.* The National Campaign to Prevent Teen and Unplanned Pregnancy, August 2012.

256–57 **A 2018 national survey of American kids found that 72 percent of boys feel pressure to be physically strong:** Plan International, *The State of Gender Equality for U.S. Adolescents: Full Research Findings from a National Survey of Adolescents.* September 12, 2018.

257 **In one disturbing study, researchers at the University of Massachusetts edited together scenes from the R-rated movies *Showgirls* and *9½ Weeks*:** Michael A. Milburn, Roxanne Mather, and Sheree D. Conrad, "The Effects of Viewing R-Rated Movie Scenes That Objectify Women on Perceptions of Date Rape," *Sex Roles* 43, nos. 9/10 (2000): 645–664.

258 **In 2016, for instance, the Harvard men's soccer team was caught rating new recruits to the women's team based on their hotness:** Andrew M. Duehren, C. Ramsey Fahs, and Daphne C. Thompson, "Harvard Cancels Men's Soccer Season After Finding Sexually Explicit 'Reports' Continued Through 2016," *The Harvard Crimson*, November 3, 2016. Accessed October 18, 2020. https://www.thecrimson.com/article/2016/11/4/soccer-suspended-scouting-report-harvard/.

258 **at Columbia, the men's wrestling team referred to the school's female students as "ugly socially awkward cunts":** Daniel Radov, Austin Horn, Christopher Lopez, and Bradley Davison, "Wrestling Team Under Investigation After Racially, Sexually Explicit Group Messages Surface," *Columbia Spectator*, November 11, 2016. Accessed October 18, 2020. https://www.columbiaspectator.com/sports/2016/11/10/wrestling-team-under-investigation-after-racially-sexually-explicit-group-messages/.

258 **and at Amherst, the men's cross-country team sent around an email that contained photos of eight women:** Des Bieler, "'The Messages Are Appalling': Amherst Suspends Cross-Country Team over Misogynistic and Racist Emails," *Washington Post*, December 12, 2016. Accessed October 19, 2020. https://www.washingtonpost.com/news/early-lead/wp/2016/12/12/the-messages-are-appalling-amherst-suspends-cross-country-team-over-misogynistic-and-racist-emails/.

258 **But as journalist Peggy Orenstein explained in her 2020 book, *Boys & Sex*:** Peggy Orenstein, *Boys & Sex: Young Men on Hookups, Love, Porn, Consent, and Navigating the New Masculinity* (New York: Harper, 2020).

259 **A 2019 study reported that the more that teens are exposed to sexually explicit material:** Chelly Maes, Lara Schreurs, Johanna M. F. van Oosten, and Laura Vanderbosch, "#(Me)Too Much? The role of Sexualizing Online Media in Adolescents' Resistance Towards the MeToo-Movement and Acceptance of Rape Myths," *Journal of Adolescence* 77 (December 2019): 59–69.

259 **Another 2019 study found that tenth-grade boys who watched violent pornography:** Whitney L. Rostad, Daniel Gittins-Stone, Charlie Hungton, Christie J. Rizzo, Deborah Pearlman, and Lindsay Orchowski, "The Association Between Exposure to Violent Pornography and Teen Dating Violence in Grade 10 High School Students," *Archives of Sexual Behavior* 48, no. 7 (October 2019): 2137–2147.

260 **As developmental psychologist Deborah Tolman wrote in a 2012 paper:**
Deborah L. Tolman, "Female Adolescents, Sexual Empowerment and Desire: A
Missing Discourse of Gender Inequity," *Sex Roles* 66 (May 2012): 11–12.

260 **When Cornell social historian Joan Jacobs Brumberg read and
compared the diaries written by adolescent girls:** Joan Jacobs Brumberg, *The
Body Project: An Intimate History of American Girls* (New York: Vintage, 1998).

260 **This focus on appearance feeds into a bigger and more pernicious
problem:** American Psychological Association Task Force on the Sexualization
of Girls, *Report of the APA Task Force on the Sexualization of Girls*, 2007.
Accessed October 18, 2020. https://www.apa.org/pi/women/programs/girls
/report-full.pdf.

260 **A 2009 study found that young women are four times more willing than
young men to engage in sexual activities they don't like:** Christine
Elizabeth Kaestle, "Sexual Insistence and Disliked Sexual Activities in Young
Adulthood: Differences by Gender and Relationship Characteristics," *Perspectives
on Sexual and Reproductive Health* 41, no. 1 (March 2009): 33–39.

260–61 **In a 2014 study, researchers asked young women to describe key
indicators:** Sara McClelland, "'What Do You Mean When You Say That You're
Sexually Satisfied?' A Mixed Methods Study," *Feminism & Psychology* 24, no. 1
(January 2014): 74–96.

261 **Orenstein encountered this issue over and over again while interviewing
girls for her 2016 book *Girls & Sex*:** Peggy Orenstein, *Girls & Sex: Navigating
the Complicated New Landscape* (New York: Harper, 2016).

263 **In her book *The Sex-Wise Parent*, Janet Rosenzweig:** Janet Rosenzweig,
*The Sex-Wise Parent: The Parent's Guide to Protecting Your Child, Strengthening
Your Family, and Talking to Kids About Sex, Abuse, and Bullying* (New York:
Skyhorse, 2012).

264 **One book that's great for introducing young kids to this topic is *Consent
(for Kids!)* by Rachel Brian:** Rachel Brian, *Consent (for Kids!): Boundaries,
Respect, and Being in Charge of YOU* (New York: Little, Brown, 2020).

266 **As clinical psychologist Lisa Damour wrote in her book *Under Pressure*:**
Lisa Damour, *Under Pressure: Confronting the Epidemic of Stress and Anxiety in
Girls* (New York: Ballantine, 2019).

268 **When my daughter was four and my son was seven, my husband and I
bought them Robie Harris's book *It's Not the Stork!*:** Robie H. Harris, *It's
Not the Stork!: A Book About Girls, Boys, Babies, Bodies, Families and Friends*
(Somerville, MA: Candlewick, 2006).

270 **Author Robie Harris has written a series of excellent books for kids of
various ages:** Robie H. Harris, *It's So Amazing!: A Book About Eggs, Sperm, Birth,
Babies, and Families* (Somerville, MA: Candlewick, 2014). Robie H. Harris, *It's
Perfectly Normal: Changing Bodies, Growing Up, Sex, and Sexual Health*
(Somerville, MA: Candlewick, 2014).

270   **"We hold on to the idea that there's a fixed quantity of sexual information adults need to keep close to the chest . . .":** Deborah Roffman, *Talk to Me First: Everything You Need to Know to Become Your Kids' "Go-To" Person About Sex* (Cambridge, MA: Da Capo, 2012).

272   **When social psychologist Antonia Abbey interviewed college students, 72 percent of women told her:** Antonia Abbey, "Misperceptions of Friendly Behavior as Sexual Interest: A Survey of Naturally Occurring Incidents," *Psychology of Women Quarterly* 11, no. 2 (June 1987): 173–194.

272   **Her work has also found that young men are much more likely to overestimate a woman's interest when they have been drinking alcohol:** Antonia Abbey, Tina Zawacki, and Pam McAuslan, "Alcohol's Effects on Sexual Perception," *Journal of Studies on Alcohol and Drugs* 61, no. 5 (2000): 688–697.

275   **In her book *Not Under My Roof*, University of Massachusetts at Amherst sociologist Amy Schalet:** Amy Schalet, *Not Under My Roof: Parents, Teens, and the Culture of Sex* (Chicago: University of Chicago Press, 2011).

276   **Although teens from both countries lose their virginity at around the same age, American teenage girls are nearly six times as likely:** "Reproductive Health: Teen Pregnancy," Centers for Disease Control and Prevention. Accessed October 18, 2020. https://www.cdc.gov/teenpregnancy/about /index.htm. "Relatively Few Teenage Mothers in the Netherlands," Statistics Netherlands, December 12, 2017. Accessed October 18, 2020. https://www.cbs.nl /en-gb/news/2017/50/relatively-few-teenage-mothers-in-the-netherlands.

278–79   **Surveys suggest that more than half of eleven-to-thirteen-year-olds have seen pornography:** BBFC, "New Research Commissioned by the BBFC into the Impact of Pornography on Children Demonstrates Significant Support for age-verification," September 2019. Accessed October 18, 2020. https://www.bbfc .co.uk/about-us/news/children-see-pornography-as-young-as-seven-new -report-finds.

281   **According to a 2018 systematic review of the research literature, more than one in four teens:** Sheri Madigan, Anh Ly, Christina L. Rash, Joris Van Ouytsel, and Jeff R. Temple, "Prevalence of Multiple Forms of Sexting Behavior Among Youth: A Systematic Review and Meta-analysis," *JAMA Pediatrics* 174, no. 4 (2018): 327–335.

281   **In a 2019 commentary, cyberbullying researchers Justin Patchin and Sameer Hinduja argued that when kids receive a sext:** Justin W. Patchin and Sameer Hinduja, "It Is Time to Teach Safe Sexting," *Journal of Adolescent Health* 66, no. 2 (February 1, 2020): 140–143.

Index